Comments on other *Amazing Stories* from readers & reviewers

"*Tightly written volumes filled with lots of wit and humour about famous and infamous Canadians.*"
Eric Shackleton, *The Globe and Mail*

"*The heightened sense of drama and intrigue, combined with a good dose of human interest is what sets* Amazing Stories *apart.*"
Pamela Klaffke, *Calgary Herald*

"*This is popular history as it should be... For this price, buy two and give one to a friend.*"
Terry Cook, a reader from Ottawa, on **Rebel Women**

"*Glasner creates the moment of the explosion itself in graphic detail...she builds detail upon gruesome detail to create a convincingly authentic picture.*"
Peggy McKinnon, *The Sunday Herald*, on **The Halifax Explosion**

"*It was wonderful...I found I could not put it down. I was sorry when it was completed.*"
Dorothy F. from Manitoba on **Marie-Anne Lagimodière**

"*Stories are rich in description, and bristle with a clever, stylish realness.*"
Mark Weber, *Central Alberta Advisor*, on **Ghost Town Stories II**

"*A compelling read. Bertin...has selected only the most intriguing tales, which she narrates with a wealth of detail.*"
Joyce Glasner, *New Brunswick Reader*, on **Strange Events**

"*The resulting book is one readers will want to share with all the women in their lives.*"
Lynn Martel, *Rocky Mountain Outlook*, on **Women Explorers**

AMAZING STORIES

GREAT CAT STORIES

AMAZING STORIES

GREAT CAT STORIES

Incredible Tales About
Exceptional Cats

ANIMAL / HUMAN INTEREST
by Roxanne Willems Snopek

In memory of our old boy Cody.
We miss you Cody-cat.

PUBLISHED BY ALTITUDE PUBLISHING CANADA LTD.
1500 Railway Avenue, Canmore, Alberta T1W 1P6
www.altitudepublishing.com
1-800-957-6888

Copyright 2004 © Roxanne Willems Snopek
All rights reserved
First published 2004

Extreme care has been taken to ensure that all information presented in this book is accurate and up to date. Neither the author nor the publisher can be held responsible for any errors.

Publisher   Stephen Hutchings
Associate Publisher   Kara Turner
Series Editor   Jill Foran
Editor   Deborah Lawson

We acknowledge the financial support of the Government of Canada through the Book Publishing Industry Development Program (BPIDP) for our publishing activities.

Altitude GreenTree Program
Altitude Publishing will plant twice as many trees as were used in the manufacturing of this product.

We acknowledge the support of the Canada Council for the Arts which in 2003 invested $21.7 million in writing and publishing throughout Canada.

Canada Council   Conseil des Arts
for the Arts   du Canada

National Library of Canada Cataloguing in Publication Data

Snopek, Roxanne
Great cat stories / Roxanne Willems Snopek.

(Amazing stories)
Includes bibliographical references.
ISBN 1-55153-777-X

1. Cats--Canada--Anecdotes. 2. Cat owners--Canada--Anecdotes. I. Title. II. Series: Amazing stories (Canmore, Alta.)

SF445.5.S66 2004   636.8'0887   C2004-903756-0

An application for the trademark for Amazing Stories™ has been made and the registered trademark is pending.

Printed and bound in Canada by Friesens
4 6 8 9 7 5

Contents

Prologue 9
Chapter 1 Lost... and Found 11
Chapter 2 The Cold, Hostile Streets................. 24
Chapter 3 The Secret of Simon Teakettle 36
Chapter 4 Prescription Pets: Cats Who Heal 47
Chapter 5 Miracle Babies........................... 57
Chapter 6 The Cat-Man of Parliament Hill 72
Chapter 7 The Making of Mister Got-to-Go.......... 82
Chapter 8 Journey's End........................... 91
Chapter 9 The Simon Years 104
Epilogue 115

Prologue

Trees turn colour early in Saskatchewan and fall is just a quick slip of a season before winter's cold arrives to stay. The veterinary teaching hospital where I worked was across the bridge from my apartment. Although the drive to work was short and pretty, my job was anything but. Until an animal health technician position opened up, where I could use my newly acquired skills, I was stuck on kennel duty and I hated it.

I quickly cleaned and fed the patients in the cat ward. Then I moved to the large dog runs. Hot water shot out of the hose, sending excrement and bits of food rolling down the trough to the drain at the end. Even with my nose clamped shut, I could taste the smell at the back of my throat and I knew it clung to my clothing when I went home.

Finally I came to the smaller cages on the dog ward. It was quiet that day and I progressed quickly until I came to the last cage. Inside, to my astonishment, crouched a tiny kitten, thin and filthy, its eyes crusted and running. Too young to be away from its mother, but not old enough to be vaccinated, this kitten was in the no-man's land of infectious disease. And he'd been abandoned.

I cleaned him up as best I could, but he was just a baby and a messy one at that. His coat was stained and matted from one end to the other, and when I set down his dish of warm gruel I saw why. He promptly climbed right in, slurping and kneading the dish with his paws as if he knew he should still be nursing at his mother's side.

I hoped he'd find a home but I knew his chances were slim. There was no way I could take him; my apartment was strictly No Pets. If he were at least cute, there was a chance someone would take pity on him. But he was sickly, dirty, noisy, and ugly. Who would want such a kitten?

Chapter 1
Lost... and Found

"Cats seem to go on the principle that it never does any harm to ask for what you want."
Joseph Wood Krutch

Mid-life is a time of change. Some people find themselves letting go of parts of their lives that no longer fit. Some discover a sudden yearning to fulfil long-forgotten dreams. And for some people it's a matter of adapting to the unexpected, both good and bad.

Barb Taylor of Cumberland, Ontario, didn't choose change in her life; change chose her. It began with a dream — to build a new home. This decision was not entered into lightly; Barb can count on one hand the number of times she's moved in 56 years. "At 19, I hopped a plane and headed west from England," she says. "I told my parents I was going to stay in Canada for two years whether I liked it or not. That was 1968. I've never looked back."

Barb's life was good, but busy. Her husband's work kept him away from home much of the time. Until recently, Barb's job as an administrative assistant in a high-tech company had kept her preoccupied with the lives of others. "The hours were long, and the pay was short," she says wryly. When she left her job she was finally able to put her energy towards managing the life she shared with her husband and Benji, her Bichon Frise dog. She was settled and content, looking forward to the next phase of her life and marriage.

"My life was my garden, my ordinary, everyday stuff, and my Benji," she says with a laugh. "I am so boring." But change was stalking her. Around that time, Barb's husband's business partner passed away, leaving a beautiful piece of property overlooking the Ottawa River. His widow wanted to sell it to them. Barb's first reaction was resistance. "It was too expensive and much farther away than we wanted to move," recalls Barb. "But it was gorgeous. And it got the building bug going in us." Once the idea bit, it hung on. Her husband broke down her initial defences and soon Barb caught his excitement. They found a different lot, in an area they liked and in the price range they'd hoped for, and started making plans to build their dream home.

It was an exciting and exhausting time. Moving out of the house they'd lived in for more than 20 years was more difficult in every way than Barb had imagined it would be. A lot of living had gone on within its walls; they'd been the backdrop for memories both good and bad, the whole range

Lost... and Found

of experiences that make up a life together. She knew it would be some time before the new house, beautiful as it was, would feel like home to them. Finally the last nail was in place and in February of 1999 they moved in. She looked forward to quiet evenings, enjoying some peace and contentment, reconnecting with each other.

But before Barb had even finished unpacking all the boxes, she was blindsided by a stunning twist: her husband of 28 years left her. The shock was devastating. Everything she believed was called into question and she found herself withdrawing, trying to hide from the pain. "It was hard," she remembers. "This wasn't supposed to be *my* dream house; it was supposed to be *our* dream house." Instead, she found herself in a new house, a new neighbourhood, and alone.

Except for Benji, her lifeline. "He was a cuddler," says Barb, "a very human sort of dog." Recurrent knee problems had made Benji dependent on Barb to carry him around and he enjoyed being pampered. He also had diabetes, which meant Barb was responsible for giving him twice-daily insulin injections and monitoring his food intake. Having Benji to care for during that time helped her get through the worst of it. She was able to push aside her own vulnerability and focus on his needs. But Benji was thirteen years old. Barb knew his days with her were limited.

In September of that year the time she'd been dreading arrived: Benji died. Now Barb was truly alone and she began to feel the full impact of the loss that walked hand-in-hand with the changes in her life. Barb forced herself to be strong and think positively. At least, she told herself, she'd had time to prepare for Benji's death. He'd had a good life. She'd cared well for him at the end, and she'd said her good-byes. Now it was time to move on. She desperately tried not to dwell on her sense of loss. She looked around her beautiful new home at the cherry hardwood floors, gleaming countertops, and black furniture, and told herself that, in spite of missing Benji, she'd be happy not to have white dog fur all over the house anymore.

No matter how hard she tried to ignore it, however, she knew something was missing from her life. "Having never had children I was finding my life, to say the least, pretty empty," recalls Barb. "However, I worked at putting away all the doggy things, returned the unused insulin, and said to myself, 'Okay Barbie, put the vacuum away. You can come and go as you please. You only have yourself to take care of now.'"

Her bittersweet freedom lasted until the following spring. It was a beautiful Friday evening in May and Barb was just about to have her supper, a symbolic meal celebrating her independence. "I'm pretty self-sufficient now," she says with a grin, "but before I'd always let the men handle the barbecue. That evening, I'd made up my mind to cook myself a steak." Much to her satisfaction, she turned out a perfectly grilled chunk of sizzling sirloin.

Her habit, since becoming single again, was to eat standing in front of the kitchen window, looking into her

Lost… and Found

backyard. But before the first tasty bite reached her lips, she saw a strange animal meandering aimlessly across her yard.

This, in itself, was no surprise. To her great delight, Barb had discovered her new semi-rural neighbourhood to be populated with many wild animals including racoons, foxes, groundhogs, fishers, and birds of all sorts. Her kitchen window provided an endlessly entertaining glimpse into the natural world. This furtive stranger, however, was not a wild animal. It was a cat, a grey-and-white tabby, and his erratic progress triggered her concern. "He didn't look like he knew where he was going," she recalls. "He seemed lost and confused, as if he'd been wandering around for awhile." As he picked his way around the pool towards the open garage door, Barb suddenly remembered the mousetraps she'd set earlier. She left her dinner untasted and ran outside to head him off.

Her reaction wasn't due to an abiding affection for cats; Barb had always felt that, when compared to Benji, cats didn't even rate. After all, they shed everywhere, they scratched the furniture, they were selfish and independent, not to mention the little issue of hairballs. "I was definitely not a cat person," Barb emphasizes. "I knew the nose and the tail, that's it." She simply reacted on instinct, hoping to shoo him away before he hurt himself. But as soon as she came near, before she'd even touched him, the cat abandoned his wily ways, dropped down, and rolled onto his side, begging her to pet him. She didn't quite know what to think. "Aren't cats afraid of strangers?" she asked herself. "From that moment," she says, "I realized this cat was different." She saw that he was a young male, not neutered, and hungry but not starved. He obviously had a home somewhere. But wherever he came from, it had been too long since his last meal. So she invited him in. "What do cats eat?" she wondered. Having no intention of sharing her very first steak, she crossed her fingers and opened a can of tuna for him. "I was worried about making him sick," she says. "Benji had had a very sensitive stomach so I was used to being careful. But this cat ate the whole can without hesitation and looked at me as if to say 'thank you.'" He seemed rather nice, she thought — for a cat.

She began phoning around to see if any neighbourhood cats had gone missing. "The Ottawa Senators were playing their final hockey game that night," she remembers, "so I knew a lot of my neighbours would be home watching it on television." One cat-loving friend asked her to bring the stray over so she could take a look at him. Barb scooped up the little cat and carried him over. He lay calmly in her arms, but when the friend reached for him, he leaped down and refused to come back. She cajoled and sweet-talked but he wouldn't come near them. "Everyone told me not to worry," says Barb. "It's a cat, they told me. It'll go home." So she went back home and went to bed, firmly ignoring her concern. The next morning it was raining and she wondered if he'd been able to find someplace dry. She called for him outside but didn't see him. He must have found his way home, she told herself. But she kept thinking about him, hoping he was okay. On Sunday morning she went out again and looked for him. This time she spotted him in the tall grass at the side of her yard; when she called to him, he came.

Barb immediately put him in a crate and took him to the veterinarian to make sure he was healthy. They looked for tattoos or microchips that might be used to reunite him with his owner but he had no identification. Worse still, they discovered an infected toe. During his travels, the little cat had somehow torn his claw so badly it was now on the verge of gangrene. He needed antibiotics. And until that treatment was finished he couldn't be vaccinated.

None of this was good news. Barb filled the prescription, paid the bill, and reluctantly returned home with the cat in his crate beside her. Neither of them was happy. Suddenly, the car was filled with a horrible odour. "He'd peed inside his little crate, all over himself. I'd covered the carrier with a towel, thank goodness, or I'd have been showered too."

The urine of an intact male cat is a powerful identification tool, used to mark territory and warn away competition. But to the human nose, especially in close quarters, the smell is sinus-searingly nasty, potent enough to take your breath away. Barb couldn't bring such a stench into the house, but she couldn't leave the cat outside with his injured toe, either. "I knew he'd clean himself off eventually, but what were we supposed to do in the meantime?" Cats aren't known to love water, but it didn't matter. They eyed each other warily, but

Barb knew there was only one solution. "I had to wash him," she confesses.

She rolled up her sleeves, plugged her nose, and hauled him to the laundry room sink. The cat didn't like it, but Barb gave him no choice. "I was bound and determined," she says. "The poor guy didn't have a chance. In the end, I won. But I had to wipe down the walls and floor afterwards." He was shampooed, scrubbed, rinsed, and rubbed until at last the odour was gone and he could be allowed into the house again. As soon as she finished, he sprang away to dry off and recover his injured dignity. They were both exhausted.

Once she had time to sit down and consider her options, Barb found herself in a dilemma. She'd found a cat rescue agency named Friends of Abandoned Pets (FOAP), but they had no foster homes available just then. Even if one had been available, this unvaccinated stray presented a potential health risk to the other cats and would be best kept by himself until his health status was certain.

Friends of Abandoned Pets first suggested that Barb sign on to be the foster home; they would then assume responsibility for his veterinary bills and look for a permanent home. "This meant," explains Barb, "that I'd probably have him for quite a long time before he was adoptable." She feared that after caring for him, she might become attached to him only to have to give him up eventually because — as a foster care provider — Barb would be ineligible to adopt him herself. Barb wavered; she wasn't about to risk opening

Lost... and Found

her heart again, only to be hurt and alone in the end. Then the FOAP counsellor suggested Barb could keep her options open by taking full responsibility (including financial) for him while she searched for his owners. "And, of course," she says, "that's what I did."

Barb continued to hope that somewhere out there a family was searching for their beloved missing pet. She was convinced he must have been something special to someone. "I spent the next couple of weeks trying to find an owner." She called several local shelters and rescue organizations, but no one had reported a missing cat of his description. She was afraid to relinquish him to a municipal shelter because, despite their assurances that all adoptable pets find homes, she knew there was a risk he'd end up being put to sleep. "He was such a nice cat. I was positive he belonged to somebody," she says.

Barb wondered why she felt such an obligation to help this unfortunate stray who'd found his way into her yard. She certainly hadn't been looking for a cat. But, for the time being at least, she was stuck with him. "I tried hard to find him a good home," says Barb. "I didn't believe mine was the right place for him." She tried not to feel any further responsibility. After all, she'd fed him. She'd paid to have him patched up. She'd even bathed him. Why should she feel obligated to give him a home, too? Surely some cat lover out there would recognise what a nice boy he was and take him into their home. She tried to give him to her neighbours. She tried to give him to family members. There had to be a way to find a good home for this lovely cat. But that would *not*, she insisted to herself, be *her* home. She wanted her freedom; she didn't want to be vacuuming up cat hair.

But the whole time she was trying so hard to foist him on someone else, she knew that deeper things were at work in her heart. She'd never forget the heartbreak she'd felt when Benji died. She was still reeling from the break-up of her marriage. She'd had enough loss recently; she wasn't ready for any more. But perhaps taking risks was part of the healing process. She knew that if she looked after this little stray much longer she'd be too attached to give him up. Her heart would once more be at risk.

So she continued her efforts to find his original home. Somewhere along the way, for no particular reason, she began to call him Sammy. Now, cat lovers everywhere know that once you name something, it's yours. The jig was up, but Barb wasn't ready to admit this to herself yet.

"I posted pictures all over the neighbourhood mailboxes," she says, "even though we aren't supposed to do that." The woman at the post office told her the area was known to be a dumping ground for unwanted animals. Thoughtless owners found the semi-rural roads a convenient place to casually 'lose' inconvenient pets. "Go ahead and put up your pictures," said the post office lady. "I'm not supposed to allow it, but I'll close my eyes."

Still no one responded. But soon afterwards, she noticed

Lost... and Found

Sammy

that someone else had posted a picture of another cat, a female, found on the same night as Sammy. Immediately, she phoned the number. The story she heard was so similar to the way she found Sammy that she began think the post-office lady might have had it right. Had someone taken two unwanted cats to the country and left them there to fend for themselves as best they could? "Who knows?" says Barb. Too many cats find themselves set free to starve or be killed by predators when their owners decide to join the spring moving frenzy. The little female cat ended up at the humane society, hopefully to be adopted, but Barb refused to take that chance with Sammy.

She continued her efforts at locating his owners, or at least finding someone who wanted to give him a good home, until finally someone told her bluntly that Sammy didn't need a good home because he already had one: with her. Barb had to face what was already evident to everyone else around her. Not only had she become a cat owner, but — without noticing it, without even wanting it — she'd become a cat lover, too. Soon after, while visiting a friend who had two dogs and two cats, she realized just how much she'd changed because of Sammy. "Normally in the past I would have gone to pat the dogs first and ignored the cats," she says with a laugh. "Now I say hello to the cats first, and *then* go pat the dogs."

"I'd never have believed I'd ever have a cat in my home. I don't even wear angora because the fluffy stuff bugs me so much. Did I realize how much fur a cat sheds? Oh, my! I have dark hardwood floors and there's cat hair everywhere." But Sammy, it seems, knew he had won Barb over. His goal accomplished, he has settled down and is enjoying the quiet life that suits them both so well. As for Barb, she finds it hard to believe how much she's enjoying this unexpected turn of events. "I think this little guy had a lucky day when he 'found' me," says Barb. "But, even more important, I'm a very lucky person."

Lost... and Found

Barb has proven herself to Sammy as well, giving a lot of security to her new companion. "He fell down the stairs once," she remembers. "It's an open-tread staircase and he was trying to jump to a window. He missed and fell about 20 feet onto the ceramic tile floor below." To her relief he wasn't injured, but that incident made her shudder to think of him taking a similar fall into one of the rocky crevasses near her home. The risks, she decided, were too great. Now Sammy enjoys the outdoors by bird watching at the windows. Pine siskins and American goldfinches give him hours of entertainment, and neither he nor his little friends are in danger.

She's also getting to know Sammy's temperament. "He's easily spooked," she says. "If he hears a strange voice in the house, even a soft-spoken female voice, he disappears." But Sammy seems to understand that Barb has accepted him wholeheartedly. It's finally safe for him to relax and just be himself with her.

Barb's heart is vulnerable once more, but the love Sammy brings is worth it. She knows there's no avoiding the twists and turns of life. But sometimes the most unwelcome changes lead to surprising joy. "Someone must have thought I needed somebody to take care of," says Barb. "In hindsight, I believe Sammy was sent to me." It seems that Barb's new house has finally become home, thanks to the little cat that insisted he belonged there too.

Chapter 2
The Cold, Hostile Streets

"Time spent with cats is never wasted."
Colette

For Linda Jean Gubbe of Saskatoon, Saskatchewan, it all started in 1996. "I was working downtown at the time," she says, "and when I left the office for my lunch break I noticed some cats hanging around outside." Two in particular caught her eye, one grey and one black-and-white. She began going outside on her breaks to look for them and soon discovered they lived beneath the building. She didn't always see them but they saw her, especially after she began putting down dishes of food. "They started to know what time I'd come, and I'd see eyes watching me."

As they became accustomed to her presence, Linda was able to observe them a bit more closely; she began to take

The Cold, Hostile Streets

note of how many there were, which ones were pregnant, and if any of them appeared ill. They didn't let her get close to them, so there wasn't much she could do but watch and bring food.

But for Linda, a fire had been lit. "You know how it is — all of a sudden one day you become aware of something, for whatever reason, and then you start seeing it everywhere?" So many cats lived in the cracks and crannies of the city. And not just her city. She began to search out organizations that worked with feral cats and discovered that many other people had the same concerns she did — and were doing something about it. If others were doing it, thought Linda, she could too. "I'm not a very patient person," admits Linda with a laugh. "I like to get things done." A few short months later, Street Cat Rescue of Saskatoon, also known by its nickname SCAT, was up and running. "We were registered at the beginning of 1997," she comments with pride.

Inspired by hope. Guided by compassion. That's the phrase above the logo on the SCAT website. Linda and her volunteers at SCAT have a two-part mission: (1) to reduce the at-large feral cat population through non-lethal control, and (2) to promote public awareness of responsible companion-animal guardianship and compassion for feral cats in the community.

They're lofty goals but Linda has a lot of support, especially from her family. Long-time animal lovers themselves, her parents knew the importance of what Linda was trying to do and that she'd do it with our without their help. "Mom was the most help at the beginning; Dad just said, 'More cats?'" But no charitable organization can survive without behind-the-scenes practical assistance, and that's where Linda's dad shone. If anything needed to be built — a shelter or a cat-run — he was there with hammer and nails. "He even became a member," says Linda, "because he was proud of his daughter." But the real surprise was when, after helping Linda feed that first colony of ferals she'd noticed beneath her work building, his heart was stolen. "He'd never had a cat of 'his own,' but this little tortoiseshell just fell in love with him. He called her Cuddles and she went home with him eventually."

The cat that personifies what SCAT is all about is a little ginger shorthair the volunteers dubbed Fantasia, because of the amazing trip they found she had survived in order to get to Saskatoon. "Sometime in July of 1997, early in SCAT's history, I received a call from a woman who said this little cat had been found up inside the motor of her husband's semi," recalls Linda. He had to take his engine apart to get at her, and when he was finally able to pull her out she was no prize: filthy, oily, scruffy, with raw, sore-looking ears. And she was very fat. But as soon as she knew she was safe, her delighted purrs made it obvious that she had once been a well-loved pet. The trucker called SCAT and put the ginger cat in his garage to await Linda's arrival. "We went over and found this very dirty, very sweet, very pregnant little orange tabby with these mysterious sores on her ears." It looked to Linda like recent frostbite. But that was hardly possible — it was the middle of a blistering prairie summer.

"About an hour later," continues Linda, "the woman called back." She reported that her husband had gone back to work and was discussing the little cat when one of the other truckers spoke up. "That must be the one that jumped out of the back of my truck." She had scurried out of the trailer and he had not been able to catch her. The last he'd seen of her, she was in among the other trucks. He'd just completed a long trip from Calgary, Alberta... hauling a refrigerator truck.

The mysteries of her frostbitten ears and her long journey were solved, but there still remained the question of where this tough little cat belonged. SCAT members began contacting Calgary shelters and rescue groups in the hope of finding her family. They wanted to get her home before she gave birth. Unfortunately, no one had reported her missing and Fantasia's kittens were born at the shelter. The volunteers felt badly for her, being separated from her home, but at least these babies would grow up with love and care, instead of on the street, wild and unwanted.

"A week or so later a call came in about four kittens, a week old, whose feral mom had been scared away and hadn't returned," relates Linda. They'd found a volunteer willing to try bottle-feeding, but round-the-clock kitten-raising is hard work and she felt she could only handle two of them. The other two orphans were brought in, on the off chance that Fantasia would be willing to add them to her little family.

"We knew there was a chance she might reject them," says Linda. "So we took the two new kittens and rubbed them alongside Fantasia's kittens before putting them in the basket." Then they held their breath as they set the foundlings next to the other kittens. "We needn't have bothered," says Linda. "We had just barely dropped them into the basket before she was trying to clean them. She immediately gave the two new kittens a complete bath and tucked them in with the others. She was an amazing mom as well as a travelling girl." Fantasia's amazing journey ended in a new life for her, and four kittens saved from a life on the street. "They have all since been adopted into great homes, but they are ever in our minds as one of our best success stories."

Today, Linda's work is more at the podium than it is in the trenches. Her vast network of 200 volunteers is more than capable of handling the work in the streets and alleys. "My area is primarily paperwork — talking to media, talking to people, going into schools, so I can find other volunteers, raise awareness, and find money and resources to pass on to the people who need it."

Many feral cats weren't always wild, they may have had human families and homes at one time. Then, for one reason or another, they found themselves out on the street. Cats, being the resourceful species they are, can often cling to survival by learning to scrounge and hunt, but this behaviour seldom endears them to people. Thieving from garbage pails, stalking bird feeders, and nipping into the food bag in the

The Cold, Hostile Streets

garage earns them little more than a bad reputation. Their soft fur and gentle demeanour quickly disappears, replaced by dirt, scars, and a watchful, lean, and hungry look. Such cats seldom receive a warm neighbourhood welcome. It doesn't take long for trust to erode, but still, these are usually stray cats, not true ferals. When these former pets not only survive, but also reproduce, the instinct to protect their offspring leads them to give birth in such tucked-away places that their babies have virtually no human contact. When they emerge with their mothers several weeks after birth, they look on the world through eyes untouched by domestication. These kittens belong to the race of domestic felines, but they are essentially wild. Unless caught and rehabilitated early, they will become true feral cats, living their short, hard lives, only to produce more kittens before dying on the cold streets.

Linda wants to break this cycle. "It's hard to reduce feral populations," she says. A vital part of breaking the cycle is preventing the birth of more feral kittens. SCAT promotes the use of TNR (Trap, Neuter, Return) whenever it's in the best interest of the particular cat but their preferred plan is something they call TNFA or Trap, Neuter, Foster, Adopt. Live-traps are used to catch the cats without harming them. Then they are spayed or neutered and evaluated for temperament. If the cats are truly wild, they are returned to their colony. If there are any indications that the cat is willing to rejoin civilization it's placed in a foster home to await permanent adoption.

"What I envision for SCAT isn't just taking care of colonies," says Linda. "I wanted a key part of our work to be providing a resource base for other care-givers." Many individuals are working quietly to care for the feral cats in their neighbourhood but they don't necessarily know the importance of doing it properly. People who don't like cats don't differentiate between feral cats, strays and the cat next door. Leaving food out, for instance, can attract unwanted wildlife and irritate neighbours. "People get annoyed by the cat that wanders into their yard and pees on their property. Ferals avoid people," she emphasizes. "They don't come into yards."

But Linda knows that improving the future for feral cats doesn't start with the cats. It starts with humans, and some humans have enough problems of their own without worrying about the needs of a cat.

The instant she answered the phone one day at the shelter, Linda had a feeling it would be bad news. The woman on the other end of the phone said she'd found a kitten starving in a dumpster. She had brought it inside but now it wouldn't eat. Could Linda do something to help? Linda sighed silently and then began explaining that this kitten probably needed urgent veterinary care. Medical care is part of responsible pet ownership, she told the caller gently. But the woman refused to take the kitten to a veterinarian. Her attitude was, "It's just a cat, and not even *my* cat. Can't *you* do something?"

Linda's biggest enemies are always ignorance, irresponsibility, and apathy; this time was no different. As soon as she

The Cold, Hostile Streets

hung up the phone she went to do what she could. "When an animal is sick or injured — especially a kitten — there's never any second thought," says Linda. "Just as soon as we have an address, we're out the door."

The address she was given confirmed her initial impression; it was a very neglected, run-down area of the city. The apartment building was even more derelict than she had expected. Linda and her partner walked up the rickety stairs, found the right number, and knocked on the door. It was partly open and they could hear the sound of a television inside, but no one came to the door. They heard whispering. Heads peered out from other doors, then quickly ducked back inside. Still no one answered. They were about to leave when someone in another apartment asked if they were there about the kitten. Once the neighbour realized they wanted to help, the atmosphere changed quite suddenly. "I think they thought we were with the police," says Linda. The relieved neighbour pointed to the right door and told them to go on in.

Inside the dingy room they found the kitten lying on a chair, too weak to even lift its head. The woman who'd called barely looked at them before turning her gaze back to the television. When Linda realized there was a toddler in the room with the woman, she guessed what had really happened. Small children often hurt kittens inadvertently by picking them up too roughly, perhaps by a limb or tail. Kittens and kids both need close supervision,

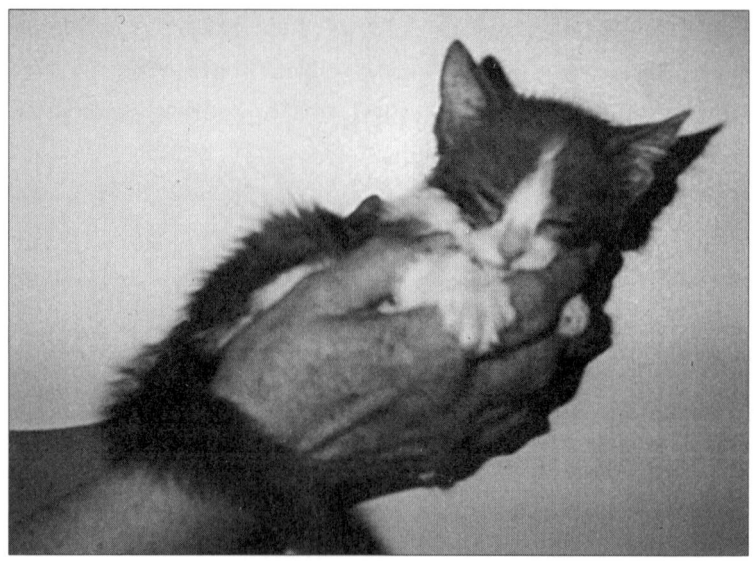

Molly Brown as a kitten

especially when playing together.

They bundled up the little female kitten and took it straight to the animal hospital. She was terribly dehydrated, malnourished, and too weak to even eat on her own. "But she had a will to live," says Linda. "When I held a spoon of food near her, her little mouth would open and close even though she couldn't lift her head, so I'd poke in some food." The kitten, who appeared to be eight or nine weeks old, needed to be hand-fed every hour for an entire week before she began to regain her strength. But she didn't give up. They began to call her The Unsinkable Molly Brown.

"She ended up at my mom's place," Linda says. Round-the-clock care brought her back from the brink of death, but it still took a full two weeks before she began to act like a normal kitten. "Then," laughs Linda, "she became a pain in the butt. Boy, did she have spunk!"

One day soon after that the woman from the apartment phoned SCAT again to find out when she could get her kitten back. Linda was torn; she knew these people wanted the kitten, but it was her responsibility to ensure they would provide adequate care. Pets cost money and she wanted them to understand that if they couldn't afford to meet the kitten's needs, perhaps they shouldn't keep her. Many people of limited means find ways to provide for their animals, even if it means personal sacrifice, because they value them as family members. Maybe this woman truly did care about the kitten. There was only one way to tell. "There was a $200 veterinary bill that had to be paid if they wanted her back," she reports. "I explained this to the woman, and we never heard from her again."

Shortly afterwards, a couple came into the shelter with an unusual request. They were looking for a kitten and they weren't particular about colour or coat or sex or any other characteristic. The only thing they wanted was a kitten to match the name they'd already chosen. As soon as she heard the name, Linda knew The Unsinkable Molly Brown had found a home. They wanted a cat named Kaos, "chaos" spelled with a K. "Boy," Linda told them, "do I have a cat for you!"

Great Cat Stories

When cats and people come together like this, Linda knows all her work has been worthwhile. "Often adoptions just seem to match, as if they were destined to be. That's so satisfying. When people phone later and tell us how well it's going," she adds quietly, "that's very nice."

But the teamwork of her fellow cat-lovers is just as satisfying to Linda. "I definitely couldn't do this by myself," she emphasizes. "There are so many others who willingly joined me with their commitment and dedication to these animals."

She even has a code-phrase to call people to action. It came about after a volunteer called Linda late one night to say she thought she smelled smoke in the shelter. Linda immediately told her to start putting the cats into carriers; then she started calling volunteers. "Every time I got someone on the phone and said the words, 'Smoke at the shelter,' there were no questions, no hesitations," recalls Linda. "Twelve volunteers were at the shelter within ten minutes." As it turns out, the smell was due to a burnt-out fluorescent light ballast in the gas station next door, but in talking with the firefighters, Linda discovered that they hadn't known there was an animal shelter in the area. "They immediately put us on their list, so if there are ever any problems in the future with a nearby business, they'll be sure to monitor the safety of our animals," says Linda.

Linda and her co-workers spend their time and energy caring for felines who will never thank them. In fact, many

The Cold, Hostile Streets

Molly Brown grown — now named Kaos

of their charges would do everything possible to avoid them. But that doesn't matter to the dedicated volunteers at SCAT. They know the cats are not to blame. Every feral cat eking out an existence on the fringes of civilization is there because somewhere, sometime, a human being has discarded a pet like so much garbage. Linda can't change what's already been done, but she's determined to try and prevent it from happening again. And in the meantime, she gives as much care as she can to those cats already living on the cold, hostile streets.

Chapter 3
The Secret of Simon Teakettle

"There are many intelligent species in the universe. They are all owned by cats."
Anonymous

Barbara Florio Graham doesn't look like a woman with a mysterious past. With over five decades of journalistic experience, one might expect the energetic Gatineau, Quebec writer to have long since lost the excitement of the creative process. But no, not Bobbi. Her love affair with writing and teaching is as strong as ever. Her career has brought not just international recognition but gifts, cards, and boatloads of fan mail.

She does, however, have a secret: her biggest success is due to an unexpected friendship with a cat named Simon.

When Bobbi moved from Chicago in 1967 she brought along her beloved cat, Mysti. But shortly after their arrival

The Secret of Simon Teakettle

Mysti died. "I felt terrible and decided I wouldn't get a cat again because the feeling was too awful when she died." However, she missed the easy companionship. Eventually she decided to get another cat, but this time not bond so closely with it. An older cat, she thought, would be much safer emotionally. She would be strict, she decided, right from the start. This cat would be just a cat to her, another creature to share her home. Nothing more. "So I answered an ad in *The Ottawa Citizen*," she recalls. The advertisement said the cat in question was a domestic shorthair, black, neutered, and free. He seemed like a good fit except for one thing: Bobbi had a perfect name picked out and this one was already named: Simon (his brother was Garfunkle).

She explains, "We had a little saying from Don Quixote when I was growing up, about the pot calling the kettle black. I'd always called a black cat a 'teakettle' and said if I ever had one I'd call him Teakettle." She shrugged her shoulders and took him anyway. Simon was very frightened at the change in his life. He slunk around the house, hiding under furniture, scuttling behind doors. Bobbi had to work to gain his trust. But little by little, Simon responded. By the time he finally adjusted to Bobbi, her battle for a reserved attitude was lost; he'd wormed his way into her heart. "The ban on sleeping on my bed was lifted," she admits. Still, she hankered to use the name she'd imagined. First she tried calling him Simon the Teakettle, but it didn't quite seem right. Then she happened upon Simon Teakettle. "As soon as I said it, I knew it was the perfect name." She had no idea the effect this name would have on her life and her career.

Bobbi had been certain of her calling early in life. Her first story, submitted when she was nine years old, was printed in *Humpty Dumpty Magazine* and earned her the grand total of five dollars. At the age of 11 she sold a story to *Jack and Jill* for $10. "That's when I decided to be a writer," says Bobbi. "I'd like to know of anyone else who doubled their income in two years — before they hit puberty!"

She knew journalism was the right path for her in spite of the challenges of being a self-employed, freelance writer. At the time Simon Teakettle joined her life, Bobbi was writing a regular column for a small community newspaper on a volunteer basis, as a favour to the editor, on top of her other writing jobs. The paper was still short of material but, in spite of great reader response, Bobbi hesitated to contribute more. Then, on a whim, she wrote a cheeky little piece from the viewpoint of her cat, signed it Simon Teakettle, and sent it in. To her surprise, the editor loved it. Bobbi made him swear to keep Simon Teakettle's identity a secret. "Originally it was so that people wouldn't realize I was writing half the paper," quips Bobbi. But it quickly turned into something more. People began to ask, "Who is this Simon Teakettle?" As the mystery gained momentum, someone on the local CBC radio station mentioned him. Soon Simon's words were quoted almost every week.

But despite his growing celebrity, Bobbi didn't receive a

penny for the columns she and her cat wrote for the paper. So she started looking at possible paying markets for Simon's material. "In 1975 I took a poem 'he'd' written and sent it to *Cats Magazine,* and they took it," recalls Bobbi. "I began sending his stuff off to other radio stations, too."

Then the axe fell. The small community newspaper was purchased by a large weekly and word came down that almost all the copy would be cut. The new owners weren't interested in any of the regular writers, except for one column: this spicy, funny column by the mysterious Simon Teakettle. "My own column was cut," Bobbi protests with mock outrage, "but they kept the Simon Teakettle column." Not only that, but Simon Teakettle would now be paid for his words, $15 each week. Simon had begun to earn his kitty litter.

In Simon Teakettle's voice, Bobbi began to write for other publications. She still wrote her own genuine articles and columns, but with the Simon Teakettle columns, something else emerged from her creativity. In her entertainment columns, for instance, she'd report properly on the highbrow events around town. But as Simon Teakettle, she'd mercilessly skewer anything pretentious. "I would be invited to these things to write seriously for my other columns, but he would take the same events and write from his humorous, sarcastic, superior-to-humans persona." And Simon got away with the most preposterous stunts, such as "sneaking under the skirts of the governor general's wife at the opening of an exhibit."

Throughout the development of this alter ego, the bond

between Bobbi and Simon continued to grow. He was more than just companionship for her; he was inspiration, a true muse. "Simon Teakettle was always the fun side of my writing," says Bobbi.

Simon Teakettle was becoming very well known, and Bobbi knew it was time to take the next step. "He was so big I worried that the name would be stolen, so I started my own company." She called it "Simon Teakettle, Ink." She explains, "'Ink' is a play on words: a symbol of the human-feline partnership. Ink means writing and ink means black." What does Simon think of this? "He owns it all. The company, the website, the e-mail and the business account are all in the company name," reports Bobbi. "*He* is the bigwig — so of course he thinks *he's* incorporated."

In spite of his upward mobility, the real person behind the classy black cat remained a mystery. The only ones to know the truth were a few local CBC executives. "Simon's 'interviews' were always handled by me, on the phone," says Bobbi. "For the Halloween shows we did I would begin by saying Simon wasn't available because he was still out trick or treating, but that he'd left a message for me to read. I handled other shows in a similar fashion."

Bobbi soon became known as "the lady who shares Simon Teakettle's typewriter." Later, as technology advanced, she became "the lady who shares Simon Teakettle's computer," and eventually "the lady who shares Simon Teakettle's office."

The Secret of Simon Teakettle

In 1981, Bobbi had Simon enter a contest on a new program from the CBC in Edmonton called *RSVP*. Host David Lennick and Simon exchanged letters, and soon Simon was a regular on the program. After four years of regular guest spots for Simon on *RSVP*, Bobbi was disappointed to learn that the show was being moved to Toronto. But soon after, Bobbi scheduled a workshop in Toronto and she and Simon decided to look up the host. "Simon wrote to Lennick and said that if he'd provide a phone number, 'The Lady' would arrange a meeting," says Bobbi. "Lennick arrived at the meeting with a delightful stuffed mouse wearing a dress and bonnet as a gift for Simon. He told me he'd finally discovered my identity just before he left Edmonton, after an exhaustive search by his staff."

Friendships fostered by Simon appeared to be long lasting; even though Lennick hasn't worked for the CBC for many years, he and Bobbi remain friends. Many other well-known people at the CBC claim friendship with Simon Teakettle as well; cards and letters from Mary Lou Finlay, Vicki Gabereau, and Jurgen Gothe are among his cherished mementoes.

Simon Teakettle's career was most definitely on the rise. He was a contestant on *The Radio Show*. He was included in Lennick's new program, *Night Camp*. He contributed to *Basic Black* and *Morningside*, and was asked to exchange on-air letters with Bill Richardson's cat on the summer program, *Cross Words*. Simon's letters appeared in *The Globe & Mail* and *The Toronto Star*. He was quoted in the Canadian book,

Purring is My Business. As well, he found his way into *The Bedside Book of Celebrity Gossip*, published in the United States by Crown Group. "Simon Teakettle was one of only a handful of Canadians quoted in the book — in company with Pierre and Margaret Trudeau — and the only cat!" says Bobbi with pride.

By the time Simon was 10 years old he was writing a regular column for the *West Quebec Post*, as well as columns for the Canadian children's magazine *JAM* and the US national newsletter, *PURRRRR!* Bobbi was being paid for all of them. He had a publicity mug shot next to his columns and became known as "The Classy Cat in the Black Fur Tuxedo."

Then, at the height of his fame, the unthinkable happened: Simon Teakettle lived the last of his nine lives. Despite her resolution years ago to never grieve for a cat again, Bobbi missed Simon dreadfully. He was more than a friend and partner; he was a Name. He had responsibilities. He had a readership that adored him. A media tour was in the offing. She couldn't let them down. Bobbi knew what she had to do.

Simon Teakettle, she decided, must go on. And that meant she had to once more take a chance with her affection. This time she knew there would be no holding back.

"I went to the SPCA," she relates, "and told them I needed a kitten to match this mugshot." Simon Teakettle was a long-time supporter of the SPCA and everyone there knew of him, so they were most helpful. But, as luck would have it, there was an unexpected shortage of black kittens that spring. There were orange kittens, grey kittens, calico kittens, and tabby kittens, but no handsome all-black kittens. Then a feral cat was brought in with her litter of five — a tabby, a spotted black-and-white, and three black kittens.

Feral kittens can have a hard time adjusting to domesticity and Bobbi wasn't sure this would work. The mother was essentially wild. The other kittens scratched and scrambled to get away from her. Then she picked up one, a little black male with a tiny locket of white at his throat. "He sat in the palm of my hand and just looked at me. And I knew. This was the one." The shelter workers were sceptical, but Bobbi's certainty convinced them. Simon Teakettle the Younger, known as Tiki, went home with Bobbi. A new chapter in the Simon Teakettle saga began.

From early kittenhood, Simon Teakettle the Younger showed unusual interest in everything human. "Although he was born in a barn to a feral mother with grey tabby markings, he appears to have a significant portion of Siamese genes," says Bobbi. "He is vocal, smart, and uses his paw like many Siamese do. He's also very Siamese in his body type: lean and compact, with a narrow face."

Since Bobbi knew Tiki would have to face the spotlights, she decided to put these personality traits to good use: she trained him. "He responds to many commands including: come, stay, sit, give me your paw, sit up, catch it and get down." But why stop there? Tiki also understands more complex questions, such as: Do you want to go on the front porch or in the backyard? (He responds by going to the door he prefers.) Would you like a fresh drink? (He goes into the bathroom, jumps on the counter where his water bowl is, and lifts his paw.) Where's your bear? (He finds his teddy bear.)

"I have also taught him the concept of ball," adds Bobbi. "He knows the word means anything in the shape of a ball, regardless of its size, colour or composition." When she asks him to "touch the ball," and identify it in an assortment of other items, he can do it, whether the ball in question is a sparkly, fuzzy green ball, a small yellow plush ball, a large patchwork plastic ball, or a purple rubber ball with a bell inside.

"He has quite a repertoire now," Bobbi says proudly. "I try to teach him a new behaviour every year." He even knows when he's been naughty. "The other day I told him, 'You better take a nap.' Off he trotted, right away." She smiles, remembering. "I'd sent him to his room!"

Bobbi also insisted Tiki learn to appreciate the local wildlife as 'paws-off' entertainment, rather than as snacks. "He's learned not to chase the birds," she says. "He knows that if he chases them, they fly away and don't come back. So he lies quietly in the foliage and watches."

He and the squirrels have even devised an elaborate game. Tiki sits and watches them, and when they start to run he gives them a head start. They scamper up the tree, he stretches full-length against the tree trunk, then he goes back to wait for them to come down so the game can start again. "When the babies first descend from the tree they're not afraid of him," says Bobbi. "He's extremely respectful of them because they don't know the rules yet. So he'll just sit six or eight feet away, quiet as can be, watching them eat their seeds."

Teaching a cat *not* to hunt isn't difficult, but it takes a great deal of patience. "I'd go outside with him on a leash," Bobbi explains. "Whenever he made predatory body postures or noises, I'd scold him and pull him back. Sometimes I'd go out and sit with him, wait for a bird or squirrel to appear, then hold him on my lap and encourage him to sit quietly and watch. He is really smart."

In fact, he's decided that if he can't chase the birds, no one else can either. "He actually keeps other neighbourhood cats away from 'his' birds. These are pets, friends — not food. Of course," adds Bobbi, "I'd never let a cat outside when he's hungry. I always tell him to finish his breakfast first."

Although Simon the Younger is a very different cat from Simon the Elder, the public persona has remained consistent. Words continue to appear under his picture and Simon Teakettle has kept his loyal followers happy. Bobbi reports that she and Simon Teakettle are currently waging an anthology war. "We're published in 21 anthologies altogether. He's in 4; I'm in 17." Their award-winning book, *Mewsings/Musings*, contains humorous essays by Bobbi as well as a compilation of the best-loved pieces of both Simon the Elder and Simon the Younger.

Great Cat Stories

Tiki is now 16 years old, a healthy, active bundle of energy. But Bobbi knows she has to cherish each day with him. Sharing her career with her cats has brought Bobbi far more than professional success. "I've always said that one of my problems is that I write for work and I write as a hobby," she says. "I really think I have learned a lot about tapping my own creativity by adopting a totally different persona." Of course, inspiration is nurtured by all of the senses, including touch. The act of petting an animal is known to have a calming effect on the body, while stimulating the creativity centres in the right side of the brain. It's hard not to smile when you're with a cat, a benefit that can sometimes be distracting. "For my very serious writing I sometimes have to wait till he's napping," Bobbi wryly confesses.

In spite of the fact that Barbara Florio Graham is a professional journalist with three books to her credit, she knows the real score. The Simon Teakettles, both the Elder and the Younger, have earned their own cat food and kitty litter from the get-go. "This is my business, but I work for him," she states matter-of-factly. "After all, I open the food. I clean the litterbox."

Chapter 4
Prescription Pets: Cats Who Heal

> *"There are two means of refuge from
> the miseries of life: music and cats."*
> Albert Schweitzer

In 1994, Al Hodgkinson sat in the doctor's office reeling from the news he'd just been given. "Put your affairs in order," the doctor said. "You have terminal prostate cancer." Al did have the option of trying radiation therapy in the hope that it might extend his life for one more year, but he was told not to expect anything more.

Al and his wife Pat looked at each other and knew they had to try everything possible, no matter how unlikely. Thirty-five radiation treatments later, Al wondered if his last year of life would be worth living. He returned home in a wheelchair, barely able to move his legs.

Great Cat Stories

In spite of the bleak prognosis Al had been given, the radiation treatment was successful; his cancer was defeated. The treatments themselves, however, resulted in nerve damage that left him with sensory deficits, mobility problems, and pain. "Until a couple of months ago, a shower was my only means of bathing," he explains. "When sitting in a tub, I could not establish whether the water temperature was hot or cold." But it was the pain that made him wonder whether the cure was worse than the disease. When the throbbing struck, even powerful analgesics didn't last long enough to control agony so intense that sometimes all Al could do was count the minutes, tears rolling down his face, until he could take another painkiller.

One night while Al and Pat were watching television the pain was especially severe. Pat sat beside him helplessly as he struggled to contain his misery until it was time for his next pill. "About 20 minutes later," Al recalls, "Pat asked me if the pain had stopped." He realized he was no longer crying and the pain had indeed subsided. "She asked me to look at what was sitting on my lap ... and purring." It was their cat, Precious.

Precious, an orphan from birth, was the only one of her litter to survive. In 1993, when her first home with Al and Pat's daughter didn't work out due to allergies, Al volunteered to take her back to the shelter. They made a brief stop at home first and within minutes Precious had endeared herself to both of them. The shelter was forgotten and Precious has been with the Hodgkinsons ever since.

Al and Pat began to notice that Precious exhibited certain behaviours only when Al's pain was at its worst. She seemed to know when the pain reached its peak, and at that point she'd leap onto Al's lap and start purring. Of course she'd hop up onto his lap at other times as well, but her manner was different at those times, and she didn't purr. It was as if she was acutely aware of Al's emotions, and recognised his painful episodes as the times when he needed her talents the most. "We started to realize that this had been happening for quite a while, even if we didn't understand why or how," says Al. One theory is that the sound waves of the feline purr are in the same range as the ultrasound used to manage pain disorders. "Gee," Al jokes, "I have my own free ultrasound machine — and it comes with a fur coat!"

Some of his medical caregivers are sceptical, but none of them can deny the improvement in Al's health. Most significantly, he has long surpassed the one-year extension that the radiation therapy was supposed to give him. "I've progressed from a wheelchair to two canes to one cane. Three years ago, I went to no canes at all. And," adds Al, "today and for the past six years, I take no prescription medication at all. If and when pain strikes, Precious seems to know, and when she comes ... pain runs away."

Al still has pain from time to time, but the intensity and frequency are now within tolerable levels — and if they get out of hand, Precious always hops up into his lap to provide her special therapy.

* * *

Experiences like Al's provide the foundation for animal assisted therapy, or pet visitation. Retired nurse Sadey Guy of Sidney, BC, knows that animals can play a role alongside modern medicine to promote healing; she's been immersed in both all her life. Born in Wales to parents who were master and matron of an English hospital, Sadey literally grew up surrounded by patients. As a child she often visited the wards, sometimes bringing her rabbits or other pets along. It was a comfortable environment for her but she never intended to be a nurse herself. "No, Mom," she remembers telling her mother, "I like people. I can't stick needles into them."

Famous last words! Sadey Guy became a nurse after all, and loved her work. When it came time to retire she couldn't imagine leaving the hospital setting permanently. Then she had an idea. In her last few years of nursing she'd been working with elderly patients in extended care. Sadey had witnessed wonderful relationships spring up between patients and resident pets. "It was the natural thing to do in those days," she says. "In the 70s, when animal therapy first began to catch on, animals weren't often allowed in acute care hospitals but they were welcomed into extended care facilities." Aquarium fish and birds were often permanent residents, but at that time even cats and dogs began to be welcomed into hospitals.

Prescription Pets: Cats Who Heal

Toby, a collie-cross who lived in the extended care facility where Sadey worked, took his job very seriously. He sat near various patients in turn, allowing them to pet him and talk to him. Toby seemed to be aware of the people whose emotional needs he could fill and gravitated towards them. Then, while outside one day, Toby was hit by a car and badly injured. He recovered but he was never the same. A staff member adopted him, and Toby continued to visit residents, but he wasn't able to live among them anymore. "I started to think it was too much for the dogs," says Sadey. "Cats love people, but they'll excuse themselves when it's time for a break. Dogs will stay by their people forever. Dogs can get worn out."

Sadey had wanted to bring animals and patients together, but wasn't sure how she should go about it. "When I retired in 1988 just after Toby's accident, I thought, 'That's what I should do!'" Sadey had already made many hospital visits with Duchess, her ageing Welsh corgi, and her black cat, Tiger. She wanted to do more.

She contacted the local Society for the Prevention of Cruelty to Animals (SPCA), because she knew the inspectors already did occasional hospital visits with dogs or cats awaiting adoption. Maybe, she thought, they would lend some of their pets out for visitation purposes. But she quickly realized that wasn't a solution. The SPCA naturally wanted their animals to be adopted, not borrowed. And patients didn't want to have to get to know a strange animal each visit. Sadey's idea was growing, but it needed structure. She continued to look for people to help her and eventually connected with Volunteer Victoria, an association that works to help volunteer groups. There, Sadey's idea gathered momentum. With the help of Volunteer Victoria, the group she envisioned became an official registered non-profit association. The Pacific Animal Therapy Society was born. When it was time for P.A.T.S. Pets, as the group is called, to find a mascot, Sadey knew exactly who it would be. Toby, who lived until the distinguished age of 17, perfectly symbolised Sadey's vision. "We adopted Toby as our logo for P.A.T.S. Pets," says Sadey, "so he lives on in love."

Knowing health care as she does Sadey solicited the input of medical administration, tailoring the program to best meet the specific requirements of hospitals, retirement homes, and other facilities in which residents could benefit from interaction with animals. "We talked to the volunteer co-ordinators at the big hospitals," she says, "and asked them what they wanted from us."

Most visits are on an individual basis, and usually last for about an hour. While the majority of animal visitors are dogs, P.A.T.S. therapy pets include cats, rabbits, birds, goats, and even more unusual guests such as a llama, a miniature horse, and a snake. "We've found that bonding forms with certain folk and all three — the pet, the owner and the patient — receive blessings through this friendship," says Sadey.

Human volunteers receive orientation regarding safety

procedures, confidentiality, and other issues relevant to the facilities they visit. Throughout the year, volunteers have the opportunity to attend workshops presented by health care professionals and receive special training in listening and support skills. They even work on a rotating schedule to ensure that this public service is available every day of the year. "Sometimes people go to a specific hospital once a week for regularly scheduled visits," says Sadey. "Other times we go as a group."

Most volunteers have one pet that they use for visitation; a few alternate between more than one. But each pet is carefully evaluated before being allowed into the program. The requirements are strict: they must be in good health, fully vaccinated, and temperamentally suitable. They must be comfortable in strange surroundings and they must not panic at strange noises or rough contact. Dogs must have basic obedience. Cats must come when called. "In a hospital basins get dropped, carts clatter and clang," explains Sadey. "Alzheimer's patients might pull an ear or tail without knowing, or a spastic person might accidentally knock into the animals when they reach out." Of course, Sadey adds, to protect fragile skin, pets' nails must be kept trimmed.

It's not a job description that fits a lot of felines. Strangers and loud noises are bad enough, let alone a weekly manicure! But Sadey doesn't waver on her rules. "You want a cat who will look around to see what's happening, but not bolt." Sadey knew that the right cats could make great therapy pets.

Great Cat Stories

The first cat to fit the bill was a big, beautiful, silver-tipped Persian named Sylvia Serina. Her owner had fostered many stray animals over the years, so Sylvia was accustomed to lots of different faces coming and going. Sadey hoped this accepting attitude would carry over to the patients she'd meet on the ward, and it did. For over three years, until she and her owner moved, Sylvia Serina spent countless hours purring quietly on the laps of her bedridden friends, comforting them with her warmth. "I think the purring helps folks realize how content and happy they are to be with them," says Sadey.

Then there was Duke, an ordinary ginger shorthair who loved to be where the action was. "Nothing worried him," says Sadey. "He'd sit in a lap, or wander around. You could take him in to visit children as well as adults." In fact, the children were his biggest fans. During his time in the program Duke worked his way through almost every hospital department, including the surgical and rehabilitation wards where many of the kids he visited were in for lengthy stays. Duke quickly became a favourite among them. Then, to the sorrow of his many friends, Duke suddenly died. Visitation days weren't quite so special anymore.

His owner, Diane Taylor, wanted to continue what Duke had started so she went to the local SPCA, hoping to find another cat to fill the void. She came home with Simon. At 17 pounds of pure muscle, he was a beautiful, powerful cat. But would he have the right personality? Duke was a hard act to follow. "We weren't sure how he would do," recalls Sadey. "We waited awhile before testing him." Time, they hoped, would help Simon adjust to his new life enough to be comfortable meeting new people. Then one day Simon was ready. They introduced him to a patient who had just finished her lunch. He sat down on the bed beside her and when she offered him her leftover milk, he politely accepted.

When Simon realized the rewards of being a hospital visitor he threw himself into the role with great enthusiasm. And, like his predecessor, he's learned to love children. At a visit to a pre-school class Simon makes himself right at home, sitting at a low table among the students. If he's in the right mood he offers them his paw, much to their delight. "Simon is coming along just fine," says Sadey. "He's become so much like Duke."

Sadey knows that not everyone likes cats. In fact, sometimes she'll be told that a certain patient doesn't want a visit from *any* of the animals. She understands and doesn't let it bother her, because more often the response is just the opposite. "Just as many say, 'No dogs, but I love cats!'" she comments. "Some people get very emotional. They hold their arms out, calling, 'Bring him here, bring him here. Leave him here!'"

That emotional reaction touches a chord with Sadey. She doesn't have a cat now, but hopes to have one again soon. "I miss my cat terribly," she admits. Until the right cat comes along she keeps busy with her dog, a Welsh terrier named

Dylan Thomas, who has seemingly unlimited energy and enthusiasm. "He is wonderful," says Sadey. "A very feeling creature. He helps many folks — including me."

Joy, like illness, can be contagious. Happiness, like medicine, can heal. Whenever a cheery visit from an animal lifts the spirits of someone sick or in pain, Sadey knows her work has been worthwhile. People like Al Hodgkinson simply reaffirm her belief that pets affect our health in far more ways than we understand. It's the kind of story that keeps the volunteers at Pacific Animal Therapy Society going back, even when their contributions come at an emotional cost. Every time they look for an old friend only to find an empty bed, they are reminded that each visit could be the last. "Still," says Sadey, "we would not change our volunteering experience. We love it, and its rewards are unbelievable."

The rewards took on a tangible form recently when Sadey Guy received the Valued Elder Recognition Award, sponsored by the University of Victoria Centre on Aging. A tree with a plaque honouring Sadey's contribution to humanity, society, and community now grows on the university grounds. What started as a bridge between Sadey's professional life and her retirement has grown into something much larger. Sharing the healing power of pets through Pacific Animal Therapy Society reminds people — volunteers and patients alike — that life is good. "There's a world outside," says Sadey, "that's worth getting better for."

Chapter 5
Miracle Babies

"Where there is great love there are always miracles."
Willa Cather

Caroline Cameron and Nancy Hutchinson knew that if they were going to breed cats, they had to do it right. That meant running it as a business and treating their cats as the valuable assets they were. So the two friends turned their London, Ontario home into the Katzanova Himalayan Cattery, breeding champion Himalayan cats — registered, health-guaranteed, and fully socialized. They quickly established a firm reputation in the competitive world of cat shows as breeders of quality, well-nurtured kittens. But behind the ambition Caroline had a secret wish. "I wanted a seal point as a pet," she confesses. "As breeders we weren't keeping any Himmies as pets. When you're a breeder you are supposed to think with your head, not your heart."

But Himalayans are a breed that appeals to the heart.

They are the result of an attempt to create a Persian-Siamese cross, an idea that proved more difficult to realize than breeders expected. The goal was to obtain a cat that combined the compact, stocky ("cobby") body and long, luxurious coat of a Persian with the colour points and blue eyes of the Siamese. Many litters were bred in which kittens that had one trait didn't have the other. Finally breeders found success and in 1950 the Himalayan breed was born. They are now one of the most popular pedigreed felines in the cat fancy, that elite group of cat-lovers dedicated to refining their chosen breeds. Seal-point Himalayans, perhaps the best known colour variety, are truly stunning: snub-nosed faces, deep blue eyes, and long beige body fur tipped with rich, dark brown on the ears, mask, paws, and tail. But as beautiful as these cats are, it's their personality that appeals to people. "Himalayans are similar to a Persian but with much more of a spark," says Caroline. "They love to follow you around like a puppy-dog!"

Caroline and Nancy loved their cats and were committed to spending whatever time, energy, and money was necessary to improve the breed. Caroline explains, "Breeding is not a big money-maker. We wanted to jump in with both feet and do it properly. If you do it right, that means registering every litter with the Canadian Cat Association and keeping very tight records: every vaccination, every time we used antibiotics, it all had to be accounted for. All the adult cats had to be tested for polycystic kidney disease, feline leukemia, and feline immunodeficiency virus."

Miracle Babies

So Caroline set her dream to one side and continued with the practical work of running a cattery. And there was a lot of it. "I quit my job to be home with these guys," she says. "I had to clean litter boxes three times a day and scrub the floors with bleach and water. To maximize efficiency and ensure the well-being of the cats, Caroline and Nancy aimed to have two males and eight to ten females in their cattery. At one time, Katzanova had 12 adults and 18 kittens, but they were definitely prepared; each room in the house had a different purpose. "One room was for mating only; the males lived there full-time," says Caroline. "We had one room as a nursery only and one room for females that don't get along with other females. Fortunately, we only had a couple like that. The others got along fantastically well, especially considering the number of cats we had."

After two years in the business they'd acquired a wealth of experience. They'd learned how to evaluate kittens shortly after birth to decide which would be raised for showing, which should be kept for breeding, and which ones would be sold as pets. So when Caroline was looking over one particular litter, she knew there was one especially good one in it. "He looked like he'd make a good breeder," she recalls, "possibly even a show cat." But they'd also learned that the breed could be somewhat delicate. When she found that this young hopeful's eyes had both opened when it was only three days old, her heart dropped; kittens' eyes don't usually open until around 10 to 14 days of age. "They were closed again by the next morning, but it was just long enough for an infection to start."

"Off to the veterinarian I went with this tiny newborn. I got ointment and medication to clear up the infection," says Caroline. "The vet instructed me to clean the kitten's eyes several times a day, and showed me how to do it, and I did exactly that." But while cleaning the area one day it became all too obvious that she was losing the battle. As she moved the swab gently across his tiny face she was horrified to see what looked like part of the eye dissolve onto the cotton ball.

The veterinarian confirmed her fears. The eye was gone. But there was still worse news: the infection that destroyed the eye was threatening to overwhelm the tiny body. Even with round-the-clock care, the vet warned, the kitten had little chance of survival. He was too small and too young to cope with such an assault on the system. In every way, the odds were against him.

But for Caroline, the smallest chance was enough to keep her fighting. She kept him in a box beside her at all times, with a heating pad and baby receiving blankets to keep him warm. Hour after hour she treated him with various remedies: tiny amounts of medication, antibiotic drops, and fluids by mouth, but there was little response.

It was touch and go. At one point the veterinarian advised Caroline to prepare to lose him. But she kept hoping for a miracle. Throughout the night she kept up her ministrations, reminding him that she was there and that he should

Miracle Babies

keep fighting. Morning came with no change but still she continued. He wasn't getting better, but nor was he getting worse; that was enough reason to keep trying.

Then, in the microscopic battle waging within the tiny body, the tide turned. Caroline's hopes surged as she saw the kitten make a few feeble movements. "Within 24 to 48 hours I noticed an improvement in him," she recalls. "He started crawling on his tummy and showing a few livelier signs." Because he was too weak to nurse, Caroline had been feeding him with an eyedropper, giving him formula specially designed to replace mother cat's milk. Hour by hour, day by day, she watched him as he fed. It wasn't just her imagination. He was definitely improving. "Once he looked stronger," says Caroline, "I put him back with his mother and he started nursing again." This was a hurdle; could he compete with his littermates and get the nourishment he needed?

Apparently he could; he continued to grow and gain weight. Then his other eye opened up. This was the sticking point. A cat with one blind eye can live a normal life; helping a cat cope with complete blindness would be a huge challenge. But to Caroline's relief the eye was normal. "The veterinarian checked it and said it was all fine. The minute I knew he was going to make it I said, 'Nancy, I've got to keep him!'"

And so the Katzanova Cattery had its very first pet Himmie. Himalayan kittens are born completely white, so Caroline endured several weeks of suspense wondering what colour he would be. To her delight, this kitten turned out to be the handsome seal point she had secretly wanted for years. He was to become her pride and joy, never to be bred, sold, or shown — a cat just for her. Patch Adams, as she named him, had survived against all odds and she couldn't let him go.

"Once Patch fully recovered, he was a real delight. What is so neat about the Himalayan is that they love the human touch and they like to be wherever you are. They will follow you from room to room, all around the house." As Patch has regained his strength and continues to grow, he follows Caroline everywhere. He sits at the stairs watching her when she goes out, and when she returns he runs to greet her.

Patch is very much a hands-on cat, accustomed to being toted around in Caroline's arms and curling up in her lap for a cuddle whenever she sits down. "Patch became my new best friend, my buddy, the love of my life," says Caroline. "He's the seal point Himmie I had so desperately wanted."

No matter how much they are cherished, most cattery cats eventually end up somewhere other than where they started. Kittens are born and raised for the specific purpose of being sold to loving homes. Retired breeding cats are placed with people who want adults rather than youngsters. Caroline and Nancy have said good-bye to many much-loved cats over the years, but one cat in particular, Patch Adams, Caroline's One-Eyed Jack, isn't going anywhere.

* * *

Miracle Babies

Birman breeder Betty Sleep of Coles Island, New Brunswick, knows the rich history behind her chosen breed. According to ancient legend in Burma (Myanmar), a white temple cat named Sinh sat on the chest of the dying priest, Mun-ha, before the statues of the goddess. When the holy man died the cat was transformed. His feet remained white like the priest's beard, but his head, tail, and legs turned a rich brown, the colour of the earth, and his eyes took on the goddess statue's deep blue glance. Today, the "Sacred Cat of Burma" is known as the Birman. Not to be confused with either the Himalayan or the Burmese, the Birman is an intelligent, gentle breed distinguished by pure white gloves on all four feet.

But romance and glamour aside, to breed and show champion Birman cats is a demanding occupation. Betty was just catching her breath after hand-rearing an orphan kitten and was anticipating a nice, quiet season in the cattery. Late one evening in August 2002, however, she realized it was not to be. Betty was finishing up some paperwork at her computer when she noticed one of her pregnant females acting suspiciously. This cat wasn't due to give birth for nearly a week, so Betty was shocked when she found what looked like a kitten's head emerging from the mother. She grabbed her delivery supplies and took the cat to the birthing box. "Once there," she says, "I discovered it was an 'old' placenta." The placenta, which links mother and baby together before birth, had detached from the uterus; without a healthy placenta, there's no way for the baby to get vital nutrients, including oxygen. X-rays had revealed earlier that three kittens would be born. Now only two would be born alive.

Hoping to save the remaining kittens, Betty rushed the mother cat to her veterinarian. She suspected a Caesarean section was the only chance for the remaining kittens, even though they weren't ready to be born yet. But either way it was risky. Cats have a normal gestation period of 63 days; even a couple of days can make the difference between full-term and premature babies. At Day 58, these kittens were scraping the edge of viability. "If you have a dead kitten," explains Betty, "chances are it will decompose, and not necessarily quickly. By the time you realize it's decomposing your queen (the mother cat) may be compromised and your other kittens dead." There was no choice. The kittens would have to be delivered surgically.

By this time it was past midnight. The veterinary team set to work, preparing to perform a Caesarean section. Soon the first kitten, a perfectly formed male, was born. But he wasn't breathing and his skin was white, suggesting blood circulation had stopped some time ago. "I could pretty much tell by looking that he had been dead for several hours," says Betty. "He had no reflexes, no reactions, nothing."

Still, you never know. Betty massaged and stimulated the little body, hoping against hope that she was wrong and this kitten might still live. Rubbing and massaging them this way mimics the mother cat's rough licking and helps stimulate

Miracle Babies

their respiratory system. "I was still working on the first one when the vet came out of the operating room," recalls Betty. "He had his hands cupped. I looked inside and he held what looked like a little purple grape. We just sort of stood there and stared at it." She passed the first kitten to someone else and laid this tiny one out on the towels to start resuscitation efforts. In a kitten of normal size, Betty would put a square of gauze over the muzzle before blowing into it to stimulate respiration. But a two-inch square of gauze was bigger than this little speck's entire body. Betty did the best she could, encouraging the heartbeat by tapping the wee chest and puffing softly into the tiny nostrils from time to time. Slowly the kitten's skin began to lose its dusky purple tinge. From the operating room Betty could hear the veterinarian yelling at her to keep going. Suddenly, the kitten's body shuddered and the tiny female began to breathe.

Newborn kittens are very susceptible to heat loss, so during her efforts Betty kept the infant on a terry-cloth covered hot water bottle. "A towel was too big to use on her," recalls Betty, "so I used the corner of a face cloth." After about 15 minutes, enough vital oxygen reached the kitten's tissues to turn her skin a more normal pinkish colour. Finally Betty was able to take a break, pull back the cloth, and examine her properly. The relief of getting her breathing quickly faded. "It was like looking at a baby bird that had fallen out of its nest," she says. "She had those big dark eyes that have hardly any tissue over them. She had some hair on the top of her head and down her back, but the skin on her abdomen was so transparent you could almost see her organs." She was such a wisp that the scale wouldn't even register a weight. They guessed she weighed maybe 28 grams or one ounce, about the size of a Cadbury Easter Cream Egg. This baby was less than a third of the size of a normal kitten.

While Betty absorbed the reality of this kitten's fragile hold on life, she heard a squeaking sound from the operating room. One kitten at least, another female, was born healthy and energetic. But Betty knew — chances were slim that she'd still have two kittens in the morning.

To her surprise, both kittens lived through the night and Betty took all three cats home. Unfortunately, the mother cat refused to have anything to do with her new family. The premature delivery meant she didn't yet have the hormone levels that trigger the feline mothering instinct. Betty forced her to lie down with the kittens, hoping they'd get a bit of colostrum, the early milk rich in antibodies. But as soon as she was allowed, the mother cat leaped away from her babies. Betty kept hoping the mother would come around, but even with drug therapy she simply had no milk. After four days she had to admit it was a lost cause. Betty, with her feeding syringes, was the best mom these kittens would be getting.

Then one night, during a midnight feeding, Betty noticed the healthy kitten wasn't as vigorous as she'd been earlier. Knowing how quickly kittens can fade, she immediately paged her veterinarian. But even before the call had

Miracle Babies

been returned, the kitten died. "We were down to the grape," says Betty. Still, one was better than none. Betty determined to do everything she could to keep this last baby alive. She made her a little nest in a carrier with a heating pad and a sheepskin covering. She put the carrier next to her on the bed, and for the next several weeks Betty barely let the kitten out of her sight.

"I was afraid to name her," admits Betty. But the kitten had to be called something. By the alphabetical naming tradition followed by the cat fancy in North America, 2002 was year "Z." Then it hit her — the perfect "Z" name for a kitten who had resembled a grape at birth — Zinfandel. The unlikely survivor now had a handle. Betty and the kitten, dubbed "Fan," settled into a routine of sorts, but it was still difficult to believe this little Zinfandel might actually survive. "The only way I could lift her was to take my thumb and forefinger and gently pick her up by the barest flap of skin," says Betty. "Touching her was like touching a rubber glove. Even at two weeks she was just starting to look like a newborn kitten. I've never seen anything like it before and never want to see anything like it again. It's the smallest thing I've ever seen survive." The rule of thumb for feeding orphan kittens, according to Betty, is 24 millilitres of formula for every 100 grams of body weight. At that time, Fan was getting about six millilitres, just over a teaspoon, in a 24-hour period.

Betty hated to see Fan all alone. Cats rarely give birth to single kittens; this one had neither littermates nor a mother to keep her warm and cosy. So when Fan was about ten days old Betty got her a soft, terry-cloth covered beanbag toy with "It's a Girl!" written on it. Fan quickly learned to crawl underneath this toy, sandwiching herself between the warm pad below and the warmth reflected from above.

Then at three weeks, disaster struck. Artificial formula, while as good as science can make it, isn't mother cat's milk, and hand-reared kittens often have difficulty digesting it properly. Fan became severely constipated, a situation that could develop into a serious condition known as megacolon, where the bowel is permanently overstretched. For five days, Betty and the vet tried everything: more water, laxatives, corn syrup, and even enemas. Finally, though she was less than a month of age and weighed a mere seven ounces, they decided to try one last ditch effort: the kitten was put on solid foods. Amazingly, Fan's condition began to improve. Syringe-fed kitten food pureed with warm water eventually remedied the problem.

They weren't over the hump yet. Lack of sleep was beginning to take its toll on Betty. She began to wonder how much longer she could carry on without becoming ill herself. Between feedings she caught what sleep she could, propped upright with Fan's carrier next to her on the bed. But two weeks later, in the wee hours of the morning, Fan began vomiting. It would be another night without rest for Betty. "At that age — Fan was 31 days old — a kitten can dehydrate and die in a couple of hours," says Betty. And at 225 grams, Fan was still less than half the weight of a normal kitten the same age. She couldn't afford to lose even a gram.

By six o'clock in the morning Betty was at the veterinary clinic again. After a few hours of treatment with fluids and medication, Fan's vomiting stopped. Although the diarrhea continued throughout the day, the miniscule kitten looked like she was getting better. Betty took Fan home and hoped she'd continue to improve. "I put her back in her carrier and she crawled under her beanie, turned her back, and went to sleep." Betty lay back against the headboard and tried to relax, but sleep eluded her. Finally, at about four o'clock the next morning, she decided to feed Fan even though it wasn't quite time yet. "I reached in to pick her up and almost had a heart attack," recalls Betty. "She didn't move. Although she was breathing and her eyes were open, she was unresponsive. Her eyes were even starting to dry." At some point during the night Fan had crossed the line between sleep and unconsciousness and by sunrise, for the second time in two days, Betty and Fan were at the veterinary hospital.

"That morning was an absolute circus," says Betty. "We filled her with subcutaneous fluids until she looked like a water balloon." Dextrose and electrolyte solutions were put by tube into her stomach. There was no explanation for her sudden stupor and little hope she'd come out of it, but as long as the kitten kept breathing Betty determined to keep trying. It didn't seem to matter what they did, Fan lay motionless, barely alive. Finally, the veterinarian left to prepare for the regular workday. Betty continued, begging the weak little mite not to give up. For a long time nothing changed. Then, within a few moments, Fan twitched and seemed to regain consciousness. She couldn't stand up or even raise her head, but she was definitely awake. Within a short time the bloated kitten rolled over, her body sloshing with all the liquids that had been injected into her. When the veterinarian returned 30 minutes later, he was just in time to see Fan get up, stagger across the blanket, and nip Betty weakly on the hand in greeting. "I wish I'd had a camera!" Betty chuckles at the memory of his amazement. "That vet just stood there and stared at her. He picked her up, checked her over, and then just shook his head." Neither of them had ever seen anything so close to death come back to life.

To this day they don't know what caused Fan's near-fatal illness. But after that episode, the road slowly evened out and she matured into a beautiful cat. When Fan was seven months of age, Betty showed her for the first and last time. "She took six finals in ten rings, and wound up as fourth best all-breed kitten in the Eastern Canada region of the American Cat Fanciers Association," says Betty proudly. "She was perfectly marked, as Birmans go, with very good body structure."

Eventually Betty had to decide what to do with Fan. In spite of the Birman's success, Betty didn't feel Fan enjoyed being a show cat. Should she keep her as a pet? "I hung onto her because I was almost afraid to let her go," admits Betty. "That little heart-string — you can only stretch it so far!" She

Miracle Babies

hadn't let anyone know that Fan was available, but then an enquiry came from a couple she knew. They'd bought a kitten from Betty earlier, a full sister of Fan's from one of Fan's mother's subsequent litters. They desperately wanted a companion for this cat and were disappointed to learn that all Betty's kittens were already spoken for. But when they heard about Fan they wanted her immediately. "There are times when people ask for a cat and you know they're going to give it a good home," says Betty. "I thought this was where Fan was meant to go."

As a breeder, Betty knows that not all kittens can be saved. But when she's presented with a kitten fighting for life, she doesn't only think like a breeder. "I can't set it aside to die naturally," she says. "If it's trying that hard to live, it's my responsibility to give it every possible chance." It's a triumph of the will to live.

And for Betty, it's bearing witness to a miracle.

Chapter 6
The Cat-Man of Parliament Hill

*"You will always be lucky if you know how
to make friends with strange cats."*
Colonial American proverb

I t's a grey day. Scudding clouds reflect off the surface of the Ottawa River behind the black silhouettes of leafless trees. Lunchtime office crowds, dodging slower-paced tourists and canoodling lovers, scurry along the concrete walkways that wind in a ribbon between stony-faced buildings. Past the Queen Victoria statue, to the left of the central building, tourists pause. Behind the wrought-iron fence a cluster of ramshackle but sturdy hutches, wooden chairs, and pet food dishes attracts their attention. They appear out-of-place in the midst of the stately Victorian- and Gothic Revival-styled Parliament Buildings, but these little shelters have become an institution in their own right.

Cats live in these shelters, but they aren't the only animals to take protection from the elements here. Squirrels nibble the crumbs leftover in the dishes and a fat groundhog scuttles beneath the boardwalk. In the branches overhead, sparrows huddle together and pigeons ruffle their feathers impatiently. The creatures seem to wait in a hush of expectancy. Local employees hurry inattentively back to their offices as the lunch hour comes to an end — this peculiar gathering is nothing new to them — but visitors peer through the bars of the fence, curious about the wildlife-tolerant cats hovering nearby.

Then the air is filled with the majestic peal of the Peace Tower clock chiming one o'clock. As if on cue, more cats — many of whom spend their days largely hidden from view — begin to emerge from their secret haunts. Tourists scramble for their cameras.

A big orange-and-white male pads delicately up to the fence and sits gracefully. A fluffy grey tabby leaps down from a branch. An old calico yawns and stretches out from inside her wooden shelter. From nooks and crannies, high and low, they materialize. And they are not disappointed. It's lunchtime and René Chartrand, the Cat-Man, has arrived.

Once upon a time the plateau now known as Parliament Hill housed troops of soldiers and was called Barracks Hill. In the mid-1800s, the plateau became the location of the nation's government, which was housed in three buildings referred to as West Block, East Block, and Centre Block. Centre Block was destroyed by fire in 1916 and subsequently rebuilt, but the other two still stand as originally constructed. Today they hold the offices of senators and members of Parliament, as well as the House of Commons and the Senate itself. In addition to the more public figures, vast numbers of support personnel — aides, clerical workers, maintenance staff, and others — go about their duties. The politically ambitious can always be seen scurrying one way or another. But back when the buildings were first constructed, other creatures were scurrying besides upwardly mobile assistants. Parliament Hill had a serious rodent problem.

As far back as 1877, according to popular local history, cats were brought in to deal with the burgeoning vermin population on the Hill. These cats did their jobs, faithfully keeping mice and rats in check throughout the many buildings. They stayed out of the way and raised their offspring to do the same. In time, a colony of semi-domesticated cats was established on Parliament Hill. They belonged to no one and answered to no one.

But the cats did their job too well; as rodents became less of a problem, the cats on the Hill could no longer rely on their hunting skills to stay fed. The colony had turned into a shifting, growing group of homeless stray cats — hungry, wild, and desperately in need of someone to care for them. Since legend has it that this colony is made up of descendants of the mousers that once worked in Her Majesty's ser-

The Cat-Man of Parliament Hill

vice, many people felt they deserved better.

In the late 1970s, a compassionate cat-lover named Irene Desormeaux decided it was time to do something about it. They didn't need much — a little protection from the weather and a bit of food. So she had two little wooden shelters built, each large enough to house up to 20 cats. Round openings allowed easy access for the occupants, as well as contributing a whimsical appeal to the shelters. The houses were built to protect the cats from the elements. Waterproof shingles made for a dry roof and a wide overhang kept wind and snow from getting in. During the coldest months they were filled with straw for additional insulation.

But caring for a couple dozen cats was a great deal of work for this elderly woman. When her health began to decline she enlisted the help of her friend and neighbour, René Chartrand. In 1987, on her deathbed, Irene begged René to take care of the cats for her. He promised her he would look after them until another permanent caretaker could be found. He's done it ever since. Now people call him the Cat-Man of Parliament Hill. It's a natural part of his life.

"There have been cats there since I was a little boy and now I'm 83. We used to go there and look for litters of kittens," recalls René.

Today there are 28 felines residing on the Hill. Every day, no matter what the weather, René gets on the bus, travels across town, and trudges up to the shelter with his bag of supplies. Every day the ménagerie greets him with an assortment

René Chartrand

of welcomes: throaty purrs, waving tails, the occasional wash with a rough tongue. They seem to understand the depth of René's commitment to their well-being. He sets down his battered backpack and begins to pull out the day's feast. A few dishes go here, some go there, and one gets tucked into the corner where the shy cat hides out. Kibble goes into the metal dishes, at least eight of them, and he doesn't ignore the squirrels, now waiting safely in the branches overhead. Handfuls of peanuts are quickly scooped up and the squirrels, as easy in the presence of cats as they are with people, sometimes eat their treats perched on René's shoulder. Lastly, René reaches for the pigeon feed. He bends down, then tosses high. The pigeons take flight, flapping madly, snatching bits out of the air before landing on the concrete to clean up the rest.

People have complained about the pigeons from time to time and René has even been asked to stop feeding them. He responds the same way he's always responded to complaints about his work with the animals. He ignores them. Although everyone on the Hill knows him, not everyone values what he does for the cats and he's fully aware of this. From the government, the best he can hope for is that they continue to tolerate the cats' presence. Official support would be too controversial, so not a dime of tax-payers' money goes towards the cat sanctuary in spite of the fact that it's mentioned in the official pamphlet and on website information: Government of Canada — Explore the Hill — 2003:

> *Cat Sanctuary*
> *Tucked away in the trees that border the rear of Parliament Hill is a small community of stray cats. This area, which has now come to be called the "Cat Sanctuary," has been home to strays since the late 1970s. A volunteer ensures that the shelters used by the cats are maintained and that the animals are fed every day.*

The contrast between these modest shelters and the formality and tradition of the Parliament Buildings is a symbol of compassion, one of the important elements of Canadian society.

This anonymous "volunteer" doesn't let such nice-sounding but essentially empty sentiment get in the way of the job he's there to do. Nor does he let resentment mar his day. He talks to the animals as he works, scolding, cajoling, and laughing, simply living in the moment, oblivious to the bureaucracy that sizzles and bubbles all around him.

Over the course of the afternoon, René fills each individual dish as often as necessary and freshens the water supply. After the first feeding frenzy has subsided, René leans against the shelter and surveys his charges, checking for signs of illness or injury. He knows each of them. The big orange-and-white male, Brownie, is the boss. If necessary, he doesn't hesitate to put another cat in its place with a well-placed swat. But even Brownie doesn't mess with Big Mama. René says she's the most senior of the bunch, at least 20 years old. She spends her days sleeping — on a chair in the sun, or inside a shelter if it's cold or wet. Fluffy, the friendly grey-and-white tabby, seems to be the public relations consultant of the group. He goes up to anyone who will pet him, giving a quick rub and purr before going on to glad-hand another member of the crowd. But Blackie hovers around René even after the meal is over. He clearly enjoys the attention from his benefactor and is reluctant to stray far from him.

The Cat-Man of Parliament Hill

The cats look a little on the rustic side — twigs cling to Fluffy's tail and when one of the calicos rolls over for a tummy rub, she reveals white fur stained yellowish from the straw — but they appear as healthy and happy as most house cats. They are certainly well fed. René makes sure of that.

In addition to dry kibble he puts down a variety of other edibles, including different flavours of canned foods and a few semi-moist treats. René spends an average of $6000 a year supporting the cats — a substantial amount on his pensioner's fixed income. The cats finish their meals, settle down for a nice after-dinner wash, and gradually melt away into the background once again.

René relies on donations to help with expenses. A lockbox is bolted to the metal fence near his area, with a sign explaining the history of the sanctuary. The offerings rarely amount to much, but he is grateful for whatever assistance he receives. One year he was excited to learn that a major pet food manufacturer had agreed to donate a substantial amount of food to the sanctuary, with the possibility of becoming long-term supporters. The long-term part didn't pan out but René isn't one to look a gift-horse in the mouth. Veterinary care, the next big expense after food, is no longer an issue thanks to the generosity of the veterinarians and staff at Alta Vista Animal Hospital. All the cats are spayed or neutered and fully vaccinated. If René suspects one of the cats may be feeling under the weather, he contacts the staff and someone comes to pick up the cat in question.

This support has ensured that the cat's health needs are looked after, relieving René of his biggest concern. But even if no one ever stepped in to give him a hand, René would keep caring for the cats no matter what. "I'll keep doing this maybe until I'm 99! I feel good." He takes a deep breath and gestures with his arm. "I'm outside, in the fresh air. When I'm with the cats I am happy."

René's calling has cost him more than money over the years. His devotion, for which he received the Heroes for Animals Award from the Humane Society of Canada, has remained unswerving even in the face of huge personal loss. "I have always been faithful to my daily obligation to the animals on the Hill," says René, "even when my beloved wife, Rita, died during the winter of 1990." But René would be the first to say that his cats have paid him back everything and then some. Every throaty greeting rich in contentment reminds him of why he comes back every day.

The big question is, who will come every day when René can no longer care for the cats? He has occasional helpers but so far no one has committed to a regular schedule, let alone considered shouldering the full responsibility.

René doesn't waste time worrying about it. Perhaps he has faith that when the time comes, the right person will feel called to the task, the same way he was over 16 years ago. He's been working with the cats on the Hill longer than most politicians will ever be in office. He's taken no sick days, no vacation time, and he's never been paid. Neither he nor his

The Cat-Man of Parliament Hill

cats have any official power or status. But René appears satisfied as he goes about his humble duties. In a culture obsessed with influence, reputation, and competition, this is no mean achievement. Some things of value, the cats might be saying, can't be measured in money.

Chapter 7
The Making of Mister Got-to-Go

"There are few things in life more heart-warming than to be welcomed by a cat."
Tay Hohoff

Situated on the sparkling water of English Bay, two blocks from Stanley Park and five minutes from downtown Vancouver, the Sylvia Hotel is a lovely place to stay — if you're on vacation. But writer Lois Simmie wasn't staying at the hotel for a holiday. It was a welcome change of pace from life in Saskatoon, Saskatchewan, but it was still work, plain and simple. She and children's novelist Cora Taylor were under the gun to complete the final edits on Cora's second novel, and the deadline loomed ever nearer. "The publisher told us, 'We're going to shut you up in this hotel and you can't come out until you're finished'," recalls Lois. She knew they had to stay on task, but as she walked through the doors into the lobby after lunch one day she noticed a grey cat sitting with the clerk behind the front desk. She'd seen him earlier and wondered where he belonged; now it was clear that he was completely at home. He looked about himself as if to say, "Of course I live here! Every hotel needs a cat like me!"

A life-long cat lover, Lois couldn't walk past him without stopping to say hello. Since the age of seven, when her father brought home a tiny grey kitten named Tom, she's never been without a cat in her life. "I just fell in love with Tom," remembers Lois. They grew up together; in fact, Tom lived until Lois had a daughter of her own. When Lois reached out to pet the friendly cat on the counter, she couldn't help but remember the grey cat who had meant so much to her.

"What's his name?" Lois asked the front desk clerk.

"Got-to-Go," the clerk responded.

"*That's* his *name*?" she asked. "How long has he been here?"

"Seven years," the woman answered, rolling her eyes.

"I went straight upstairs and wrote the story of *Mister Got-to-Go* that afternoon." She recalls, "I kept hoping Cora wasn't writing the same story!" Fortunately, Cora was busy working on her novel. When Lois read it to her the next morning, she loved it, but they both knew they had to complete their current project, so *Mister Got-to-Go* was put on hold.

"It sat for at least two or three years in my file cabinet," admits Lois. She submitted it to two or three publishers, but each time the response was the same: no one was interested in another children's story about a cat. Lois wasn't too worried; a veteran of the Canadian writing scene, she was already well acquainted with the slow wheels of publishing. With a stack of books to her credit already, she knew it was a matter of persistence. Most books rack up dozens of rejection slips before finally being accepted. Even a successful track record such as hers didn't guarantee an easier time with the next manuscript.

"I've been all over the map with my writing," Lois admits. In addition to her award-winning children's books, poetry, and plays, she's published short stories, full-length fiction, and non-fiction. It was one of her adult books, the biography of an RCMP-officer-turned-murderer, that taught her not to take negative comments to heart. *The Secret Lives of Sgt. John Wilson* is an early-west story of obsession and retribution, and Lois was justifiably pleased with how it had turned out — until she read a particularly nasty review of it in *MacLean's*. The reviewer condescendingly tore it apart, mocked her credentials, and finally dismissed it by saying that this book would probably only be read by a handful of people interested in esoteric prairie history. Adding to her chagrin, a very similar book reviewed at the same time received a glowing recommendation from the same critic.

She tried not to be discouraged but secretly she wondered if she'd lost the ability to judge her own work. Then, on a flight to Vancouver, she read in *The Globe and Mail*, that her

The Making of Mister Got-to-Go

book had been short-listed for the Arthur Ellis Award in the true crime category. Named after Canada's last hangman, this coveted prize is given by the Crime Writers of Canada; Lois had heard of it, but it had never occurred to her that her book could be nominated. Then she noticed that also among the short-listed titles was the book the reviewer had raved about in the earlier review, after panning hers. But the best part was when the awards were announced. "Both books were short-listed for the Arthur Ellis," she says, "and mine won. Sweet!"

Finally, in 1995, Red Deer College Press recognized the potential in Lois' story. They commissioned award-winning children's artist Cynthia Nugent to draw the accompanying illustrations and before she knew it, Lois was proofing the final manuscript. *Mister Got-to-Go: The cat that wouldn't leave* was about to become a reality.

"One dark and rainy night at the edge of a city on the edge of an ocean," the book begins, "a stray cat came walking down the beach. Across from an old hotel covered with vines, the cat stopped. As he looked at that place, he got a strange, warm feeling inside him. 'I think,' thought the cat, 'I am tired of being a stray cat.'"

The manager, called Mr. Foster in the book, feels sorry for the cat and decides to let him come in out of the rain — but just for one night. The next morning, he emphasizes, that cat has got to go! But every time they put him out, he finds a way back inside.

Lois was delighted with how perfectly Cynthia Nugent's

pictures suited the text. The illustrations faithfully portray the character and dignity of the Sylvia Hotel, complete with Virginia creeper-covered terra cotta exterior, but it was Cynthia's ability to reveal the cat's emotions that delighted her most. According to the Sylvia Hotel's real-life manager, Axel De Verrier, Got-to-Go was not a cat that suffered fools gladly. Fawning and mincing might earn a hapless admirer a swat on the hand — unless that hand held a tuna sandwich or perhaps a European wiener! He knew how to work a crowd and wasn't above a bit of play-acting if it looked to be worth his while. This wasn't a soft, fluffy lap-kitty. He was a street cat with a tough edge and Cynthia captured him perfectly. "The reason these books appeal to kids so well, and to such a wide range of ages," explains Lois, "is that they can tell by looking at every illustration what the cat is thinking."

She immediately phoned Cynthia to tell her how pleased she was with the artwork. "I said, 'Obviously, Cynthia, you are a cat person.'" But the illustrator's reply took Lois by surprise. "She answered, 'Hell, no! I had to rent a cat from the SPCA!'" Perhaps this unsentimental viewpoint is what allowed her to so successfully capture the essence of the grey cat's tenacious personality.

The staff of the Sylvia Hotel were naturally pleased to see a book about their cat, but they had no idea how his story would touch the hearts of readers. The hotel had already earned a reputation for pet-friendly accommodation. Built in 1912 and named after the owner's daughter, it was the tallest

The Making of Mister Got-to-Go

building in Vancouver's west end for over 30 years and is an attraction in its own right. In 1975 the well-known landmark was given heritage status, ensuring that visitors will be able to enjoy its hospitality for years to come. Now the story of Got-to-Go added a new aspect to its appeal. "They've had busloads of kids come through the hotel to see the cat," says Lois. "There's a whole gallery of Got-to-Go pictures drawn by kids." When the buses pull up to the front doors, the cooks know it's time to put on the hot chocolate.

Lois and Cynthia decided they weren't finished yet; in 2001 Raincoast Books published the sequel, *Mister Got-to-Go and Arnie*. This time, the book describes how the big grey cat's world is turned upside down by the arrival of Arnie, a small, noisy dog whose character is based on the Yorkshire terrier owned by hotel manager Axel De Verrier. Humour and compassion leap off the pages, along with the spectacular West Coast scenery, as Got-to-Go learns to deal with this pesky nap-interrupter. The cat, of course, triumphs in the end.

Lois emphasizes that, while she's taken creative license with the facts, all adventures are taken from true-life events. No one knows exactly where Got-to-Go came from originally. But Axel clearly remembers his arrival. "Picture this," he says. "English Bay on a rainy October day, a cat enters the Sylvia Hotel and firmly decides to make that place its new home." Employees fell all over the poor cat, fussing about how wet he was, how hungry he looked. Axel told them to get the cat out of there. The cat looked plaintively at the employees and meowed. From then on, Got-to-Go had the upper hand. "I eventually lost the game," says Axel, "and the cat moved in and made the Sylvia Hotel its residence." But he admits he didn't put up much of a fight; he capitulated in a matter of hours.

It was a fortuitous decision for them both. Almost immediately Got-to-Go began to tailor the job description of "Hotel Cat" to fit himself, giving people one more reason to visit the Sylvia. Local residents often stopped in to say hello and give him a rub, which he might or might not choose to receive graciously. He preferred to greet visitors from his vantage point on the desk while they registered.

"His schedule was very simple," recalls Axel. "He slept during the day, got food from the maids downstairs, woke up in the evening, and waited in the old manned elevator until the bellman brought him up to Lobby level." From there the cat went out to see what trouble he could drum up in the neighbourhood, usually staying out for most of the night. Several times he returned battered and bloodied from his nighttime revelries, after which someone would cart him to the animal hospital to be patched up. He often returned to the hotel in the early morning at the same time the newspaper delivery truck pulled up to the front doors. Reminiscently, Axel says, "Then he had a long, extravagant stretch in the middle of the lobby as he waited for the housekeeper to arrive and take him downstairs." Sometimes during warm afternoons the cat drowsed in one of the lobby's sunny windowsills, enjoying the guests' many admiring comments.

It was a golden time in the history of the Sylvia. "Nowadays, a cat wouldn't be allowed in a public eating area. But you always could tell when Got-to-Go came into the dining room because all the diners' heads would turn down at the same time as he wound his way between the tables," remembers Lois.

Discovering and sharing stories like this one is one of the best parts of Lois's work as a writer. "This has been so much fun," she says.

Cats are a recurring theme for Lois. She's presently working on a book entitled *What About George?*, about feral cats and Linda Jean Gubbe's work with the Street Cat Rescue Program in Saskatoon. And Got-to-Go was far from being the first significant cat in her life. Like many writers, she has reserved some desktop space for a number of feline muses. "My former cats have all been great lovers of lying under the desk lamp, watching me type," she says.

Today Lois has a tortoiseshell cat named Alice and a grey-and-white kitten called Amelia Ann Higgins. Alice had given birth while at the SPCA, and as her kittens grew and found homes, she became lonely. "When her own litter was all adopted out, she kept reaching through the bars towards these cages with kittens in them," says Lois. "So they started letting her care for orphaned kittens." By the time Lois decided to give Alice a home, the cat had fostered about 20 motherless tykes. She'd also developed a great reputation as a mouser. "No wonder she was bored when she came to my place," Lois adds. "She needs company."

Cats have a way of insinuating themselves into a life, regardless of whether or not they are expected. All we can do is accept them for the gift they are, and be grateful.

Got-to-Go may have started his life as a vagabond but he ended it in the lap of luxury, surrounded by friends. As he got older, he found it hard to keep up his duties as Hotel Cat. "The last time I saw him," says Lois, "they brought him up from behind the furnace and he was all dusty and annoyed." He craved peace and quiet and tended to spend more and more of his days sleeping in tucked away places, but he never lost his spirit.

"Despite the fact that he did not like to be petted," adds Axel, "and despite his departure for cat heaven in 1993, our guests still talk about Mister Got-to-Go!" Got-to-Go, the cat that wouldn't leave, had become far more than an old cat. He was a beloved friend who brought something special to thousands of travellers and readers all over the world.

"It's seven years since that dark and raining night the stray cat came walking down the beach to the Sylvia Hotel," the book ends. *"Every so often, Mr. Foster says, 'My word, is that cat still here? He's got to go, you know. As soon as it stops raining, that cat's got to go.'*

Sometimes the sun is shining when he says it."

Chapter 8
Journey's End

"He makes his home where the living is best."
Latin proverb

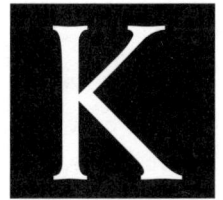

Karen Barker stood in the doorway of her new home and looked around. It was July 25, 2003. She'd moved only a few kilometres from her old neighbourhood in Calgary, Alberta, but the house was a huge change. It was newer, bigger, and more private. Her mind was filled with plans. First on her list was a backyard fence so her cat, Theo, could explore in safety.

Karen had tried to convince Theo that this new house was a good move, but he wasn't having it. Everything about him oozed resentment, from his luxurious tail, twitching in annoyance, to the glare in his golden eyes. Even his magnificent caramel-and-cream fur looked rumpled and put out. "Here I was all excited," says Karen, "and Theo wouldn't even come out from under the dining room table."

She'd expected it would be traumatic for him. The old

neighbourhood where Theo had lived with Karen for the past nine years had been very sheltered and safe. "When Theo went outside there, all the neighbours knew him. In fact," she adds, "they all fed him." He'd always been a very confident cat, unafraid of strange noises or new people. Nothing, from the hum of a treadmill to the roar of an engine, caused him to bat an eye. His size, his coat, and his easy-going temperament even made Karen wonder sometimes if he was part Ragdoll, a breed with a reputation for becoming extremely relaxed when being stroked. "A typical position for him was to lie half on the couch and half hanging off of it."

A bit of upset was to be expected, but Karen was confident Theo would get over it as soon as he discovered how nice the new place was. Gently she encouraged him to explore the yard, carrying him outside with her. But he wasn't interested. As soon as she set him down, he dashed for shelter beneath the nearest object and refused to come out. "It wasn't like him to be so out of sorts," she says. Karen was beginning to realize Theo was seriously upset by this move.

"Before, you could tell he didn't know what to do with himself, but at least he'd been affectionate," she recalls. "That day he kept glaring at me, as if he was angry." When she reached out to stroke him, he grumbled at her and stalked away. Karen hoped he'd soon come around. Even if Theo didn't realize it, Karen knew he didn't really have a choice. They weren't moving back. Giving him to a friend from the old neighborhood wasn't an option. Seeing him so miserable made her feel wretched too, but to be apart from him was unthinkable. She didn't know what to do; Theo simply had to adjust. "I don't have any family nearby," explains Karen. "My half-sister lives on the other end of the country, and my parents are dead. This cat is my everything."

But on August 5, his annoyance moved into a whole new realm. It had been a fairly typical day: Karen had gone to her job as a service co-ordinator, come home, and then gone out to do a bit of shopping. "I came home about 10:15 that evening. As soon as I opened the door, Theo dashed out between my feet." She was surprised, but told herself not to worry. He'd been outside a few times with her, so she knew he was at least somewhat familiar with the area. She put down her shopping, hung up her jacket, and then went around to the backyard, hoping to find him there and cajole him into returning to the house. But he wasn't there. She went back to the front. No Theo. Where could he have gone in such a short time?

Karen walked all around the house, calling and shaking the cat food box. Finally she decided to wait inside for him to come back. "I thought I'd leave the back door open and run the can opener a couple of times," she says, "because that usually worked." Still he didn't come home. Finally, at about 2 a.m., Karen went to bed, a hard knob of dread forming in her stomach. She might as well have stayed up, because she couldn't sleep for listening. Each hour she got up to check the doors, and even went out to walk up and down the alley. But there was no sign of him, nothing to indicate he'd even been there. "It was as though aliens had picked him up off the face of the earth. He was just gone," she says.

When Karen got up to go to work the following morning, the full realization of Theo's disappearance hit her. His food dish sat untouched. His favourite spots lay empty. "Nothing worse could have happened to me," she says. Panic began to set in but she pushed it down and tried to focus on her responsibilities.

Karen co-ordinates support services for people with disabilities. Her network of friends and colleagues is wide and it didn't take long for everyone in her office to hear the news that Theo had gone missing. Newcomers only had to look at the pictures on Karen's desk to know Theo was important to her. Karen tried to concentrate on her work but worry kept intruding.

Locating Theo became the nucleus of her life, and working to bring him home kept her from despair over his possible fate. Her first task was to get the word out. Across the city of Calgary Karen's posters began to appear, all bearing the same message: MISSING! The posters had a picture of Theo, his tattoo number, and Karen's contact information. The same poster hung on her office door where everyone who passed by would be sure to see it.

Then she picked up the phone. Karen contacted the Calgary Humane Society, as well as every shelter and veterinary hospital she could think of, to give them Theo's identi-

Journey's End

fication details. She signed up with CanadaStrays.com and PetLynx.net, two on-line lost-and-found pet services. Her heartfelt messages drew sympathy from many people, as did her persistence.

Day after day, Karen posted the same plea: "I have lost my beloved cat, Theodore. I check your phone line every day, and have since he went missing. If you see my cat come through your doors, please please please call me, or e-mail me. Theodore is a nine-year-old ginger-and-white tabby longhair, with four white feet and a white mane. He is a tad bit overweight. He has a tattoo in his right ear: CH563. He is the love of my life, my only family."

As the days turned to weeks, Karen established an unvarying morning routine. She'd get up, log on to the websites, and scan the photos of any cats that had been found. Then she'd phone the City of Calgary animal services department. Each time she was given the same answer: Sorry, haven't seen him. Finally, she'd make the phone call she dreaded most, to the city's road maintenance department. "Sometimes I couldn't actually phone road maintenance, I'd have to get someone else to do it," confesses Karen. If Theo had been killed in an accident, she needed to know. But hearing such news from a harried municipal clerk didn't bear thinking of. Their business-like attitude towards animals found dead on the road was more than she could take.

"I dreaded getting those e-mail messages that started out with 'Sorry Karen, but...'" says Karen. "My hope constantly waffled. Some days I'd tell myself that Theo was spoiled rotten — a mama's boy who wouldn't be gone long." Then she'd remember Nose Hill Park, the nearby wilderness that's home to a variety of wildlife including deer, coyotes, and wolves. She tried not to think of the stories she'd heard about coyotes coming into residential neighbourhoods to prey on pets, but as the summer waned and fall approached, she knew it was a very real possibility for Theo.

It had been over a month since he disappeared. "After Theo went missing, I'd go to the humane society every day," says Karen. "First I'd check the room with the lost and found pets, then I'd check the ones for adoption." She came to recognise some of the animals, especially those who stayed longer, but she was too focused on finding Theo to be tempted by any other cat. Then one day while she was making her way through the room, a beautiful little cat named Mini caught her eye. She looked at the cage card and discovered that Mini was 10 years old. The shelter workers told her no one wanted Mini, in spite of her sweet personality, because she was too old. "I thought, 'This is a cat that Theo could get along with ... if he comes home,'" says Karen. "And I missed having a cat around. So I adopted her."

Mini was a great comfort, but loved ones are irreplaceable; Karen's grief, anxiety, and fear for Theo continued to grow. "One night I just absolutely broke down," she recalls. "I went and sat down by the back door, where I kept checking to see if he'd come home. I sat there till it was dark and just

Journey's End

cried and cried."

As she sat weeping in the darkness, Karen realized one thing. If she knew for sure that Theo was dead, she'd be able to mourn. But without that certain knowledge, she couldn't give up, even though the constant bouncing between hope and anguish left her emotionally exhausted. Through her tears, Karen begged every power in the universe for something, anything, to keep her hope alive. "I said, 'I don't know who's running this, God or energy or whatever, but could you just give me a sign that he's okay and that he's going to come home.'"

The next day at work Karen was surprised to find, addressed to her, a little gift in the inter-office mail from a co-worker she knew only casually. It was a keychain and on it were the words: *I Love My Cats.* "It wasn't like her to buy me something," says Karen. "But she told me she'd seen it in the store and immediately thought of me, so she bought it." Karen read it again. Cats. Plural. Suddenly her senses went on full alert. It was the sign she'd been looking for, a nudge from the universe telling her to hang in there.

Karen still had many reasons to give up hope. Theo had been gone for more than two months. It was nearing the end of October and the weather was getting cold. Even if he were alive, he was likely to be ill or injured. But she set those thoughts aside. Instead, in her heart grew the small, insistent belief that she simply had to keep faith and be patient. "I understood then what people say about getting through something a day at a time, or an hour at a time," says Karen. "It was just a matter of getting through it."

Then the calendar turned over. Again. November had arrived and Theo was still missing. The cold air swirled in from the mountains, adding a welcome crispness to the air and warning of snow soon to come. Some people were already beginning to talk of Christmas. Karen continued her unvarying routine of phone calls and checking websites, and she continued to believe. But with each day and each drop in temperature, it became harder not to grow frantic.

By this time, Theo's disappearance was also registered with the Meow Foundation, *The Calgary Herald*, Shaw Cable, and Pets for Life. Karen took out ads in the paper, and while none of the people who read them phoned to say they'd found Theo, she got many calls of support. Some callers were in tears, just wanting her to know they were thinking of her and praying for Theo's safe return. Karen was grateful for every response she got, even the negative ones, because it meant that people were looking. Who knew what chance observation might bring him home again?

Remembrance Day arrived. Karen's parents had been in their early forties when they adopted her. Because they'd both been through World War II, Remembrance Day always had special significance in their lives. Even after they'd passed away, Karen honoured the day because she knew how important it had been to them. Throughout the day she said little prayers, hoping that somehow, somewhere, her parents

Journey's End

could hear her and send their love to strengthen her. She'd never needed it more.

When she returned home after work that day, the message indicator was flashing on her phone. Karen still has the message. It was from a woman in Okotoks, a small town about 18 kilometres south of Calgary. "My name is Gabby," the voice said in a thick German accent. "I am calling about a cat named Tee-o-dore. Tattoo number CH563. If you are the owner of this cat, please call me. He's very thin and he's not very happy." As soon as Karen heard the name and tattoo number, she began leaping up and down. As she dialled the number with trembling fingers, the thought uppermost in her mind was, "This is a cat that grew up with a silver spoon in his mouth and he's been roughing it all this time. No kidding he's not happy!"

Gabby, who ran the Okotoks Pound Rescue, gave directions and then Karen ran out of the house, forgetting her purse in her haste. All she could think of was getting to Theo as soon as possible. Unfortunately, in her excitement she made a few wrong turns and the trip took about three times longer than it should have. Karen ended up in a nearby town and had to ask for more directions. Finally she pulled up to the right building. Her prayers were about to be answered but instead of the surge of emotion she expected, she felt calm and peaceful. She didn't know what condition Theo would be in, but at least he'd be back with her. "Gabby met me at the door," remembers Karen. "She took me into a little room and there was Theo, hiding under a bench." The Theo she'd known in her old house didn't hide; he was more likely to lay on his back with all four feet in the air. She called to him, but it took several tries before he responded. He tentatively peered out, as if unable to believe his eyes, then edged a bit nearer. Softly, Karen started singing to him, something she'd done all his life. She sang, "Who's Afraid of the Big Bad Wolf," and suddenly Theo was purring. "Gabby couldn't believe it," says Karen. "He had been terrified. Then I come in and after a couple of words, he's mama's boy again."

Gabby explained that Theo had shown up at a farm in Okotoks in October. A kindly couple brought him into their garage, fed him, and started trying to find out where he came from. Finally they called Gabby, who put her own network into action. Soon after, the trail led to Karen. Karen and Gabby speculated on the many things that could have happened to Theo. Perhaps while Theo was out he had been caught in a cat-trap, driven out of the area and dumped on a country road. Or maybe, during his angry spell, he'd made his way inside one of the many RVs or campers in Karen's new neighbourhood and gone for an unexpected ride. They had no way of knowing and Karen didn't care. All she knew was that her little boy was finally back with her, safe and sound.

His adventure had taken its toll, though. His body had gone from 17 pounds of muscular feline grace to an emaciated 6 pounds. All his bones were clearly visible beneath his skin, and his once glorious fur was now little more than strag-

Journey's End

gly tufts. He looked fragile, beaten. "Normally," says Karen, "he's a big cat with a lush coat. He looks like he's got bloomers on his legs. When I finally found him, his legs were like sticks and there were no bloomers anymore, just matted bits of fur." Would her old Theo still be there inside this pathetic shell? Karen drove home slowly and carefully with Theo curled up quietly in her lap the whole way, hoping he hadn't been irreparably damaged. "When we got home and I opened up the door, he went in immediately and recognised the place," says Karen. "He went straight to his food dish. He got the bare essentials in — food and water — right away."

"And then he saw Mini." Theo stopped dead in his tracks, assessing the interloper. Perhaps in his time away he'd learned that resisting change is a risky proposition; maybe he was just tired. Either way, he had more important things to do than fight. The cats exchanged unpleasantries, then studiously ignored each other.

Over the years, Karen and Theo had developed many rituals. Their usual nighttime routine had always included a cuddle, a wash, and a game of "Tent" under the covers; then Theo would settle down for the night. But would Theo remember this much of his old life? Karen watched him, hoping he hadn't forgotten their customary game. "I got ready for bed and he got into bed with me," says Karen, "and then it was like he hadn't even left. He wanted to play 'Tent'."

Theo was finally home. Karen's ordeal was over; her life returned to normal. "Of course, I was so happy. I don't think

I've ever been so happy!" Then came the welcome task of informing everyone that Theo was home. She immediately tore down the MISSING! poster on her door and put in its place a banner saying FOUND! The entire office celebrated with her. "Everyone had taken it very personally," she says.

Unbelievably, Theo had no health repercussions from his time on the run. His weight gradually returned to normal and if anything, he's a little overweight again. Karen says it's as if he's afraid to let himself get hungry and keeps continually trying to make up for the weeks of starvation he lived through.

Theo turns 10 this summer. He was gone for 99 days. He returned home on Remembrance Day. It's little details like these that Karen remembers with gratitude. She's kept many of the messages of hope sent to her by friends and strangers and she's also kept the messages she sent herself. In her darkest moments, when her faith was weakest, affirming the love she shares with Theo was the only thing that helped her through.

Mummy misses her little boy,
And Theo needs his mum,
But he is safe and he is sound,
And home he soon will come.

Mum will feel his soft warm fur,
And hear his sweet meows,

Journey's End

Theo will lie in mummy's arms,
Again in our new house.

Fate will bring my boy to me,
Love will bring him home.
He'll be fine and he'll be happy
No more will he roam.

Chapter 9
The Simon Years

*"No, heaven will not ever heaven be,
unless my cats are there to welcome me."*
Unknown

One morning, as I worked my way through the wards of the veterinary hospital in Saskatoon, Saskatchewan, changing litter pans and filling food and water dishes, I asked myself for the millionth time if this was what I went to school for. "I'm a veterinary technician. I should be doing treatments, anaesthetics, laboratory analyses. Instead," I muttered to myself, "I'm cleaning kennels."

I came to the area where the smaller dogs were hospitalized. At the back of one cage crouched a tiny kitten, its striped orange fur matted with food. When he saw me his mouth opened soundlessly and he tottered over to the bars. He was perhaps four weeks old, too young to be vaccinated. That explained why he was in the dog ward instead of with

The Simon Years

the other cats — to protect him from the organisms carried by his own species. The kitten sneezed violently, falling off his feet with the effort. He had a serious respiratory infection but his health was the least of his problems. I glanced at the cage card: STRAY. "Oh, boy," I murmured to the little face pressing itself against the bars. "It doesn't look good for you."

The kitten stayed on the ward and recovered slowly, but he remained bedraggled. At first sight, little about him was appealing. His coat was sparse, his face a splotch of ginger on white. Mackerel tabby markings etched hollow flanks and climbed a thin crooked tail. His front end was caked with food, his back end with diarrhea. He smelled terrible.

But every morning when I came to clean, feed, and medicate him, he met me with unmistakable welcome. A disproportionately loud purr rattled from his tiny throat as he tripped over himself in eagerness to rub my hand. He was the ugliest kitten I'd ever seen, but he had character.

His health improved eventually but he still had no home to go to, no owner to take responsibility for him. One day I overheard the clinicians discussing euthanasia. "I'll take him," I blurted, without thinking. I wasn't supposed to have pets in my apartment but I figured I'd only keep him until I found him an owner. That evening I trekked across campus to the bus stop with a kitten nestled in my backpack, bouncing gently against the towel I'd tucked in with him. Once settled in my seat, I peeked in to find him curled up contentedly, totally unconcerned about the jostling and bumping.

He looked up at me calmly as if to say, "I know I'm in good hands." That night he slept wedged up tightly against my side, his purr reverberating throughout my small apartment.

Within a few days I knew for certain that no one would ever want this kitten. At the shelter even the cute ones don't always find homes; an ugly, scrawny one like this had no chance. My heart ached for him. Love pours out in abundance to the pretty, the talented, the strong, and smart. But what about the ones who stumble on the cracks of inadequacy, overlooked and bypassed until even a mere trickle of affection is too much to expect? Eventually, they learn that all life holds for them is rejection. They give up hoping for anything more.

Well, this creature simply refused to give up. He was blissfully unaware of his outlandish appearance and general lack of appeal. When he scrambled awkwardly into my lap at the end of the day, his raucous purr high in his throat, he seemed convinced that he was the best thing to ever happen to me. It didn't take long before I began to believe it, too. I knew that there must be some reason he'd fallen into my life. Rules or no rules, I'd found him a home. With me.

If he were to stay with me he'd need a name. That was a poser. Nothing cute or fluffy, obviously. Nothing overly regal or cool. He needed a solid name, not fancy but sturdy, something that would reflect the character I sensed within. One day it just popped into my head: Simon. That was his name. It fit like a glove.

The Simon Years

Intensely food-oriented, Simon loved to investigate my meals. One day he stuck his nose into my bowl of hot chicken soup. Sneezing mightily and licking his scalded muzzle in surprise, he retreated, glaring at me as if I should have warned him.

He quickly learned my routine, complaining loudly whenever I gathered my coat and keys to leave. Running from door to window, he would watch me walk away, yowling with forlorn persistence. When I returned at night his strident call was the first thing to greet me. His warm body winding around my legs was a welcome change from the quiet apartment I was used to, and I discovered I liked my demanding new roommate. He was my buddy, my Simey.

Other changes were happening in my life that winter. I was transferred to the veterinary surgery department and began to really enjoy my work. And a young veterinary student caught my eye: Ray, with his easy laugh and gentle touch with the animals, soon held all my attention. Poor Simey was relegated to the back burner.

It was the start of a long love-hate relationship for Simon and Ray. Slimy, as Ray called him, delighted in ambushing Ray from around corners and behind doors. Grappling with all four paws, he'd pummel poor Ray's ankles then dive back under the couch, waiting for the next attack opportunity. Every encounter ended in a new scratch for Ray. He tolerated the abuse, but he was convinced I had a seriously demented cat. I figured Simon was something of an acid test; if this guy stuck around in spite of my cat, maybe he was a keeper.

Within months, I had my answer. Simon and Ray became buddies and I knew Ray and I were meant for each other.

As soon as Ray graduated, he and I left the prairies for Ontario. My parents were elected to watch over Simon until we sent for him. Unfortunately, we'd no sooner arrived than I had to go into hospital for a badly needed tonsillectomy. Homesick and in pain, I was lying on the couch when Ray arrived home from the airport with my cat. Doped up on painkillers I hadn't noticed how late they were. Simon, it turns out, had gotten misplaced at the airport. His crate had been shunted around from terminal to terminal, while Ray frantically chased down the clues, always a few steps behind, hoping he wouldn't have to return empty-handed. Finally they located him and Ray loaded him into the car. The whole way back, Simon sat plastered against one end of the crate, his eyes wide with fright.

When they walked through the door, Simon took one look at me, dove for my lap, and went to sleep. He stayed there the full week I was recuperating, uncharacteristically calm and sedate, seeming to know I needed him. But as soon as I had recovered and was back at work, Simon returned to his wild ways.

Before we knew it, we were married and expecting our first child. One day Ray brought home a most beautiful kitten, a long-haired male we named Cody. He'd been found on the

The Simon Years

side of the road with a broken leg and brought to the clinic where Ray worked. Ray fixed the leg, knowing that if no one claimed him he'd have to bring him home. Simon loved him. In fact, he loved him so much we had to protect Cody from Simon's exuberant embraces in order to let Cody's leg mend. By the time the little bones had knit and the hair had grown back, he'd grown into a graceful, stunning orange-and-white prince, the perfect foil for his bumbling adopted brother.

Soon life changed again with the birth of our daughter Stephanie. I was worried how Simon would behave around the baby, but he dispelled my fears. He was so happy to have me around during the day, it was worth sharing me with a noisy little human. Although I missed the animals and my co-workers, I loved being home with my child and my Simey.

Time passed. We moved to British Columbia and had another daughter, Andrea. Simon casually reigned over the multitude of pets that collected in our home over time, from cockatiels and baby crows to a retired racing greyhound. Our unusual, unwanted, and much-loved cat continued to dip his crooked tail into every teacup, startle every visitor, and lick any available chin. He was irritating, always trying to get outside, jumping up and knocking things over. But he'd become part of the fabric of our lives. I couldn't imagine life without him.

Then one day he disappeared.

I was horrified. Simon, my innocent, indoor cat, had escaped unnoticed. His knowledge of the world was limited to the view from the window, and now he was lost. He must be cold and afraid. Perhaps he was injured, or even dead.

"Have you seen Simon?" I asked Gertrude, my next-door neighbour.

"It's the weirdest thing," she answered, frowning. "I saw a cat just like him on my way to work yesterday."

In fact, Gertrude had witnessed an altercation between Simon and her own cat in her carport. After a bit of hissing and spitting, Simon had run beneath her car and that was the last time she'd seen him. Several hours later Gertrude left for work. At a busy intersection, she'd heard the thump of something hitting the pavement underneath her car. When she looked in the rear-view mirror she saw an ugly orange cat darting through the traffic. "What a coincidence," she thought. "That cat looks just like Simon."

With growing horror, I realized what must have happened: Simon had climbed onto the underside of her car, and clung on in fear when it began to move. The area where Gertrude heard the noise was a well-travelled commercial district, with four lanes of busy traffic at all times. If this had been Simon, and he'd survived, he must be lying somewhere nearby, badly injured.

I was newly pregnant with our third child at that time and feeling less than energetic. But there was no question what we had to do. Stephanie and Andrea and I dashed into the car and headed to the area Gertrude described. We walked up and down the sidewalks, peering under every

The Simon Years

bush. We rattled his favourite treat can, called his name, and asked every person we found.

But no one had seen him. Up one street and down the other we went, all the while dealing with the fears of two little girls who loved an ugly cat that had been with them their whole lives.

Then, success! An ugly orange cat with a skinny, crooked tail? Yup, a woman told us, she'd seen one hiding under the garbage cans behind her house. She'd noticed him because he looked a bit like her own cat — except for his scraggly tail! I moved the cans around and there he was. He greeted me with a plaintive cry, as if to ask, "What took you so long?" He crawled up onto my shoulder, tucked his head under my chin and firmly shut his eyes. If this was freedom, he wanted home.

Stephanie, five, and Andrea, three, were giddy with relief. The bigger miracle, however, was that, after riding underneath a car for six blocks, running through four lanes of traffic, and spending the night outside in a strange neighbourhood, Simon had not a scratch on him.

From that day forward he had no desire to go anywhere near a road. We could let him outside safely now, knowing he'd stay nearby.

As Simon got older he didn't race to go outside anymore. Instead, he ambled. He no longer jumped from the floor onto my shoulders and there was a certain stiffness in his hips when he walked that suggested arthritis.

Then, one day, Simon didn't come for breakfast. Alarm bells went off. Simon was not a cat to miss his meals. Ray took him in for tests, and x-rays revealed fluid in his right lung. My husband tried to calm me but I knew this was a bad sign. He drained some of the fluid and sent it to the lab for analysis while I waited at home, hoping against hope for good news.

The results were unmistakable. Cancer.

Many times I had been on the clinical end of a bad diagnosis, had helped treat sick pets and end the suffering of those beyond hope of recovery. But never before had it been my pet.

I needed to know for sure how sick he was, so we scheduled more tests. An ultrasound revealed that Simon had something wrong in virtually every system of his body. He had heart disease, fluid in his lungs, enlarged kidneys and liver, and bowel and bladder abnormalities. The radiologist said that while Simon's cancer probably originated elsewhere, it had spread to his lungs and possibly to other organs as well. His cardiovascular system couldn't tolerate surgery to find the primary tumour, nor was there any purpose in looking for it. There was nothing to be done. It was just a matter of time now.

It was October when we learned the sad news. "I don't think he'll make it to Christmas," I told our daughters, over the lump in my throat. We decided to hope for my birthday, less than a month away.

So began our last days with Simon. Except for the

The Simon Years

shaved patch on his chest, he looked relatively normal. He'd never been pretty, so his debilitation wasn't immediately noticeable. But as he got sicker, his appetite dropped more and more until he was barely eating anything. He took to sleeping in warm, tucked-away places, trying in vain to chase the chill of cancer from his bones.

In mid-November, on the morning of my 33rd birthday, Simon climbed onto my husband's chest as we awoke, licked Ray's chin, and purred as if all was well. We lay together, stroking his frail body, savouring his loving friendship. It was the last time he ever purred.

Two days later we awoke to a treat — snow, in our warm province. All day it fell thick and fast, covering the ground as quickly as we could shovel it. The girls were thrilled to have a chance to go sledding and build forts. I picked up Simon to show him the snow and when I put him down, he could walk only two steps before resting. I picked him up again and carried him to the bedroom, choking back sobs. It was time.

That night after the girls were tucked into bed, I brought Simon downstairs. There, at our kitchen table, Ray brushed back tears and slid a needle into the fragile vein of this ugly cat we'd grown to love. I stroked the ginger fur and kissed the bony head as Simon slipped peacefully from this world. Simon, my Simey, was gone.

It was hard to adjust to his absence. As much as I missed him, it was worse for me to see my daughters grieve. One day, not long after his death, we were talking about Simon. Andrea began to cry and could not stop. We talked about what he had meant to us and how we'd like to remember him. I tried to console her but my own feelings were still too strong.

Finally, for distraction as much as anything, I suggested we go visit the cats at the local shelter. We dried our eyes and got into the car. As soon as we entered the shelter's cat room, I spotted our reason for coming on that particular day — a four-month-old orange tabby with white markings, a nasty cut on his ear ... and no time left. If he weren't adopted immediately, he'd be euthanised.

We named him Mylos and brought him home.

Mylos quickly moved into our hearts. Some days I see him sitting in the window, just like Simon did, and the resemblance takes my breath away. He's not a replacement for Simon; he's a reminder that life, and love, goes on. Change and loss will always be with me, much as I resist it, but I've learned this truth: when the Simon years come to an end, it means the Mylos years are just beginning.

Epilogue

We sprinkled Simon's ashes beneath his favourite cedar hedge, where the birds he loved to watch still nestle in fragrant safety. In January 2004, Simon's old friend Cody joined him at the rainbow bridge; next spring the scent of lilac blossoms will be rich with memories of our other special old cat.

Our cats have been with us through a lot of living. These days the kingdom of Simon and Cody belongs to Tabitha, Mylos, Sophie, and Bryan, and I've no doubt other cats will pass through our home in years to come.

But Simon was special. He was the first cat of my adult life, a link between the carefree world of youth and the responsibilities of maturity. The best things in my life all came to me after I opened my home and then my heart to an ugly cat that no one else wanted.

For More Information

For more information about SCAT Street Cat Rescue Program Inc, of Saskatoon, SK, please visit:
http://www.quadrant.net/streetcat/index.html

To read more about Simon Teakettle, please visit:
www.simonteakettle.com

For more information about Pacific Animal Therapy Society of Sidney, BC, please visit:
http://members.shaw.ca/patspets/

For more information about the pedigreed cat fancy, please visit:
http://www.fanciers.com/

For more information on reporting or locating lost animals, please visit:
www.canadastrays.com and www.petlynx.net

For More Information

To help support the cats of Parliament Hill, contact the Cat-Man at:

> René Chartrand
> 1207-160 Charlotte St.
> Ottawa, Ontario
> K1N 8Z5

Acknowledgements

So many feline aficionados contributed to the making of this book! My thanks to Barb Taylor, Linda Jean Gubbe, Barbara Florio Graham, Al and Pat Hodgkinson, Sadey Guy, Caroline Cameron and Nancy Hutchinson, Betty Sleep, René Chartrand, Axel DeVerrier, Lois Simmie, and Karen Barker for sharing the lives of their cats with me.

An even bigger thank-you to my family: Ray, Stephanie, Andrea, and Megan. You've fed the cats, made supper, cleaned up the hairballs, vacuumed the floors, walked the dogs, and generally supported me royally as my deadline approached. Thank you! (And next time, let's not have any car accidents, dislocated elbows or emergency appendectomies, okay?)

Credits

Excerpts from Mister Got-to-Go with permission by Red Deer Press.

Chapter Nine, The Simon Years, originally appeared in Reader's Digest and appears in this book in altered form. Copyright © 2002 BY THE READER'S DIGEST MAGAZINES LIMITED. REPRINTED BY PERMISSION FROM THE MARCH 2002 ISSUE OF READER'S DIGEST and the author, Roxanne Willems Snopek.

Photo Credits

Cover: Photos.com. Carmen Breitkreutz: page 35; Linda Jean Gubbe: page 32; Stephanie L. Snopek: page 119; Roxanne Willems Snopek: page 76; Barb Taylor: page 21.

About the Author

Roxanne Willems Snopek lives and writes in Abbotsford, BC. She has over 100 published magazine credits. Some of her articles and essays have been reprinted in several languages in a dozen different countries. This is her second book for Altitude Publishing and she's currently working on a third Altitude animal book, as well as completing her first novel. In her spare time, she enjoys yoga, gardening, reading — especially mysteries — and training her poodle to do higher math. She shares her life with one husband, two dogs, three daughters, four cats, and numerous tropical fish but, happily, neither a partridge nor a pear tree. If you enjoyed this book, she'd love to hear from you. Contact her through her website at www.roxannesnopek.smartwriters.com.

OTHER AMAZING STORIES

ISBN	Title	Author
1-55153-943-8	Black Donnellys	Nate Hendley
1-55153-947-0	Canada's Rumrunners	Art Montague
1-55153-966-7	Canadian Spies	Tom Douglas
1-55153-795-8	D-Day	Tom Douglas
1-55153-982-9	Dinosaur Hunters	Lisa Murphy-Lamb
1-55153-970-5	Early Voyageurs	Marie Savage
1-55153-968-3	Edwin Alonzo Boyd	Nate Hendley
1-55153-996-9	Emily Carr	Cat Klerks
1-55153-973-X	Great Canadian Love Stories	Cheryl MacDonald
1-55153-946-2	Great Dog Stories	Roxanne Snopek
1-55153-942-X	The Halifax Explosion	Joyce Glasner
1-55153-958-6	Hudson's Bay Company Adventures	Elle Andra-Warner
1-55153-969-1	Klondike Joe Boyle	Stan Sauerwein
1-55153-980-2	Legendary Show Jumpers	Debbie G-Arsenault
1-55153-979-9	Ma Murray	Stan Sauerwein
1-55153-964-0	Marilyn Bell	Patrick Tivy
1-55153-953-5	Moe Norman	Stan Sauerwein
1-55153-962-4	Niagara Daredevils	Cheryl MacDonald
1-55153-945-4	Pierre Elliott Trudeau	Stan Sauerwein
1-55153-981-0	Rattenbury	Stan Sauerwein
1-55153-991-8	Rebel Women	Linda Kupecek
1-55153-956-X	Robert Service	Elle Andra-Warner
1-55153-952-7	Strange Events	Johanna Bertin
1-55153-954-3	Snowmobile Adventures	Linda Aksomitis
1-55153-950-0	Tom Thomson	Jim Poling Sr.
1-55153-976-4	Trailblazing Sports Heroes	Joan Dixon
1-55153-977-2	Unsung Heroes of the RCAF	Cynthia J. Faryon
1-55153-959-4	A War Bride's Story	Cynthia Faryon
1-55153-948-9	The War of 1812 Against the States	Jennifer Crump

These titles are available wherever you buy books. If you have trouble finding the book you want, call the Altitude order desk at 1-800-957-6888, e-mail your request to: orderdesk@altitudepublishing.com or visit our Web site at www.amazingstories.ca

New AMAZING STORIES titles are published every month.

Comments on other *Amazing Stories* from readers & reviewers

"*Tightly written volumes filled with lots of wit and humour about famous and infamous Canadians.*"
Eric Shackleton, *The Globe and Mail*

"*The heightened sense of drama and intrigue, combined with a good dose of human interest is what sets* Amazing Stories *apart.*"
Pamela Klaffke, *Calgary Herald*

"*This is popular history as it should be... For this price, buy two and give one to a friend.*"
Terry Cook, a reader from Ottawa, on **Rebel Women**

"*Glasner creates the moment of the explosion itself in graphic detail...she builds detail upon gruesome detail to create a convincingly authentic picture.*"
Peggy McKinnon, *The Sunday Herald*, on **The Halifax Explosion**

"*It was wonderful...I found I could not put it down. I was sorry when it was completed.*"
Dorothy F. from Manitoba on **Marie-Anne Lagimodière**

"*Stories are rich in description, and bristle with a clever, stylish realness.*"
Mark Weber, *Central Alberta Advisor*, on **Ghost Town Stories II**

"*A compelling read. Bertin...has selected only the most intriguing tales, which she narrates with a wealth of detail.*"
Joyce Glasner, *New Brunswick Reader*, on **Strange Events**

"*The resulting book is one readers will want to share with all the women in their lives.*"
Lynn Martel, *Rocky Mountain Outlook*, on **Women Explorers**

AMAZING STORIES

WILDLIFE IN THE KITCHEN

AMAZING STORIES

WILDLIFE IN THE KITCHEN

...And Other Great Animal Tales

ANIMAL/HUMAN INTEREST

by Roxanne Willems Snopek

PUBLISHED BY ALTITUDE PUBLISHING CANADA LTD.
1500 Railway Avenue, Canmore, Alberta T1W 1P6
www.altitudepublishing.com
1-800-957-6888

Copyright 2005 © Roxanne Willems Snopek
All rights reserved
First published 2005

Extreme care has been taken to ensure that all information presented in this book is accurate and up to date. Neither the author nor the publisher can be held responsible for any errors.

Publisher	Stephen Hutchings
Associate Publisher	Kara Turner
Series Editor	Jill Foran
Editor	Deborah Lawson

We acknowledge the financial support of the Government of Canada through the Book Publishing Industry Development Program (BPIDP) for our publishing activities.

Altitude GreenTree Program
Altitude Publishing will plant twice as many trees as were used in the manufacturing of this product.

We acknowledge the support of the Canada Council for the Arts which in 2003 invested $21.7 million in writing and publishing throughout Canada.

Canada Council for the Arts   Conseil des Arts du Canada

National Library of Canada Cataloguing in Publication Data

Snopek, Roxanne
  Wildlife in the kitchen and other great animal tales / Roxanne Willems Snopek.

(Amazing stories)
Includes bibliographical references.
ISBN 1-55439-008-7

1. Wildlife rehabilitators--Canada. 2. Wildlife rehabilitation--Canada. I. Title. II. Series: Amazing stories (Canmore, Alta.)

SF996.45.S64 2005   639.9'6'0971
C2005-901167-X

An application for the trademark for Amazing Stories™ has been made and the registered trademark is pending.

Printed and bound in Canada by Friesens
2 4 6 8 9 7 5 3

To the many people who selflessly use their abilities and expertise to rescue and rehabilitate wild creatures injured by human activity. The world is a better place because of you.

Contents

Prologue 11
Chapter 1 Baby Season in the Bird Ward 13
Chapter 2 Wolf Watching 23
Chapter 3 Lionheart 36
Chapter 4 Rock and Peep: A Love Story 48
Chapter 5 Saved at Sea 59
Chapter 6 When Polar Bears Come to Town 70
Chapter 7 Wildlife in the Kitchen 85
Chapter 8 The Last Wild Horses in Canada 101
Epilogue 122

Prologue

By the time she was dropped off at the wildlife shelter it was too late. Dried blood stained her bristly white guard hairs, matting the dark fur below. The lips above the long narrow muzzle were pulled back in a final grimace, exposing daunting canine teeth. She was a young opossum, hit during a nocturnal roadside ramble by a passing motorist. She'd dragged herself to cover at the side of the road but it was probably hours before a kind-hearted Samaritan found her and rushed her to the shelter. Now, as early morning sunshine streaked the sky, the last spark of life left her broken body.

Elizabeth laid her out on a soft towel and examined her quickly. Time was, after all, of the essence. The prehensile tail lay still, its furless skin cool to the touch. Eyes once dark and glistening now stared sightlessly, half-closed and dull. The woman manipulated the limbs, now flopping limply, felt through the fur over the soft, still-warm abdomen, searching, probing. There. That's what she was looking for.

Through a vertical opening in the opossum's belly, she felt a quiver of movement: babies. They'd survived the impact. She gently removed them from their mother's body and laid them in a warming basket, tiny pink hairless creatures no bigger than mice. She shook her head. They were living embryos,

Wildlife in the Kitchen

needing the warmth, security, and rich milk found within their mother's pouch for several more weeks at least. Could she give them what they needed? Or would they suffer the same fate as their mother?

She gave a last stroke to the dead mother and turned her attention to the living. She'd done it before. With any luck, she'd do it again. But these babies were so young; could any of them become strong enough to make it back to the wild?

All she could do was try.

Chapter 1
Baby Season in the Bird Ward

It's spring once again, the time of year when fledglings venture out of the nest, on their own for the first time. At Elizabeth's Wildlife Centre in Abbotsford, British Columbia, Elizabeth Melnick makes her way through a maze of flight cages, caring for babies whose first journey might very nearly have been their last.

A tidy outbuilding adjacent to her home houses her primary clinic, the treatment area where the most seriously injured birds and animals are cared for. She bends over a baby incubator, opens the porthole, and strokes a miniscule killdeer chick. "This one came in weighing 6 grams," she says, reaching for an insulin syringe minus the needle. She pulls a slurry of food mixture into the syringe and holds it above the gaping maw of the orphan. He gulps it down greedily, cheeping for more, but that's all he gets for now.

Next in line are two baby waxwings. "These birds are 90 percent fruit-eaters," she says, "so they get a mixture of canned puppy food, vitamins, strained blueberries, and applesauce." Her ability to recognize different species of birds is just as important as knowing their dietary requirements. Like human infants, many of them look very different from their adult counterparts but, unlike humans, they can have vastly different nutritional needs. There's no such thing as generic baby bird food. "People phone me up and ask what to feed this baby bird they found," Elizabeth says. "I try to get them to bring it to me instead, because I know it's probably going to die."

Few people know it's against the law to confine a wild animal for longer than 24 hours, even for the purposes of helping it. Elizabeth's Wildlife Centre Society is a licensed facility, with special permits from the British Columbia Ministry of Environment, Lands and Parks, as well as the Canadian Wildlife Service, that allow her to care for injured wildlife. The permits are necessary because the animal is the one who pays the price for amateur rescue attempts. Elizabeth regularly attends courses in wildlife rescue and is a member of numerous organizations for professional "rehabbers." Unfortunately, when people happen upon a wild animal or bird that needs help, they often want to try to save it themselves, maybe to keep as a pet, maybe simply for the inherent romance.

Baby Season in the Bird Ward

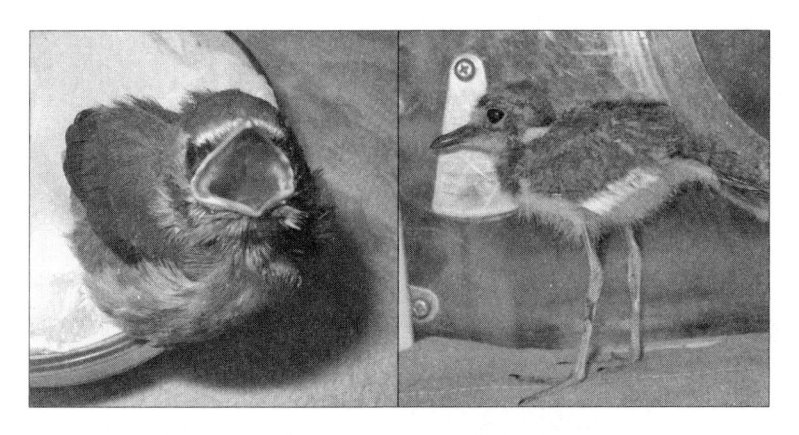

Patients at Elizabeth's Wildlife Centre:
(l) a cedar waxwing fledgling; (r) a baby killdeer

But the romance wears off quickly when the creature doesn't respond. "I'll get calls from people who have had a bird or a bunny or a squirrel for a couple of days, and it's not doing well," Elizabeth says. "By the time they bring it to me, it's nearly dead."

Elizabeth is very careful to make sure she meets or exceeds every requirement for her facility. Being in a residential subdivision, the last thing she needs is complaints from her neighbours. So her heart sank one day when one of her neighbours approached her to ask if she'd recently released a jay. Steller's jays, commonly seen west of the Rocky Mountains, are intelligent, beautiful birds with deep black-blue plumage, but they are raucously loud and can be persistent thieves. Elizabeth cringed to think that perhaps a bird

Wildlife in the Kitchen

she'd cared for might be becoming a neighbourhood pest.

The neighbour explained that her husband liked to go out onto the deck and enjoy a cigarette in the evenings. But recently, a jay had swooped onto the deck, snatched the cigarette out of his hand and flown to the roof with it. Elizabeth closed her eyes in horror at the image, envisioning the whole block of houses going up in smoke, but the neighbour quickly reassured her that the cigarette had gone out and the roof hadn't caught fire. "She told me that now her husband takes a piece of bread outside with him and the bird lets him finish his smoke in peace. Thank goodness!"

But she can't always predict her neighbours' reactions. "I had a little bantam rooster once," she says. "He was just a baby but then he started to crow, a really awful, pathetic noise." She knew once this jaunty little bird properly found his voice he'd be crowing at the break of dawn each day and that his urban neighbours might begin thinking he'd be a lot cuter in a pot. So she found him a home on a farm. Before she knew it, though, neighbours were asking her what had happened to the rooster. They'd enjoyed the morning serenade and missed it! "They told me that the next time I get a rooster I'm supposed to keep it," she comments wryly.

Elizabeth continues around the side of the building to where the stronger birds convalesce. In one cage, a grosbeak with a bad leg hops awkwardly from perch to perch, a jay with no tail waits for new feathers to come in, and a robin drags a damaged wing. Without protection predators would

Baby Season in the Bird Ward

easily pick off each of these birds, but a little time to heal will give them a chance to make it. Five young pigeons coo and cluck in the next cage. "See the fluff on their heads?" she points out. "They're still babies." Three juvenile wood ducks rest quietly together in a shady pen beneath the shrubbery. Many of these birds are just here for a brief stopover to rest and regain some strength. "I released eleven yesterday," she says. "It's really quiet right now. It's like a holiday for me."

A total of 87 wild animals and birds reside in her shelter at the moment, during this "lull" in activity. "Sometimes I have 60 calls a day," Elizabeth says of the busy times. "I'll be running all day long." A slight, energetic woman, with bird-like quickness of movement, she confesses that she'll often lose 10 or more pounds when rescue season bursts to life in early spring and doesn't begin to gain it back until the temperatures drop and migratory birds leave for warmer climes. Each and every creature that enters her centre is recorded in the logbook, and she makes note of every telephone report of an animal or bird needing help. "I usually stay up until 1 a.m. or 2 a.m. working on records and logbooks," she says. "But I don't get up until about 8 a.m., so that's okay."

After the work involved in caring for the individual birds and managing the shelter, her next most important task is educating the public on what should and should not be done for wildlife. Each person she talks with is one less person who will inadvertently harm a baby bird, thinking it needs help. Baby birds found on the ground, she explains, are often simply at the beginning of their training. "They have to learn to fly from the ground up," says Elizabeth.

It's a natural stage of development where the young birds strengthen their muscles, she says, and the parents are vigilantly guarding them. Unfortunately, people spot the ungainly babies hopping around, and think they've fallen down and are helpless. They wave off the parents to pick up the youngsters and put them into a nearby nest, but the birds soon hop out again.

Elizabeth suggests that before approaching an apparently orphaned baby bird, people should first check to see if it appears injured. Is it hopping around? Does it have feathers? Is it really alone? Look around the area. Chances are, the parents are watching from a nearby perch. Finally, make sure there are no cats or dogs waiting to pounce on the baby. If it appears healthy and there are no predators stalking it, the best thing is to leave the young bird exactly where it is and let its parents tend to it. "As long as it can hop and has good feathers, it's going through a natural learning process," she summarizes.

Whenever possible, Elizabeth does what she calls a "soft-release," giving the birds a protected area in which to readjust to the great outdoors and freedom before setting them loose for good. At the back of her property is the pre-release flight cage, tucked next to a lush belt of deciduous and evergreen trees, salmonberry bushes, blackberry vines, and salal. Full-height, the cage is furnished with a variety of

Baby Season in the Bird Ward

branches and twigs, allowing the birds to practise their take-off and landing skills in safety.

Once Elizabeth is sure they've got the skills they need to survive, she packs them into a transport cage and takes them to a protected area where they can start over again, in the wild. "We try and release the birds early in the day," she says, "when their food sources will be most plentiful." Release sites are carefully chosen based on the needs of the birds. Robins, for instance, can be fiercely territorial. Young robins released into an area already claimed by adults might be at risk of attack.

• • •

Jackie Ward, team leader of animal care at the Wildlife Rescue Association of BC, in Burnaby, British Columbia, remembers the large male Canada goose brought to their animal care centre one spring. A concerned passer-by had noticed him at the side of the road, injured and unable to get out of the way of traffic. Somehow, the man managed to capture the large bird and transport it to the shelter. "He'd likely been hit by a car," says Jackie. "He had soft tissue damage to his leg — nothing major but he was too sore to walk. He needed time in a protected environment."

Although many Canada geese are accustomed to the presence of humans, sometimes even dependent on them for food, captivity is extremely stressful for them. Many are

Wildlife in the Kitchen

so upset they refuse to eat. Because this gander's injury was relatively minor, everyone had high hopes for his quick recovery and release. But after a couple of days at the shelter, it became apparent that his convalescence was not going well; the bird wasn't eating or drinking and he seemed depressed. Instead of the steady improvement they expected to see, his condition was deteriorating quickly. They checked him carefully for additional injuries that might have been missed on the initial examination but found nothing. This mysterious malaise seemed to be caused by something else, something outside the realm of medical science. Staff members try hard to keep their emotions from clouding their judgment, but to several of the caregivers, he seemed to be pining, lonely. Was he missing his companions?

It was a reasonable theory. Canada geese are extremely social birds that form very close pair bonds. Once they mate, it's for life. Captive geese will honk loudly if they see others of their kind flying overhead, clearly wishing to join them. "When we've only got one in captivity, it can be very difficult for them," says Jackie. If this gander had been inadvertently separated from his mate, it would explain why he'd apparently lost his will to live. Several calls later, they discovered that after the male was brought in, a female goose had been seen in the same area, wandering around and calling. Could it be that the gander they'd been caring for was her mate? There was only one way to find out.

Jackie and her co-workers went to the area and set about

Baby Season in the Bird Ward

capturing the goose. That's when they discovered that not only had the gander been separated from his mate, but they had a clutch of goslings as well. No wonder he was anxious.

Many bird species are extremely protective of their young but none exemplify this like Canada geese. Both male and female Canada geese are very involved parents, and both are highly protective of the goslings. While the female tends to stay back and shield the young, the male is usually the more aggressive, actively chasing off threatening individuals. But this time rescue workers had to catch them in order to reunite the family. So they set out on a literal wild goose chase, rounding up mom and babies to go visit dad in the hospital. After much honking, hissing, cheeping, fluttering, and flapping, the noisy group was cloistered in a transport pen and loaded into the vehicle. They hoped they'd found the right goose; if it wasn't his mate, the gander could react with aggression.

But the instant the goose and goslings came near the pen where the gander was being kept, they knew they were witnessing a family reunion. The birds clustered and milled around each other, desperate to be as close as possible. "The change in the male was immediate," recalls Jackie. "They started to communicate once they were together again, standing in front of each other, lowering their heads and necks, opening their beaks, and making little noises." He was once more the picture of a strong, healthy Canada goose.

The best care in the world can't heal a broken heart. But when the heart is healed, everything else often follows suit.

Wildlife in the Kitchen

With his family back again, the male's appetite returned, his energy level increased, and his leg quickly healed. Shortly after, the entire family was released back to the area in which they'd been found. The male flapped his wings and thanklessly hissed at his caregivers, warning them away from his little family. But they understood. He was just doing his job.

Chapter 2
Wolf Watching

The gymnasium goes quiet. Over 100 kids sit cross-legged on the floor, wide-eyed, mouths hanging open. The object of their attention is the massive 50-kilogram wolf lounging casually on the stage next to his handler, Shelley Black. From the tip of his nose to the end of his tail, he measures about one-and-a-half metres. And he's only two years old, not completely full-grown. "This," says Shelley, "is Wiley." Wiley yawns, his cavernous jaw stretching to reveal a daunting set of gleaming white teeth, and the audience chuckles nervously.

Shelley and Wiley are from the Northern Lights Wildlife Wolf Centre in Golden, British Columbia, visiting the school to help educate children about the vital environmental importance of the wolf. Each presentation — to students

Wildlife in the Kitchen

as young as kindergartners — incorporates animal biology, ecology, sociology, plus the chance to meet a wolf, up close and personal! But before any face-to-face meeting occurs, Shelley makes sure all the children understand this is no ordinary house pet. "We cover all safety procedures with the students prior to introducing the wolf," emphasizes Shelley. The underlying principle is always to avoid triggering the wolf's innate predatory drive. In essence, children are taught not to act like prey — no running, no screaming or shrieking, and no sudden movements. Cooperation is rarely an issue but, just in case, Shelley adds a final caveat: *everything* is on the wolf's terms. The animal stays in the classroom only if the class behaves.

Then, and only then, does the lesson begin. Starting with the anatomy of a predator, Shelley teaches children about the special adaptations of wolves that make them good hunters. Then she describes the intricate relationship between predator and prey. "The wolf is classified as a keystone species," explains Shelley. "Our goal is to teach people that we need the predator in the environment." Wolves, she continues, are at the top of the food chain. They prey on small mammals such as field mice, rabbits, and beaver, as well as larger animals like deer, elk, and other ungulates (hoofed mammals). This controls the populations of these animals, most of which eat only plant material. Without such population control, these species tend to increase in number until the land is overgrazed, trees and bushes are stripped,

Wolf Watching

and, in short, the balance of nature is disrupted.

"In Yellowstone National Park in the 1950s, they studied this problem," says Shelley. "It started in the 1800s and by 1930 there were no wolves left in Yellowstone." The wolves were wiped out in the hope of protecting domestic livestock, as well as the wild ungulate populations. But what they discovered was that without the wolves, the park couldn't survive. Several dozen wolves were eventually brought in from Canada and reintroduced to the park. According to Shelley, a healthy wolf population checks the herds of herbivorous animals, which allows plants like willows and other trees to thrive, which in turn allows beaver to thrive and complete the circle by providing a food source for the wolves. Without a keystone species like the wolf, all of nature suffers.

Everyone is in favour of maintaining the balance of nature — in theory. But when faced with the real-life presence of wolves, many people react with raw fear, a type of panic that Shelley insists is unfounded. "There has never been a documented case of a vicious attack on a human by a healthy wild wolf, outside of captivity," she states. Fatal attacks by bears and cougars are common in North America, but there is no verified report of anyone being killed by a wolf. In every situation where a human has been injured by a wolf, she adds, there have been mitigating circumstances: captive wolves protecting a food source, a hurt or sick wolf acting defensively, or wild wolves that have been habituated to humans by thoughtless contact.

Wildlife in the Kitchen

Wolves are characteristically secretive and will normally run away when they encounter people. Unfortunately, when well-meaning, curious, or ignorant wilderness visitors provide food and encourage the wolves to come ever-nearer for that elusive Kodak moment, the result is wolves that have become so habituated to human contact that they're no longer afraid of people. Such wolves are dangerous, to people as well as to themselves.

A tragic case on Vargas Island off the west coast of Vancouver Island in British Columbia illustrates Shelley's point most vividly. Populated by only a handful of permanent residents, Vargas is Clayoquot Sound's third-largest island, and one of the closest to the village of Tofino. The isolated island had long been a peaceful home for wolves. But when it was discovered as a beautiful destination for campers, day-trippers, and adventure seekers, things changed. As it became more popular with wilderness tourists, the wolves grew accustomed to the presence of humans. Instead of avoiding people, they became attracted to them — and the food they often offered. Local residents could do nothing but shake their heads. Year after year, the wolves took handouts from thoughtless picnickers and gradually their inherent fear of people turned to expectation.

It was a situation just waiting to go bad, and on one trip in the summer of 2000, it did. A group of kayakers had set up camp on the beach. During the night, a curious young wolf approached a camper sleeping on the beach and began

Wolf Watching

nosing around, probably looking for food. The activity awakened the camper, who reacted with understandable alarm. When he yelled, he startled the wolf, and the wolf — just as understandably — reacted to defend himself. Then he turned tail and fled, leaving the man with severe facial and scalp lacerations that required dozens of sutures. But he was alive. "If the wolf had intended to do damage," says Shelley, "that man would be dead."

But fears ran high and intentions don't count in such situations. Conservation officers immediately went on the hunt, with the predictably tragic outcome. BC Parks put up signs at Vargas and other new provincial parks in Clayoquot Sound announcing: "People have been injured and wolves have been destroyed. Don't be the next victim!" The notices claimed that wildlife had "suffered the consequences of people's actions."

It's heartbreaking — and preventable. That's where Wiley and his buddy Moab come in. "They are travelling ambassador wolves," says Shelley. "Their job is to help save their cousins in the wild."

When Shelley and her husband, Casey, first set up their centre it was for the explicit purpose of teaching people about wolves, and about how humans and wolves can coexist on the same planet. But their own education started much earlier. Casey had worked for many years as an animal wrangler for the film industry. "He did some training," says Shelley, "but mostly he cared for wolves and the other

Wildlife in the Kitchen

animals used in the movie industry." His knowledge of wolf behaviour began there but soon he wanted to take it further. And in a different direction. Instead of using wolves for entertainment, he wanted their wolves to play a role in educating people about wild wolves and how we can protect them.

"Our minds got changed," says Shelley. "We learned about other places that were teaching wolf awareness and we thought, 'We're in the Rocky Mountains, near Banff and Lake Louise, it's the perfect opportunity for us.'" They decided to do something to change public opinion and today they make their living working to keep wild wolves alive and safe in their natural habitat.

"We are an interpretive centre," says Shelley. "We have five wolves, all born and raised in captivity for the movie industry." Aspen, their first wolf, is actually a wolf hybrid, one-quarter husky, three-quarters grey wolf. She was a year old when Maya and her big brother Tuk arrived. From the beginning, the Blacks focused on giving their wolves the best life possible and making sure they would be safe around visitors. "Ours are the only wolves in the world that go for walks," says Shelley. "They go on trails outside the compound, off-leash, for 2 to 3 hours at a time."

A few years later, 10-day-old Wiley joined them and the Blacks discovered the joys of hand-rearing an infant wolf. It apparently agreed with them because in May 2004, the youngest member, Moab, joined their pack. The offspring of a white arctic wolf mother and a grey-brown male wolf from

Wolf Watching

Quebec, he arrived at the centre at the tender age of 24 days, weighing a mere two kilograms. Bottle-fed on goat's milk, little Moab received constant nurturing from both his human caregivers and his adopted wolf family.

By the time Moab was 10 weeks old, he'd more than quadrupled in size. Shelley and Casey had exposed him to people with extreme care and diligence, hoping he would become a valuable tool in their educational school programs. And it seems to have worked. "Weighing 10 kilograms, he is 50 centimetres high at the shoulder, and 75 centimetres long from nose to bum," says Shelley. "He has already met hundreds of schoolchildren from British Columbia and the United States, and hundreds more people from around the world."

With their mandate of conservation, Shelley and Casey Black are meticulous about doing everything right. "We do have a functioning wolf pack," says Shelley. "We have created our compound so that they aren't separated; they live together like a wild pack would live." The wolves live on one-and-a-half acres of fenced woodland, and they go outside the compound regularly with their human escorts. "At least two to three times a week the wolves go for a hike," says Shelley. "We go from one to four hours depending on the day and we only take two at a time — maybe three now, with Moab in training."

But no matter how well these wolves are cared for, the Blacks are quick to point out that it's not a natural life, and any puppies born to them would only end up in captivity. This is a prospect they refuse to consider. "All our animals are born in other zoo facilities," says Shelley, "and all are spayed and neutered."

So their little pack of five, plus Shelley and Casey, functions as a reasonable facsimile of a wild wolf pack. Wolves are among the most social animals in the world, and their lives revolve around the extended family of the pack. Wolf packs typically include a dominant pair, their offspring (including older pups from previous litters), and aunts and uncles of the young. The number of wolves in a pack is directly dependent upon the food available, and pack members co-operate in hunting and caring for the next generation.

Social structure within the wolf pack, as in many other animal groups, is strictly organized on the basis of a dominance hierarchy. And when it comes to dominance, size matters! Dominant wolves are unmistakable: everything about them appears large and formidable. They carry themselves tall and erect. Their ears are up and forward. Their tails are carried high on their backs. Because Aspen was full-grown when Tuk and Maya arrived, she naturally assumed the role of alpha wolf, or leader. Even though they've now outgrown her, Aspen remains the dominant wolf. None of the others question her authority. Wolves lower in the social order have very different body posture. They lower their bodies, tuck their tails and put their ears back. "Maya has always been the most submissive of our pack," says Shelley. "In the wild she would be called the 'beta wolf.'"

The main difference in this little pack is that, even for

Wolf Watching

Aspen, the ultimate leaders are the humans. "We act a lot like the alphas would in the wild — showing them food sources, protecting them, and making decisions for them," says Shelley. "We have raised them all from pups. Plus we control their food, and that has a lot to do with why they look up to us as the alpha pair."

Wild wolf packs have two separate hierarchies, male and female, and aggression is generally directed toward same-sex wolves. In a pack, everything — rank, food, the right to mate — comes with the price tag of competition. Wolves who lose such competitions can be driven out of the pack or even killed. For a wolf, being alone means being vulnerable to starvation. Most solitary wolves skulk hopefully at the edges of other packs, looking for a chance to once again be part of a family. "In over six years we've learned the social behaviour of the wolves, and we explain to people how similar it is to that of humans," says Shelley.

The wolf's co-operative nature is most strikingly demonstrated in pup rearing. Virtually all pack members contribute in one way or another. Pups are born helpless and utterly dependent, weighing about half a kilogram. The mother spends most of her time in the den with the pups for the first week. They need their mother not only for nourishment, but to regulate their own body temperature. With her every absence their tiny bodies become chilled; if she's gone long enough the puppies will die of hypothermia. When Wiley and Moab arrived at the centre as tiny pups, it was Maya, the submissive one, who stepped in as caregiver. "Maya's maternal instinct is strong, and she has taken on a protective and nurturing role," says Shelley.

Because puppies represent their future, pack members hunt and bring back food, allowing the mother to spend her time snuggling and feeding the new babies. Other females also nurse pups, sometimes even competing for access to them. If more than one litter is born, all surviving pups are usually put into one combined litter, tended and nursed by all the mothers.

When Wiley arrived at the centre, Maya immediately began digging him a sleeping area. When Moab was added to the family, Maya did what many parents do: she renovated, digging another den for the baby. "Maya was extremely loving to all our pups," says Shelley. "She became very possessive of the pups and didn't even allow me to be close to them. I think that that female would have lactated if she could have!"

When Moab was introduced to the pack upon his arrival at Northern Lights, the older wolves all eagerly sniffed at him through the fence, even before Shelley and Casey brought him inside the enclosure. Their responses were as individual as they are. "Aspen tolerates little ones," says Shelley. "Tuk keeps his distance, but he's the first one to regurgitate food for a new puppy."

Wolf pups develop rapidly and start venturing out of the den at about three weeks of age. At this time the other pack members, including adult males and yearlings, begin

Wolf Watching

to help feeding them. In the wild, young wolves don't accompany the adults on hunting forays so the adult wolves carry food back to the den from a kill the only way they can: in their bellies. They gorge themselves on the kill then return to feed the younger wolves by bringing up the partially digested food. Even though this isn't necessary, thanks to their human caretakers, the adult wolves at Northern Lights still do their part to make sure the youngsters get sufficient nourishment. "When the pups are really young the adults don't hold back at all," says Shelley. This usually continues until the puppies are about three or four months old, but some wolves have an overly developed sense of responsibility. "I have witnessed Tuk regurgitate for Wiley when Wiley was a year and a half old," she remarks.

The mother usually resumes hunting after the pups emerge from the den and will often leave them alone or in the care of other pack members, sometimes yearling "babysitters," while she's out. All pack members seem to greatly enjoy playing with and caring for pups. "Wiley was a nervous and gangly teenager at first, forgetting where his feet were and stepping on the pup a few times," says Shelley. "Now he is rather like a big brother and spends half the time playing, and the other half trying to get away from a pesky young brother."

Even with this tender, loving care, only about half of all pups born in the wild survive to their first birthday. Shelley and Casey are grateful for the privilege and responsibility of raising their wolves, but they've earned it. To keep wild animals in

Wildlife in the Kitchen

captivity requires special licences. They pay several hundred dollars per animal, per year, to maintain their status.

The feeding alone of wolves is a formidable task. Northern Lights wolves are fed a variety of food, much of it donated from hunters, farmers, and ranchers. Wild wolves eat when they can, depending on the availability of prey and their ability to hunt successfully. To simulate life in the wild, the Blacks only feed their wolves every second day, and each wolf consumes 5 to 10 pounds at a time. Their diet consists primarily of wild game, but they also get beef, chicken, bison, and, for a treat, dry dog kibble. "Nothing is fed alive," emphasizes Shelley. "We even use road kill — although we have to pay for it! A hundred pounds lasts approximately 48 hours between the four adults. They eat everything."

Wild wolves are naturally afraid of people, and so are captive wolves if they aren't socialized at a young age. Tuk and Maya received minimal human contact as pups and, as a result, they remain shy and aloof with strangers. "We use Tuk and Maya as prime examples of what wild wolves are like," says Shelley. Because of their early hand-rearing by Shelley and Casey, Wiley and Moab are familiar with humans, making them the best candidates for public relations. "We allow kids to see just how large they are. We talk about the centre but the kids get to touch the wolves." Being face to face with a creature so close to the wild stimulates unbelievable reactions from the kids. "Some of the kids are scared, some are just amazed," she says, smiling. "Even the adults' reactions are pretty cool."

Wolf Watching

It's an unforgettable experience and that's what the Blacks are counting on. The more people that learn to care about wolves, the better their chances for survival in the wild. "In all of Canada," says Shelley, "wolves are not protected outside of parkland. A wolf gets less respect than a rat. They are officially classified as vermin."

The Blacks are passionate about wolf conservation. Watching the antics of their little family, it's easy to see why. "After living with them and being with them all the time," Shelley comments affectionately, "they grow on you."

Chapter 3
Lionheart

The feathery touch of a breeze stirred the pampas grass, nudging the lazy air, but only for a moment. As soon as the zephyr died the air settled again, onto a still plain crackling with heat. Against the setting sun the expanse of grass quivered like a calm, golden ocean, the smooth surface bewitching the unsuspecting zebra to come closer, closer.

Hidden within the grass the lion lay motionless, muscles poised, watching his prey. All nerves strained toward an unseen signal that would indicate the time had come. He waited, eyes and ears sorting information, preparing. His prey moved closer, almost within range. The lion shifted and leaned forward but it wasn't quite time yet. Wait a bit longer; let it get a bit closer. Patience, patience.

Lionheart

Suddenly, the moment arrived.

"Go!" urged the man beside the lion. The animal exploded into action; a predator had been unleashed. But would he be successful? The man ran behind, hoping against hope that this time the king of beasts would capture his prey. It was his only chance. Soon they would return to Canada and hunting season would be over forever.

Just east of Toronto, off the beaten track on the Old Kings Highway, tucked away in the little town of Bowmanville, Ontario, is North America's oldest private zoological park. Established in 1919, the Bowmanville Zoological Park (BZP) sprawls over 42 acres of gentle rolling hillside, mature shade trees, ponds, and meadows. It's home to over 300 exotic, non-human inhabitants. By day, zoo director Michael Hackenberger deals with the day-to-day minutia of administration, staffing, and public relations. But his true passion is training the animals, and the bigger the challenge, the better. The Bowmanville Zoo is a home for trained animals with "careers" in film and television. "This is the food for my soul. I love spending time with animals on this level. If I could do this 24 hours a day, I would. Instead," he says comically, "I have to be a crummy zoo director."

The BZP is an accredited member of CAZA, the Canadian Association of Zoos and Aquariums, and winner of the prestigious Thomas Baines Award for outstanding excellence and achievement, known to those in the field as the "Academy Award" of zoos.

Wildlife in the Kitchen

But for Michael, pride has a much more poignant meaning. In early December 2001, four little bundles of fur were born, an unlikely and lasting legacy to Bongo, a lion who touched him in a way no other animal has.

When Michael got the call, over a decade ago, that the Ringling Bros. and Barnum and Bailey Circus in the United States had two young males they no longer needed, he decided to check them out. The cubs, born in the Maritimes at a now-defunct zoo, had been with the Ringling show until the circus obtained another big lion act. At 7 months of age, Bongo and Caesar were suddenly obsolete.

The tranquil, placid, unchanging scenery of a zoo can make it very difficult when animals, for whatever reason, must move to a new location. But Michael knew at first sight that Bongo and his companion Caesar were up to the move and would be coming home with him. He instantly recognized their potential suitability for the Bowmanville Zoo. "Right off the bat I saw big-boned, large-bodied, up-front animals," he recalls. "In captivity you often see poor quality animals but these were physically beautiful. And they were interested in people. I knew they were going to work." So Bongo and Caesar returned to Canada, the land of their birth.

"They were both superb animals genetically, with a well-laid basic foundation of training," says Michael. They'd also been very well socialized, something of a rarity in captive exotic animals. Michael knew these lions had what they needed to succeed on the world's stage. Or, as it turned out,

Lionheart

to shine as stars of the big screen.

In 1996 Bongo and Caesar were chosen to play the title roles in the movie *The Ghost and the Darkness*, co-starring Michael Douglas and Val Kilmer. With great excitement, Michael and the lions embarked on a seven-month adventure in the Songimvelo Game Reserve in Mpumalanga Province on the border between South Africa and Swaziland. "I mean, taking lions to Africa," says Michael. "How does it get any better?" But challenges quickly appeared. Everything new was fascinating to the lions. Without the insight of native-born lions, they didn't see threats; the terrain was simply full of exciting things waiting to be explored. For Michael, this meant constant vigilance and another round of training for these big cats. If they discovered a spitting cobra under a bush, for instance, they needed to learn quickly that cobras are neither toys nor food.

Until then the training he'd done with the lions had been fairly regimented, focusing on accuracy and precision of movement. While this is perfect for live shows, on film it didn't look natural. "This type of training is of great benefit when you're working with potentially dangerous animals," says Michael, "but it made them look too choreographed. So I had to let go, behaviourally."

Bongo, who played the Ghost, had the majority of screen time and Michael had to step back and trust that Bongo could do what was required of him. "There are inherent risk factors," he admits, "but we had absolutely no issues

Wildlife in the Kitchen

on that level." Very few lions have been reliably trained to simulate viciousness against humans but even the breathtaking attack scenes came off without a hitch.

After a hard stretch of acting like a wild lion, Bongo got a fabulous reward: he got to go zebra-hunting. It was tremendously gratifying for everyone to see the animal they knew so well letting his inner carnivore have free reign. But rest assured, no zebras were ever harmed in the making of the film — or afterwards. "Bongo had a great time," says Michael, "but he was really bad at it. After he'd chase the zebras he'd lumber up to us for a scratch, looking all disappointed and sad."

The African people were fascinated by this white man and his Canadian lions. "We'd head into the townships with the lions in cages on the back of the pickups," recalls Michael. "I'd go in to get a Coke, and when I'd come back out there would be huge crowds of curious Africans, asking me to tell them about my lion." He opened the truck and had Bongo jump up on top of the cage so everyone could see him and he began to answer questions. Every time he spoke, voices immediately began translating into three different languages. "Where's he from?" they asked. "Canada," he answered. "Where's that?" "Far away in a land where snow falls on the ground," he explained. With disbelief and amusement, they responded, "No way!"

They were desperately poor people and yet their delight at seeing these strange lions was so great, they tried to pay Michael. "They wanted to give me a cow or a pig or a daughter," he says. "I had to insist that it was okay, there was no charge."

But one night near the end of the filming, he realized just how much impact these lions had had on the African people. Several thousand native labourers were hired as extras for the movie. They'd been working on the night sequences for three weeks, which meant trying to sleep during the full heat of the day. Work conditions were less than ideal; lighting up 20 acres required massive lights mounted on skyjacks, which attracted insects, which in turn attracted bats. Everyone was getting testy and frequent breaks for water and rest were essential. "I'm lying in the back of the pickup, with Bongo's head in my lap," remembers Michael. "The Zulu headboys came up to talk to me. They said they wanted to pay honour to me." Michael didn't quite know what this meant, so he responded by offering them passes to his zoo in Canada. But no, what they wanted was to touch him. "It's 45°C at night there," he says. "They touched my face and then wiped my sweat on their bodies."

Michael had no idea what to make of this. "I said to one of them, 'You gotta help me with this. I'm a Caucasian Canadian — what's this about?' They told me 'We've watched you, you work with lions, so you must have very strong magic.'"

Three days later the film was finally completed. Michael and the lions were on their way to the airport, eagerly anticipating their trip home. Michael was sitting on top of the cages as they pulled out onto the tarmac toward the plane. On top

Wildlife in the Kitchen

of the buildings, they saw armed guards watching them. "As I would go by they'd all clench their fists in the air," says Michael. While he was unhooking the cages, he commented to one of the helpers that the military must really think a lot of Bongo and Caesar. "It's you," the man corrected him. "'He Who Walks With Lions.'"

Michael will never forget the generous appreciation given him by the Africans, people who know lions as westerners never can. Even though his lions were born on Canadian soil, their hearts beat to the ancient rhythms of the jungle and their heritage is the savannah of their ancestors.

Everything that helps him understand his animals, allows him to train them more effectively. "I do all my training with positive food reinforcement," explains Michael. "Predators have an extremely well-developed food drive." Working for food rewards allows Michael to achieve an authoritative relationship with the animal without domination. "It's the equal relationships that are always the most appropriate and most successful," he says. "Both partners are bringing the same into it." He never forgets, however, that his work is extremely dangerous. "Whenever I am dealing with a large predator there are safety issues," he says matter-of-factly. "They kill other male animals to establish territory. You have to keep in mind, it's what they do. Don't take it personally." Knowing what makes the animal tick, he says, allows a trainer to predict behaviour, to see conflict before it erupts. It doesn't always work, he admits, but when problems arise, the responsibility lies squarely in the lap of the trainer. "Problems are of your own making," he emphasizes. "You know they're wild animals."

Michael speaks with the voice of experience. On a sweltering August night in 1998 Bongo was performing a show at Canada's Wonderland in Toronto. Even the most placid personalities in the troupe were getting a bit twitchy. The trainers were watching Bongo especially closely, as he always got a bit more contentious in summer. "Lions go through aggressive periods at around age four and age eight," says Michael. "In the wild, at four they'd be looking to take over a pride and at eight they'd be getting kicked out of a pride." Bongo was 10 but he appeared to be expressing that same sort of testosterone-driven territoriality, centred around — of all things — a roll of carpet.

The trainers had already used several tactics to try and get him away from the carpet and off the stage, but Bongo wasn't having any of it. He'd scarfed down the meat and bounded back to the rug before anyone could intervene. "I moved in and closed a couple of exits to contain the situation, but I could see that the carpet was his piece of earth to protect," says Michael. He put a pedestal in front of Bongo, to create a barrier between him and his object of desire. Usually this defuses the situation nicely. Not this time. Bongo rushed at Michael and before anyone knew what was happening, Michael's wrist was between those massive jaws. Later, Michael would learn that several bones in his wrist were cracked. But it was nothing compared to what Bongo could have done if he'd truly intended harm. It was a warning and Michael took it as such. He knew he had to keep his distance.

"I was about 20 metres away, farther than I've been with wild lions, when he charged me again." Bongo wasn't aiming for his hand this time; he was aiming for his face. Michael got the training pole in front of him and managed to push Bongo away but he knew there wouldn't be a third warning. "Next time, either I'd lose or he'd lose," he says. "I stepped out of the ring and we darted him." He'd been trying to avoid using the tranquilizer gun because Bongo had eaten about 30 pounds of food in their earlier attempts to mollify him. With a full stomach, even light sedation can lead to vomiting and choking. "So there I am, pulling food out of his mouth, and he's still trying to bite me," Michael remembers. He can laugh about it in retrospect; in 14 years with Bongo, it was his only scare and even then, Michael insists, it was his own fault. "Bongo was as honest as the day is long. He was never sneaky. Sure, he broke bones. But he could have killed me."

In most such situations intervention would have ended the conflict. This time, as soon as Bongo was recovered from the sedation and ready to rejoin the show he immediately ran to where the rug had been. He hadn't forgotten anything. But once he realized the rug was gone, he decided to give up the battle. Nothing else, it appeared, was quite worth fighting over.

In the summer of 2001, Bongo was being readied for

Lionheart

a scheduled trip to Argentina to film a commercial when Michael realized the big cat wasn't well. Some time earlier, Bongo had had a lump removed from his hip and he just hadn't bounced back from the surgery. They cancelled the trip and took him instead for MRI, magnetic resonance imaging. Unfortunately, Bongo turned out to be too big for the machine and they weren't able to do the procedure. But when they x-rayed his chest, the culprit was revealed: lung cancer. Bongo's time was quickly running out.

Michael was devastated. But that was when he made his toughest decision. He knew that if Bongo formed an attachment with a mate, he'd view all males — even Michael — as threats. Nevertheless, he decided to let Bongo live out his remaining weeks with a female lion, in the unlikely hope that Bongo's line would continue.

They chose a lioness from the Granby Zoo in Quebec, a young one that would be most likely to get along with Bongo. Because she was born at Granby during an ice storm, they had named her Gresil, a French word that loosely translates to "hail." Often known by her Anglicized name, Gracie, she quickly became Bongo's best friend, supplanting Michael for the first time in their relationship.

Bongo and Gracie were friends, but they didn't seem to be anything more than friends. It looked like Bongo's age and illness meant cubs weren't on his agenda. However, thanks to modern reproductive technology, there were other options. Bongo's caretakers collected semen for artificial

Wildlife in the Kitchen

insemination after his death.

In October it became apparent that Bongo's illness had progressed to the point where the majestic lion was no longer enjoying his life. "We'd set up a number of criteria," says Michael. "Loss of appetite, lethargy, that sort of thing. We knew it was time." Bongo died early in the morning, peacefully, surrounded by people who loved him. "It was a very sad period for us," says Michael. They'd been keeping the media informed about Bongo's deteriorating health and had released an announcement of his death to the press. "I was driving into Toronto that morning when the 8:30 news came on and they read about his passing," recalls Michael. "I pulled over and just bawled my eyes out." Michael may have been Bongo's closest human companion, but people from all over the world sent notes, flowers, and pictures when they learned of his death.

Shortly after Bongo's death they discovered he'd left one last surprise. Gracie was pregnant after all, the old-fashioned way, and in early December 2001, she gave birth to four cubs.

Today, a young male named Bowman stars in the shows at the Bowmanville Zoo. He looks just like his dad but he will never replace Bongo in Michael's heart. "I can count on one hand the great animals I've worked with," he says. "Bongo was a great lion. I can develop a lion so far but after that it's a gift ... Bongo was a gift from the gods."

Because of the great many lives Bongo touched, his final resting place is in an area of the zoo open to the public.

Lionheart

A tree grows above the stone that marks the spot. On the stone are these words: "He was a star. He was a king. He was our friend."

Chapter 4
Rock and Peep: A Love Story

In the backyard, the birds are just settling in for the night. The last feeding is finished and Joan Biggs is covering, closing, and latching the cages. Inside, on perches and branches, are songbirds of all sorts, from starlings, blue jays, and crows, to robins, cardinals, orioles, chimney swifts, and tiny finches. "We haven't had a hummingbird yet," says Joan. "But I know what to do when we get one."

Joan and Neil Biggs have been rehabilitating wild birds for the past decade and their For the Birds Sanctuary has the necessary licence and permits to ensure that birds passing through their Sarnia, Ontario, facility receive the best possible care. As a registered charity, there's a great deal of paperwork involved. "We have to report to Canadian Wildlife Services at

Rock and Peep: A Love Story

the end of each year and tell them how many birds we've had, what type, how old they were, and what happened to them," explains Joan. "It's a lot of work." The administrative work is a hassle, but it's worth it because of the birds. She notes this with a certain pride because 10 years ago she couldn't have imagined feeling this way. "I didn't like anything flying or fluttering around me," she says. "Not even butterflies!"

Then one spring her husband, Neil, took care of a fledgling starling. "They leave the nest before they can fly and just need some assistance," she says. Neil sheltered the little bird until it was ready to fly off on its own and that was that. But word got around that he was someone who knew about wild birds; before long they were landed with an entire nest of starlings. Joan didn't know what to think. She felt sorry for the tiny orphans but it wasn't easy to let go of her squeamishness. "Then Neil told me I had to just get over it," remembers Joan. "So I did."

From then on she was hooked. They soaked up as much knowledge as they could — from other wildlife rehabilitators, from veterinarians, and from books and newsletters. But still, when Joan went to the Humane Society in response to their call about a baby bird, she didn't recognize the gangly, funny-looking creature they presented her with. "I said 'What's that?' and they told me 'It's a pigeon! Are you still going to take it?'" She and Neil had never cared for a baby pigeon before but she didn't hesitate, and the baby went home with her.

Pigeons, who belong to the same family as doves, are

sometimes known as rock birds or rock doves. While this family has a multitude of subspecies, the term *pigeon* usually refers to larger birds that have rather square or rounded tails, while *dove* refers to the smaller ones with pointed tails. The birds often seen roosting in the ledges of high buildings, commonly known as pigeons, recently had their name officially changed by the American Ornithologists' Union to *rock pigeon.*

The rock pigeon is one of the oldest domesticated animals, and was used as food by Egyptians as far back as 2600 B.C. In some Islamic countries pigeons and doves were protected on religious grounds.

The French introduced this bird into North America at Port Royal, Nova Scotia, in 1606. Rock pigeons have flourished throughout North, Central, and South America, the Hawaiian Islands, and parts of the West Indies. These birds naturally inhabit the rocky cliffs of coastal areas, so they find the ledges of high buildings a perfect substitute and have become abundant in cities, towns, and rural areas all over the world, wherever humans are close by.

Humans and pigeons, it seems, have a mutual attraction. Joan and Neil were about to learn just how strong this attraction could be.

Pigeon parents produce a very nutritious "pigeon milk" that they feed to their young by regurgitation. This baby bird would squeal for the substitute formula Joan and Neil had mixed up for her, its wings flapping rapidly above its head as

Rock and Peep: A Love Story

it bowed down and drank from the notched baby bottle nipple. "We were always amazed at the amount this bird could drink," Neil says. "It would push along the table top trying to catch the bottle as we were taking it away, even though it was so weighed down by the fullness of its crop that we were afraid the crop would burst."

They had no way of knowing if their new baby was a male or a female, so they named it Rock. But the fledgling grew quickly and, before long, they began to suspect she was a female. She had a definite personality — "avianality," according to Neil — and felt protective and possessive about what she saw as her territory. "We'd take her outside with us and watch as she chased other birds around the yard," says Neil. Rock was turning into a beautiful bird and they expected that soon she'd be ready to move out on her own. "We didn't really expect her to stick around," says Joan. "Our other birds usually joined the wild flocks that come by our house. But Rock didn't. She wanted to stay."

It wasn't long before the reason became clear: Rock was in love with Neil!

"We really don't know how she figured out which one of us was the male, but it became very apparent she saw me as a prospective mate and my wife as a threat," says Neil. Pigeons may not look intelligent or valuable, but they're commonly used in laboratory experiments in biology, medicine, and cognitive science. They can be trained to distinguish between cubist and impressionist paintings, for instance, and have

Wildlife in the Kitchen

been shown to be more effective than humans in spotting shipwreck victims at sea. "Rock was obviously smarter than me," says Neil sheepishly, "because for the first six months she was around, I was sure her belligerent, dominating ways indicated she was a male. How silly of me."

Rock's jealousy was unmistakable. She routinely flew at Joan, biting at her and pulling on her clothing, clearly trying to drive her away. Then she'd turn to Neil, bowing and cooing.

Joan couldn't help feeling a bit put out. After all her work with the bird she hadn't expected Rock to reject her so blatantly. "Here I lovingly cared for her and worried about her, and what does she do?" queries Joan. "She dumps me and goes for my husband!"

When Rock was old enough to move out of the house they decided it would be prudent to encourage some distance. It was time she realized Neil wasn't the one for her. "We set up a covered pigeon coop in the backyard with an opening big enough for her to have some freedom during the day, and a heat box for warmth at night," says Neil. But Rock wasn't about to let her true love go so easily. Back and forth she flew, from window to window, trying desperately to find a way inside the house, back to her chosen mate. "The whole neighbourhood was talking about that crazy pigeon's attempts to get into the house after we locked her out," says Neil. "She just didn't understand at all. She had selected me as her partner and now she couldn't reach me."

Around the same time, another fledgling pigeon arrived.

Rock and Peep: A Love Story

Peep, as they named him, was old enough to know he didn't want to be a pet. But he was still too young to care for himself; an adult pigeon's diet consists of fruits, seeds, berries, and small insects, but Peep wasn't quite ready for that yet.

It soon became apparent that young Peep was smitten with Rock. She, however, wanted nothing to do with him. He began to follow her around, lovesick and persistent, but all she could think of was finding Neil. "Whenever I had to go some place she'd follow me," says Neil. She'd land on the windshield wiper of his car and refuse to leave. Her persistence nearly caused her death many times, but she didn't even appear to notice. When he finally gave in and let her inside the car, she'd sit on the headrest beside him. "It was the only way not to risk her life," he says. "She would ride on the roof until the wind blew her off, then stare at the car from where she landed, which was usually the middle of the road." Neil would have to pull over and pick her up so other cars wouldn't hit her. Incredulous drivers slowed to watch. Neil was just glad he never caused a collision, stopping to pick up his lovelorn bird from the road. He watched one passing motorist try to drive while gazing open-mouthed at his unusual passenger. "I thought an accident was going to happen when a woman noticed Rock on the headrest as she was turning," he says. "I thought she'd go up the curb."

Peep continued to pay court to his lady-love and Rock robustly continued to remind him that not only was she not interested, but she also found him irritating in the extreme.

Wildlife in the Kitchen

"When birds don't want anything around," explains Joan, "they flick their wings, like you do with a towel. Peep did his song and dance and Rock just wing-flicked him and then flew up to Neil. Poor Peep looked so dejected."

Eventually Peep's persistence wore her down and Rock decided to move into the nest box with him. "She followed me around for two years trying to entice me to her nest," laughs Neil. "Then she was reintroduced to the pigeon world by Peep. Finally realizing she wasn't human, she settled for second-best with her pigeon mate." She continued to fly down to sit with Neil whenever she could, but in time her attitude seemed to be that if you can't be with the one you love, love the one you're with. "Poor Peep didn't know what he was in for," says Neil. "It probably wasn't a normal pigeon relationship."

Apparently it was normal enough; before long, there were eggs in the nest. Both pigeon parents work to guard the nest and incubate the eggs, a process that lasts about 18 days and although she'd never done this before, Rock did her share. When the eggs hatched, however, it was another story altogether. "She stood up, stepped aside, and just looked at them as if to say 'What are these things and where did they come from?'" remembers Joan. Although pigeons also share parenting duties, that first time Peep did double duty while Rock went through a brief identity crisis. A couple of times Joan and Neil had to drag out the ladder and step in to make sure the babies were being kept warm enough. But before

Rock and Peep: A Love Story

long Rock figured out her motherly responsibilities. As time went by, Rock settled into a routine with Peep and the wild pigeons in the neighbourhood.

And then Rock went missing.

Despite not being migratory birds, pigeons' outstanding homing capabilities have gained them a long and rich history of delivering messages, including during the times of Caesar and Napoleon. It's thought that they use magnetic fields to return to their home lofts, but this was cold comfort when Rock disappeared.

"A couple of times we thought we'd lost her because she didn't show up for a few weeks," says Neil. "I think one time somebody probably tried to keep her as a pet until they tired of her or she escaped." This time, though, she must have wandered farther than usual and been unable to fly back. Joan and Neil were grief-stricken, thinking she'd been hurt or killed. Even though Rock had so thoroughly rejected her, Joan wished aloud that the feisty pigeon would find her way home. "Within half an hour," says Neil, "I got a phone call from the Humane Society wondering if we would look after a rather vicious pigeon that needed time to regrow her flight feathers. I went outside and told Joan I was going to the Humane Society to pick up Rock." Joan didn't believe him. But Neil knew that since all the workers at the Humane Society were women, Rock wouldn't exactly be on her best behaviour. "I came out of the back room of the Humane Society with Rock riding on my shoulder, to an incredulous bunch of women

Wildlife in the Kitchen

saying, 'You're kidding, this is your bird?' I keep telling Joan to wish for riches," Neil teases, "because her wishes do come true sometimes."

Another spring arrived and now the little sanctuary had a flock of seven pigeons with more eggs under Rock. As spring wore on, their birds took to the air more and more and before long they were being accompanied by other pigeons from the wild flocks. "Our flock was growing in numbers," says Neil. "Luckily, Rock and Peep kept the rest from nesting at our place so our flock was a visiting one rather than a resident one." Of course, the more birds they had visiting their yard, the more food they needed to put out. The more food they put out, the more the birds visited. And the more birds they had, the more predators began to lurk in the background. "We ended up with hawks visiting the yard looking for easy prey," Neil commented soberly.

One evening near dusk Joan was working at her computer. Peep and Rock's nest box was just above the window near her desk. The birds were coming back to roost for the night when Joan heard a sudden thud, and saw feathers fluttering to the ground. With dread, she recognized the signs of a hawk attack and ran outside, hoping against hope that it wasn't one of their birds. "I kept thinking, 'Don't let it be them, don't let it be them!'" she remembers. "But it was Rock."

Pigeons mate for life. Even though Rock had never shown Peep anything in return, he had loved her with his entire being. Now Peep was grief-stricken. He mourned his

Rock and Peep: A Love Story

lost mate for over a week, going between the peak of the roof and the nest box, calling for her and crying. "He just stood there and howled," says Joan. "This was no loving coo, it was more like a growl, but really loud and constant."

Eventually, Peep joined the wild flock. Once he left, he never returned to the nest box he'd shared with Rock and eventually he found another mate. "He brought her over and you'd see them both walking through the backyard, eating peanuts," says Joan. "He wouldn't live here anymore, but he'd still come back to visit."

For Neil and Joan, who'd raised their bold little bird by hand, the loss hit hard. The only consolation they had was that, of all the ways she could have died, this was the most useful. Hard as it was to think of, Rock's death helped bring life to a nest of young hawks somewhere. Her life hadn't been long, but it had been much longer than it would have been without human intervention. And she got to experience everything but growing old. Instead of starving to death as a baby, or becoming a cat toy due to bad molts, or becoming a slave in a cage for a well-intentioned human, Rock had fulfilled her destiny: living, flying, and breeding. Her three successful clutches meant that another six rock pigeons and their offspring fly around the Sarnia area, all of which still visit the Biggs' sanctuary for food, water, and a measure of safety in an otherwise harsh world.

In addition, Rock introduced Joan and Neil to another species of bird they might not otherwise have known. They

Wildlife in the Kitchen

happily take in other orphaned pigeons now. And when fledglings are ready to leave, the visiting flock is perfect for reintroducing them to the wild.

Rock will never be forgotten at For the Birds Sanctuary. "We still think of her often, and we have video, sounds, and pictures to remember her by," says Neil. "When we get nostalgic, we play the video of her attacking Joan and nuzzling up to me. I really wish I knew how she figured out I was the male." Rock brought laughter, love, and the reminder that things aren't always what they first seem.

Chapter 5
Saved at Sea

A booming crack slices the air. It sounds like a gunshot, but it's not. It's the spring ice break-up on the frigid waters at the mouth of the Churchill River, and it's music to the ears of Mike and Doreen Macri. They operate Sea North Tours in Churchill, Manitoba, where, when the warm sun of July and August finally drives the chill of winter from the water, beluga whales arrive in droves.

Beluga whales live in the arctic and subarctic regions of Russia, Greenland, and North America. Among all whales, only the beluga, the bowhead, and the narwhal spend their entire lives in arctic waters. Most beluga pods are migratory, heading north to the Hudson Straits in the fall when the ice forms and returning south to the river estuaries in the spring

Wildlife in the Kitchen

to feed in the warmer waters where river meets ocean. The return of the belugas always brings excitement to Churchill.

Mike has always loved the sea, and he and his wife Doreen are year-round residents of Churchill. Since 1977 they have turned this love into a business, specializing in marine tours. They take up to 30 tourists at a time out on their custom-made, 12-metre boat to look at whales, polar bears, pelagic (open-sea) birds, seals, and other marvels of the northern waters. But 24 years ago, Mike was just another whale-watcher. "I've always liked being around animals, especially whales," Mike says. "All week I'd be at work, but on weekends I'd be out with my dog on the boat." There weren't very many tourists then, but he often saw people standing on the rocks, looking at whales through binoculars. Now and then he invited them to come with him on the little 6-metre boat he had at the time. He enjoyed sharing his love of the sea and his attraction to these hypnotic cetaceans. And although it's never easy to predict where the belugas might be found enjoying a meal, if anyone could find them, it was Mike. "Word got around," he says, "and people started to pay me. Soon I was making more money on the weekends than I did at my job."

That's when he knew it was time to make a change. He needed a bigger boat, made especially with whale-friendly viewing in mind. So he consulted a naval architect and had one built. "It's propelled by jet pumps. No moving parts are exposed beneath the surface, so whales can come underneath without being harmed," says Mike. "It's quiet too, with very little underwater noise, so it disturbs the whales as little as possible."

As Mike discovered, beluga whales feed in open water and on the sea bottom, in the shallows and in the depths. They dine on a variety of sea-life, including capelin, a variety of crustaceans, plus small char, white fish, cisco, and sea-run speckled trout. An adult beluga consumes approximately 12 to 14 kilograms of food in a day. They may even have some sense of taste, but they don't have the brain receptors or olfactory structures for a sense of smell.

Belugas can grow up to six metres in length. So having a group of belugas within arm's reach is beyond exciting. When they're occupied with feeding they completely ignore nearby boats. But when they're not feeding, Mike and his passengers become *their* entertainment. "They come right under the boat," he says. "Last week nine of them took turns pushing the boat with their heads, scratching their backs on the hull." Is this just the whales' way of being super-friendly? Not exactly. During their annual summer molt, when belugas shed their outer layer of skin, they love nothing better than a good scratch. The bottom of anything that floats is just the ticket. Even after all these years, Mike still feels the excitement of it. "Especially on the zodiac," he comments. "You don't feel it quite so much when they're bumping the big boat."

Mike sees the whales every day, all summer long, from the time the first ones arrive in spring until the last ones leave

Wildlife in the Kitchen

in fall. "I still like watching whales, but what I really like is watching people see them for the first time," he says. "Some people scream. I think everyone's surprised there are so many of them, and that they get so close. People don't realize these things until they're actually in the boat, surrounded by the whales."

Female belugas and their young tend to favour areas of calm, shallow water with sand, gravel, and mud bottoms, while pods of adult males and females prefer deeper, colder waters. They can remain submerged for 25 minutes at a time and may travel 2 to 3 kilometres on one dive. And they're known to have excellent vision, both in and out of water. Belugas often travel in large groups. Mike estimates that, during whale season, anywhere from 2000 to 3000 of these magnificent creatures are in the area on any given day.

Beluga whales are sometimes called "sea canaries" because they are extremely vocal, and scientists speculate that the moveable, melon-shaped area on their heads is used in communication. Mike's boat is specially equipped with stereo-hydrophones, a type of underwater microphone, so his passengers can enjoy the whale sounds. No matter how often he listens to them, he always hears something different. "Whistling, chirping, sometimes they sound like chimpanzees or chickens or even cows," he says. "Yesterday there was this melodic whistling noise I'd never heard before. It was really quite nice."

Beluga whales are very social creatures, and a group of

them can be quite loud. Like bats, belugas use echolocation to identify and navigate their surroundings. Their underwater clicks and whistles bounce off objects in the water, giving the whales a sort of "sound-map" of their environment. These clicks have a distinctive static-like sound; divers and snorklers often know whales are nearby because of the unique physical sensation these sound waves create in their chests.

Besides sound, these whales have many other subtle forms of communication. They are unusual among whales in that they have full range of motion in their necks, allowing them to nod, shake their heads, and even look perplexed.

Although Mike watches them closely, it's difficult to identify individual whales. Belugas don't have dorsal fins, a helpful identification tool in other species, nor is there any colour variation among adults. The name "beluga" comes from the Russian word *belukha*, which means "white one." They're born dark grey and gradually turn white by the time they are anywhere from three to eight years of age. Unless they have deep scars or physical peculiarities, any identifying marks disappear when they shed their skin.

But there's one whale Mike would very much like to meet again.

"I was coming back from a tour one time," he recalls, "when I saw something white bobbing out in the bay." He had no idea what it was, so after he took the last tourists back to shore he headed back out to take a look. It turned out to

Wildlife in the Kitchen

be a bleach jug and beneath it was an arctic net. Jumbled up amongst the mesh Mike saw a young beluga whale, about 5 metres long, struggling for breath. "He was tangled up in the net," recalls Mike. "Occasionally he'd come up for air but the weights on the net kept dragging him down. He was drowning."

Unless they fall prey to killer whales or polar bears, beluga whales have a lifespan of 35 to 50 years. Their affinity for shallow coastal waters makes them vulnerable to dams, off-shore petroleum exploration and extraction, and the effects of pollution. Getting caught in ice or nets is often fatal as well, since it prevents these sea mammals from reaching the surface to breathe. Mike wasn't about to watch this one die as a result of a discarded net.

Arctic nets are made of thin but extremely strong monofilament. Mike knew that if he attempted to move the net, and the whale struggled, either he or the whale could be badly cut. He couldn't do much on his own so he raced back to shore, picked up a friend, and together they hurried to save the young whale.

For about five minutes, they held the net up high enough so the whale's blowhole was above the surface, allowing him to catch his breath. They hoped he wouldn't panic. "We knew that if this guy decided to go, we wouldn't be able to hang onto the net," says Mike. "It would rip our fingers off."

But the whale seemed to know they were trying to help. "I took my knife out with one hand and started to cut

Saved at Sea

the mesh around his head," says Mike. "He was completely wrapped in it, right around to his tail." Mike continued cutting away at the net, working to free the animal from the mesh that bit deeply into his flesh in some places. Then he got to the tail, the trickiest part. If the whale began to struggle it would be dangerous for them all. To Mike's surprise, he let them continue cutting until the very last mesh thread was severed. "Then he very slowly started to move away," Mike says. "This guy had no problem letting us help him."

Mike may never know what became of this young beluga, but he'll always remember the silent plea in his eyes, and how honoured he felt that this desperate creature trusted him with his life.

• • •

In the tiny community of Kyuquot, situated at the very edge of the open ocean on the far west of the country, another ocean creature owes its life to human assistance.

No one reaches Kyuquot by accident. Getting to the village requires a four-by-four to cross the rough logging roads of northern Vancouver Island, followed by a boat or a seaplane. But in spite of these inconveniences, visitors still come to Kyuquot, lured by pristine wilderness and great fishing. When they do come, chances are they'll stop in at Miss Charlie's Restaurant and Lodging. Chances are they'll see Charlie, sunning her sleek 160-kilogram self on the dock of Walter's Cove.

Wildlife in the Kitchen

And if they leave their salmon unattended on the dock, they might see Charlie helping herself to a snack, for Charlie is a seal.

Sandra Kayra, known to her friends as Sam, is the proprietor of Miss Charlie's and she never tires of telling people about her business's namesake. No one knows the story better than Sam does; she grew up with Charlie. About 40 years ago, she explains, the government paid a bounty for seals — five dollars per seal, a significant reward at the time — counted by the number of noses turned in. A group of seal hunters working their bloody trade in the area had a particularly macabre way of making an extra fee: when they came across an obviously pregnant seal they would remove the baby after killing the mother, and get two bounties for the work of one. Sam's mother, Lucy Kayra, knew of this practice and told the hunters that if they found such a seal, she'd pay the bounty herself, in return for the living pup. It wasn't the first time Lucy had cared for a wild creature. "Growing up," says Sam, "we had eagles, seagulls, mink, otter, anything injured or orphaned."

So in the summer of 1964, the Kayra family expanded by one 10-kilogram newborn seal pup. "We proceeded to pack her up and put her in the bathtub," remembers Sam. "We had a lot of the community in our bathroom that night!"

Lucy contacted the Vancouver Aquarium for advice and was given a recipe for a very rich, high-fat "baby" formula, suitable to replace the high-calorie, nutrient-dense seal milk.

Saved at Sea

"Mom would heat it up in a baby bottle — *my* baby bottle — and feed her," says Sam.

A visiting cousin named the seal Charlie and by the time they learned their little baby was a girl, the moniker had already stuck. But it didn't matter; the name Charlie suited her perfectly.

As Charlie grew, the family moved her outdoors and began teaching her the skills she'd need to survive in the sea. "Dad built a net-cage we could put in the water," says Sam. "He didn't want to just let her go without preparing her." By pulling the net-cage out a bit deeper each day, they helped their little seal learn to swim. "Mom taught her to catch fish," says Sam. "She put herring on a rope and let Charlie chase it, playing with her." Sam affectionately recalls the seal's rather picky eating habits. "Dad brought her salmon. She preferred sockeye — but Charlie only wanted it if it was filleted, and all the fins were off."

Charlie grew quickly and soon acquired the basic skills needed to live as a seal. But she never went far from her home. "She always hung around the bay, staying near the dock," says Sam. "She loved kids, and whenever she heard young voices she'd show up to swim with us. If we were paddling the canoe she'd come by and tip us out. She even considered herself something of a guardian; when other seals came into the bay, she'd chase them away from *her* people. She thought she was human."

But *her* humans were determined to let her live a

Wildlife in the Kitchen

natural life and they expected that, as she reached maturity, she would be drawn to her own kind. They knew they'd miss her, but they wouldn't think of depriving her of a wild seal's life. So the first mating season after she was fully grown, Sam's father, Esko, packed Charlie into the boat, took her to a seal colony in the outer Bunsby Islands, about 16 kilometres to the west, and said goodbye. "There was a floating logging camp about a kilometre away, so Dad swung by and notified the loggers in case Charlie showed up, recognizing humans," says Sam. But she never did.

The bay was quiet without her and the dock seemed empty. Then, a full week later, Charlie swam her way into their lives again. "She looked tired when she arrived," says Sam, "but it was amazing that she found her way back to Walter's Cove."

Charlie, apparently, had made her choice.

In the nearly four decades she's been part of the Kyuquot community, the seal has become something of a mascot. Everyone knows her and everyone feeds her. Charlie, who used to slim down in the cold winter months, stays fat and healthy all year round now, thanks to the regular handouts she gets from her human friends. "She's now blind," says Sam, "and her hearing isn't as good as it used to be. But the local people love her."

Charlie has already lived longer than most seals will live in the wild. The 170 residents of Kyuquot know she won't be around for very many more years. But, taking pride of place

Saved at Sea

on the walls of Miss Charlie's Restaurant and Lodging, photos are displayed of the seal that chose to stay. Clearly, the community will never let Charlie be forgotten.

Chapter 6
When Polar Bears Come to Town

Shrieks of laughter compete with the crunching of frozen ground under dozens of small, boot-clad feet as the late afternoon light wanes. Excitement mounts as more and more well-bundled youngsters fill the streets, anticipating the annual candy-fest of Halloween. But here in Churchill, Manitoba, something is a little different. In the sky above the haunted streets, a Jet Ranger helicopter flies a pre-dark patrol. Vehicles from Manitoba Conservation, the Royal Canadian Mounted Police, Churchill Ambulance, and Parks Canada prowl slowly from one street to another, throughout the entire small town. Churchill Volunteer Fire Department trucks and Canadian Ranger vehicles sit motionless, guarding the perimeter. Why, on this traditionally spookiest night of

When Polar Bears Come to Town

the year, does Churchill require such heightened awareness?

It has nothing to do with the supernatural. The town pulls out all the stops so that, on this one night, it will be safe for its children to be out after dark. It's the height of the polar bear migration — and no one wants them crashing the Halloween party. The helicopters, with Polar Bear Alert crew members on board, are simply advance scouts in the search for any polar bears that come too close to town. And any bear that poses a threat can expect a "trick" in the form of a tranquilizing dart.

Richard Romaniuk, district supervisor with Manitoba Conservation, has been with the department since 1983. This is his fifth bear season in Churchill and polar bears are his department's primary responsibility. "We protect people from bears and we protect bears from people," says Richard.

Churchill's relationship with bears is due to one simple thing: location. The polar bear, whose scientific name, *ursus maritimus*, means "sea bear," is found throughout the arctic seas. Churchill, on the edge of Hudson Bay, just happens to lie at the southern limit of their range. These bears, the world's largest land carnivores, truly are at home in the frigid northern waters. They can swim close to 100 kilometres at a stretch, equivalent to crossing the English Channel three times without a break. They can dive five metres beneath the surface and stay under for two minutes at a time. Underwater, they have the ability to close their nostrils and flatten their ears while keeping their eyes open to hunt. And

Wildlife in the Kitchen

it's not uncommon for them to leap two or three metres out of the water, straight up into the air, during a seal ambush. They'd happily stay on the sea ice all year long. But that's not an option for the polar bears of the Churchill region.

By the end of July or early August, the Hudson Bay ice melts, forcing the bears ashore. Instead of hunting during their stay on land, these huge bears wander lazily over the brushy tundra in what's called a "walking hibernation," burning off the fat reserves built up over the winter and conserving energy until they can get back out to sea. As summer wanes and the air begins to chill, they follow the banks of the Churchill River toward the salt water of the bay. By October they've gathered on the outskirts of town, waiting for the bay to ice over and give them access to the ocean once more.

Ice first forms along the western coast of Hudson Bay, and usually runs north along the coast from Cape Churchill. In the past, bears seldom made it further than the Fort Churchill military base, where they were shot on sight. But after the base closed down in the early 1970s they were free to continue on to the tiny town of Churchill. Throughout the fall, and especially just before freeze-up, increasing numbers of bears move toward the coast where they gather within easy viewing access of their human neighbours. Hundreds of them pass by or through Churchill during their fall migration, earning the town the title of "Polar Bear Capital of the World."

Fortunately, even during their migration, most polar bears prefer to avoid confrontation with people. These arctic

When Polar Bears Come to Town

A polar bear on the Canadian tundra

giants have few natural enemies; they occasionally kill each other, and adult males will not hesitate to kill cubs if they get the chance. But for the most part, polar bears reign at the top of the food chain. Their greatest threats are humans and human activity.

Even when a bear becomes a hazard, every alternative is attempted to avoid destroying it. But if humans are at risk, there is no option. A problem bear can be a very *big* problem. The huge animals can reach a height of three or four metres when they stand on their hind legs, and adult males can weigh over 450 kilograms. The largest bear captured in the Churchill area tipped the scales at an awe-inspiring

Wildlife in the Kitchen

712 kilograms. Adult females are comparably smaller, but even a small bear is a formidable adversary.

In the past, dozens of bears were killed each season. But as environmental awareness has grown, attitudes have begun to change. Polar bear hunting has been outlawed entirely since 1983. "Everyone knows a live bear is worth more than a dead bear," says Richard Romaniuk. "You can photograph a bear a hundred times, but you can only kill him once."

Today, natural resource officers have better options than killing a bear. Their number one tool is the Polar Bear Alert program. "If a bear comes into town and we're not johnny-on-the-spot already, a member of the public calls us," explains Richard. "It's like calling 911 anywhere else." Conservation officers then attempt to frighten the bear into leaving the area. They use 12-gauge shotguns, but instead of regular shells, they use firecracker shells. "When the firecracker blows up it makes a loud bang, and that usually gets the bear moving," says Richard. "But some bears have heard that sound often enough that they're not scared anymore, so we use another gun, like a starter's pistol. And we can fire screamers, whistlers, and bangers. This generally gets them going." They can also fire rubber slugs, causing the bear to associate the place with a distinctly unpleasant charley-horse pain, and hopefully making him want to avoid it.

Most bears promptly decide that town isn't the place for them, but each year a few take more convincing. "If a bear persists on coming into the town, at that point we have to

When Polar Bears Come to Town

immobilize him," says Richard. The animal is darted with a tranquilizer called Telezol, a restricted drug powerful enough to knock down a 450 kilogram bear. If the dart hits a muscle, the drug is absorbed in about five minutes, but if it hits fat, it takes about 10 minutes. The time difference can be crucial. "This time of year, we have to be very careful when darting bears," Richard adds. "Once a bear is darted his natural tendency is to run to water, but if he happens to make it to the water before the drug takes effect, he could drown." So instead of free-ranging (darting them from the ground) they use a technique called "heli-darting." They dart the bear from above, then use the helicopter to steer the bear away from water until he's down.

"Once the bear goes down we transport it to the polar bear holding compound," Richard says. "We try not to refer to it as a 'jail' because that insinuates the bears are being punished, and that's not the case." The compound was originally part of the military base, Building 20 in section D at Fort Churchill. Most people still refer to it as D20. Confinement in D20 keeps the bears away from people and people away from them. "The compound can hold 23 individuals, and last year we handled 176," says Richard. "But not 176 different bears. There were about 140 individual bears handled in 2003. If they come back a second time in the same year, they're put in the holding compound until ice forms on the bay and then released." If the facility is nearing full capacity, the bears are relocated by helicopter to an area some 65 kilometres north.

Wildlife in the Kitchen

The length of time a bear remains in D20 varies. "One time we had six bear calls in town over three days. Turns out they were all for the same bear, a sub-adult 'teenager,'" says Richard. "We tried to scare her out, but she kept coming back. When we get one like this, we hold it in the compound for a 30-day time-out before release."

Occasionally a bear warrants extra-special attention. Perhaps he insists on returning or shows a tendency toward aggression. Such a bear gets a number painted on his rump. "We had one bear that was chasing vehicles in the dump," Richard recalls. "If that bear comes back we want a number on him, because his history tells us we should dart him right away. So far this year, out of 26, we've numbered one and plan on numbering two more on release."

Any time a bear is handled, Manitoba Conservation adheres to a strict protocol in conjunction with the Canadian Wildlife Service. Each new bear captured is tattooed with a number on the upper lips (or lip, if it's a cub born that year) and given ear tags with corresponding numbers. Length, girth, and fat index measurements provide an estimate of the bear's weight. All data is turned over to the Canadian Wildlife Service. "Right now the population is estimated to be around 1200," says Richard, "but we'll have a better idea at the end of next year when the CWS completes its three-year population study."

The annual gathering of polar bears at Churchill is a unique opportunity for researchers to study them and their

When Polar Bears Come to Town

behaviour. In fact, Canada's polar bears are among the most studied on earth, providing important insights into the bears' annual wanderings — migrations that can take individual animals across thousands of kilometres of tundra and ocean and then back again. Biologists from all over the world look to Canada for information on these animals.

Churchill's Polar Bear Alert program has worked extremely well, but Richard is quick to give credit to the townspeople. "There hasn't been a mauling or death for over 20 years," he says, "and it's because of the public's co-operation that we've been so successful." Even when he's not working directly with bears, Richard's job is still mostly about bears. Public education on bear safety is a large part of it and nothing ranks higher in importance than the pre-Halloween safety briefing for schoolchildren. They hear the same basics taught to children everywhere: stay on lighted streets and avoid dark alleys. But the kids of Churchill get something more. "I always tell them that if they see a bear they should drop their candy, because that's probably what the bear wants."

Problem bears are almost never killed anymore, but on the rare occasion it still happens. And if the bear is a mother, her death creates another problem: orphans. Polar bear cubs need their mother's care and protection until they are about a year-and-a-half, so without her they are destined to starve or be killed by predators. In the past, orphaned polar bear cubs had only two options: zoo placement or humane euthanasia.

Wildlife in the Kitchen

No more. Thanks to a collaboration between Manitoba Conservation and the Born Free Foundation, a private organization in the United Kingdom, when a cub is orphaned it still has a chance at life in the wild. Born Free believes that polar bears suffer badly in zoos and so they are happy to partner with Manitoba Conservation to find an alternative. Kim Daley, now in her eighth bear season in Churchill, is a foundation researcher. She's also the on-site caregiver for a unique plan attempting to solve the problem of orphaned polar bear cubs: the Polar Bear Cub Surrogacy Program. "Born Free initiated the project as a viable option to euthanizing orphan cubs or locating them in zoos," says Kim. The concept of fostering orphan polar bear cubs illustrates how much public opinion has changed over the decades.

Inspired by the true story of Elsa the lioness, Born Free is an animal welfare and conservation charity that campaigns for the protection and conservation of animals in their natural habitat. The foundation was established in 1991 and has been instrumental in numerous projects to improve animal welfare (including Zoo Check, which monitors the welfare of animals in captivity).

Theoretically, a female bear with only one cub should be perfectly able to adopt another cub — if she can be convinced to accept it. Kim and her colleagues attempt to turn theory into practice. When an orphan is identified, officials contact Kim and the program leaps into action. "The orphan is held at the compound until a surrogate female is found,"

When Polar Bears Come to Town

explains Kim. To maximize the chances of success, they look for a female with a single cub of similar age and size to the orphan. "We try to match the cubs as closely as possible," she adds. "Her natural cub and the introduced cub should be almost identical."

Then they use an age-old trick known to cattle and sheep ranchers everywhere: Vicks VapoRub. A generous layer of the camphor-and-menthol laden ointment on the head and neck masks all other odours, allowing the orphan to take on the familiar smells of the natural cub and making the mother more likely to accept the newcomer as her own. The biting aroma is a nice change for the humans from the bears' natural odour. What do bears smell like? "They smell bad!" Kim exclaims. "They smell like rancid fat most of the time. The best comparison would be a really bad wet dog smell. Their diet of seal is very rich in fatty acids, and mother's milk is extremely strong and rich, so the cubs have a sour smell to them. Seal is one of those smells that once you get it on you, it's hard to get it off." It's so bad that when they fly out to check up on their bears, pilots often make them leave their field jackets in the cargo area at the rear of the helicopter.

After the initial introduction period has passed successfully, the newly formed trio is released. Twenty-four hours later, Kim and her colleagues follow up on the new family. They know there are no guarantees but they always hope for the best. On a return visit after their very first adoption, they saw gratifying confirmation that polar bear surrogacy

Wildlife in the Kitchen

works. "We were actually able to observe the female nursing both cubs," Kim remembers. "This hadn't been documented before. Attempted adoptions hadn't been monitored by a return flight to check on them."

Their first experiment was a rousing success, but it doesn't always work so well. When Kim received a call about a nine-month-old pair of orphans, she and her co-workers immediately began searching for suitable surrogate mothers. But the ones available only had smaller cubs. They chose the closest mother-cub duos they could find, introduced the orphans, and sent them off. For several hours they monitored the expanded families closely from the ground. One mother promptly disappeared with her cubs. Subsequent search expeditions weren't able to find them, but neither did they find evidence that the adopted cub had been abandoned.

They did find the second mother and cub — but no orphan. They feared he had succumbed to a pack of wolves or perhaps an adult bear, and their fears were almost justified. "A week later he turned up in town by himself and we tracked wolves tracking him," says Kim. "He'd had a tough time of it." So they chose a different female and attempted another adoption. Once again, they set them free together in a safe location, but again, when they flew out to check on them they found the mother and her natural cub, but no orphan. "At that time the bay was frozen, and you can only fly out so far to check on them," Kim says with regret. Perhaps the mother refused to accept the newcomer; perhaps the cub

When Polar Bears Come to Town

refused to accept her. Perhaps he simply wandered away. In the unforgiving landscape they call home, a young bear has next to no chance of survival alone. Their best hope is that his death provided sustenance for some other animal. "The result of this," says Kim, "was the introduction to the next year's protocol of using drop-off radio collars on the females. So far, this protocol has not been tested."

The discouragement can weigh heavily at times. "We sacrifice a lot personally and professionally to do this work," Kim admits. "You can get pretty run-down. The temperatures are cold, the weather isn't always co-operative, and politics and logistics are hazards we deal with everyday." But even in the midst of disappointment and difficulty, she doesn't forget the good parts, the reasons she chose this life. "Some of the best parts of my job?" Kim doesn't even need to think about her answer. "I get to work outside and I get to spend hundreds of hours watching bears, all day long."

• • •

The people of Churchill feel strongly about the bears, too, and give their yearly visitors a warm — if watchful — welcome. Dave Daley (no relation to Kim) runs the Wapusk General Store and Wapusk Adventures in Churchill. A lifelong resident of the area, he considers polar bear encounters to be simply part and parcel of life in the north. "We don't really change our lives when the bears are here," he says. "We're just

Wildlife in the Kitchen

a little more cautious, I guess. My opinion is that they were here first and this is their territory. We have to let them have the right of way and try to protect them."

This laid-back attitude comes from more bear experiences than he can count. "One of my earliest memories," Dave reminisces, "is seeing my older sister meet a bear 'too close for comfort.' We used to live at Hudson's Square and my sister worked at the store. Out here, the wind is always blowing. One day she was on her way to work, walking with her head down against the wind, and I was watching her through the window. Then, there on the street, I saw a bear and she was headed right for it. I started banging on the window and yelling but she couldn't hear me because of the wind. She kept on walking and bumped right into him! She screamed, the bear ran one way, and she ran the other. Needless to say, she didn't go to work that day."

It might be an accepted part of life, but beneath his casual manner is a bone-deep knowledge of the seriousness of bear safety. Dave, who keeps and races sled dogs, takes tourists on dogsled adventures over the snow-covered tundra and out onto the ice to watch seals. During the day his dogs work hard for him, and at night they curl up snugly in the kennel Dave keeps out of town at a place called Joe Buck's Ridge. But when the dogs are in need of special care, Dave brings them to his home kennel to keep an eye on them. He'd brought one of his dogs home with him one evening, a pregnant female named Tiffany, thinking he'd be able to supervise her labour if necessary.

When Polar Bears Come to Town

But at 3 a.m. Dave and his wife, Valerie, were awakened by Tiffany — and not because she was in labour. "She was barking and barking!" he recalls. Valerie prodded him to get up and find out what was wrong. He quickly threw on the first things he could find and tromped outside to investigate. Clad in nothing but cowboy boots, boxer shorts, and a jacket that was two sizes too small, he bent down on the snowy ground to quiet the dog. "That's when I heard the bear stomping and snorting behind me," he says. "I thought, 'Oh, no!' because whenever you hear that sound it's a good hint that you're way too close." Dave looked behind him and there they were, a mother bear and two cubs, barely 10 feet away from him. He dashed around the corner of the kennel and climbed up onto the deck of the house from there. When he looked down, the mother bear was standing exactly where he'd been crouching just moments before.

"My experience is not to panic when you see a bear, but when it's breathing down your neck and snorting and chomping its teeth, you want to get away as fast as you can. I'm not sure this is the right thing to do," Dave suggests with a nervous laugh, "but it seems to have worked for me so far."

He doesn't always react the same way. One day, when he'd gone outside the store to collect firewood, Valerie opened the door a crack, peeked out, and softly said, "Dave, don't look behind you. Just come inside." Naturally, he looked behind him. There, near the store and much too near him for his liking, stood a large male bear. "I continued to pick up my firewood and then came inside," he says. "Valerie asked me, 'Dave, why didn't you just drop the wood and make a dash for the door?' I told her I didn't want the bear to know I'd seen him."

During a hunting trip one summer Dave and a friend were calling for moose on the riverbank. Dave kept hearing a snorting noise that sounded suspiciously like a bear to him, but saw nothing around them. He told his friend what he thought he'd heard, but his cautions were waved away. "The next thing I know, I'm upside down with my feet up in the air. When I land, I look down and the bear's head is right between my feet!" The bear had been beneath them the entire time, in a den built into the bank. Fortunately, the bear was as frightened as they were and no one was hurt. The hunting trip, of course, continued as planned. Around the campfire that night they relived the experience, laughing shakily about their close call. "My friend said, 'I keep on seeing you on the bank! What would I have done if that bear had grabbed your leg?'"

Perhaps his many run-ins with Churchill's famous visitors have earned Dave the right to be nonchalant. Recently, at the height of the bear migration, he was awakened by the sound of "crackers." Although they were clearly coming from right next door, he wasn't alarmed. "I didn't even get out of bed to look," he says.

Chapter 7
Wildlife in the Kitchen

At Elizabeth's Wildlife Centre in Abbotsford, British Columbia, four baby opossums hesitate at the opening of a small cardboard box. They blink their black eyes against the light, then stumble over the lip toward Elizabeth's outstretched fingers. These "joeys," rescued from the pouch of their dead mother, owe their unassuming lives to her intervention. They aren't exactly cute — they look more like small rats than anything — but they are certainly helpless. They aren't nearly ready for release into the wild yet and they still need regular, round-the-clock feedings, so instead of residing in the nursery or the clinic building, these babies live inside the house. Elizabeth has never been able to separate her life as a nurse from her work with animals.

Wildlife in the Kitchen

Inside the cage on the floor of Elizabeth's spacious breakfast nook, the joeys meander obliviously amongst each other. The kitchen, it seems, is a completely natural environment as far as they're concerned. "I never cook," Elizabeth admits, "so it's a good place for them." They poke around among the straw in their cage, twitching their long noses and reaching their pink fingers toward the grapes she offers them. Although they look extremely young, she guesses that they are as old as three months. "It's deceiving," she explains, "because they spend so much time developing after birth, inside the pouch."

The gestation period for opossums is less than two weeks. At birth the babies, each the size of a navy bean, climb up through the hair on the mother's abdomen and enter the vertical opening of her pouch. Each takes one of the mother's nipples in its mouth and holds on for dear life, remaining attached for two months. As they grow and the pouch gets crowded, the babies emerge to ride on the mother's back until they are old enough to go out on their own. When Elizabeth pulled these opossum babies from the pouch of their dead mother, they were still pink, with only the slightest bit of fluff beginning to grow over their skin. Constant warmth and endless feedings were the only way to keep them alive. Now that they are mobile, furry, and eating solid food, she feels they have a good chance at making it in the wild. But they will remain with her for several more weeks at least, until she's sure they're ready.

Wildlife in the Kitchen

Elizabeth is passionate about opossums. She's passionate about all the wild creatures that come through her doors. She has to be, because there's no money in wildlife rescue. But opossums have a special place in her heart.

At the back of the property is a large aviary, a holding pen where growing birds prepare for release. Elizabeth lifts the latch and walks inside. She bends down to a little shelter in the corner and calls, holding out her hand. "Here's my boy," she says, smiling. A mature opossum waddles out, stepping deliberately and slowly. He takes the morsel of fruit she offers him and continues on his way, climbing carefully up a branch onto a shady ledge on the other side of the enclosure. This fellow is her mascot. Unlike the little ones in the kitchen, he came to her as an injured adult. Because he's unlikely to survive in the wild, he'll remain with her indefinitely. He's become quite accustomed to her presence and has even become something of a "public relations" 'possum. "He comes with me when I go to the schools," Elizabeth says. "I like kids to learn about opossums because they are great animals that have a bad reputation."

About the size of an average house cat, opossums are the only true marsupial of North America and can be found throughout most of the United States and parts of Canada and Mexico. The name comes from the Algonquian Indian word *apasum*, meaning "white animal," and while there are over 65 species of opossums, only one, the *Didelphis virginiana* (or Virginia opossum, named after the state where

Wildlife in the Kitchen

British colonists first saw them), is native to North America. *Didelphis*, which means "double womb," refers to the pouch where infant opossums, like kangaroos and koalas, nurse and continue their growth.

Opossums are regular visitors in urban settings, often living very near humans. They are attracted to residential areas by the availability of water, pet food left out at night, and overripe or rotting fruit that has fallen from trees. They prefer to nest in sheltered places like hollow logs, fallen trees, or burrows that have been abandoned by other animals, but they'll happily set up house beneath a sundeck or up a shade tree. A solitary, nocturnal animal, the opossum's prehensile tail and opposable thumbs make it an agile, if slow, climber. Although it does not hibernate, during very cold weather it may take refuge in a tree for several days at a time, only seeking food when hunger strikes.

These animals have little physical appeal. Although their colour, body shape, and hairless tail give them a rat-like appearance, the two are completely unrelated. Opossums actually eat rats and mice when the opportunity presents itself. When threatened, they can put on a good show, hissing, screeching, drooling, and opening their mouths widely, showing off all 50 of their teeth — more than any other North American land animal. But it's little more than a good façade. They are relatively harmless creatures whose main defence when threatened is to "play 'possum," or pretend to be dead, by rolling over, shutting their eyes, and letting their tongues loll out.

Wildlife in the Kitchen

Opossums, sometimes nicknamed "nature's little sanitation engineers," have great environmental value. They are scavengers and their typical diet is opportunistically omnivorous. They'll eat anything, depending on what's available, including all types of insects such as cockroaches, crickets, and beetles. They also love snails and even help clean up carrion. Many opossums are accidentally killed on highways while attempting to feed on some other hapless animal killed by traffic. It's Elizabeth's mission to inform the public that opossums help keep neighbourhoods clean and free of harmful garden pests and unwanted rodents. Whether rural, residential, or in the wilderness, opossums are a benefit to any area they inhabit.

Elizabeth Melnick never imagined her love for wildlife would lead to the facility she now runs. She hadn't exactly intended to pursue this line of work. But in retrospect, it's a natural fit. Born with a love for all animals and trained as a registered nurse, wildlife rescue and rehabilitation work allow her to put all aspects of her skill and personality to good use.

Although she's been a licensed wildlife rehabilitator for over 18 years, she only recently gained official non-profit society status for her shelter. Now she can provide tax-deductible receipts for charitable donations and she has greater leverage for the thankless task of fundraising. But money is always an issue, although you might not guess it from the quality of her equipment. Elizabeth works in palliative care at the local

Wildlife in the Kitchen

An opossum at Elizabeth's Wildlife Centre

hospital during the winter. Any time the hospital upgrades, she is given access to a host of materials deemed unusable by human standards but still perfectly usable to her: intravenous fluid pumps, incubators, hospital cribs, medical and surgical supplies, and expired medications, among other things. "They give me stuff that would either be shipped out or thrown away," she says. "It's perfect!"

Up until two years ago, Elizabeth's Wildlife Centre operated out of her home on a typical city lot in the middle of a busy subdivision. Examinations and treatments were carried out in the garage and the kitchen. The small backyard was

Wildlife in the Kitchen

wall-to-wall cages, and included a tiny waterfowl pond. It was tidy, clean, organized — and cramped. But it was the home where she and her husband, Bill, had raised their children and he was especially reluctant to move. Bill had lived with Parkinson's disease for many years and the house was comfortable for him.

"But he came to me one day and said, 'I don't know how much longer I'm going to be around, and I want you to be happy,'" Elizabeth remembers. So they began to watch the real estate listings. When they found their current location, they knew immediately it was perfect.

Walking up the path to the front door, visitors see a painted wooden sign that tells them they've come to the right place. "Nature's touch makes the world sing." The property features a large home on 1.11 acres of land bordered on three sides by a vast spread of designated green space. Elizabeth has room for several separate buildings, spacious flight-cages, and protected outdoor pens. "I had to take a mortgage again," she says wryly. "Our other house was paid for."

In spite of the upheaval, Bill loved the new place and was thrilled to see Elizabeth so happy. He spent hours sitting on the sundeck, just gazing at the endless view. But within a year he was diagnosed with cancer. "He always hated hospitals," Elizabeth says, "so I took care of him at home." Although it's work she's uniquely qualified for, this time it was personal. "We were married for 34 years," she says. "Bill hadn't wanted to move, but he did it for me. So I made sure he didn't have to spend a single day in hospital." In March 2003, Bill died peacefully at home.

Elizabeth shakes her head in wonder, remembering the weekend of the funeral. March is the start of her busy season but that year the phone didn't ring once. Of course she knew she could have just turned off her phone, but she couldn't stand the thought of people having nowhere to turn. "It's like somehow the word just got out, 'Don't call Elizabeth right now.'"

In the months to come, she coped with her grief by immersing herself in the care of the needy animals around her. "It saved me," she says. There was little time to think or remember. But she will always be grateful that Bill had the foresight to encourage her to pursue her dream before he died.

The larger property comes with increased expenses, but she knows she can provide better for the animals now and that's all that matters. Recently the centre received a grant of $5000 from Shell Canada and she knew exactly what to do with it. At the back of her property, near the large aviary, she's built a duck pond with a trickling waterfall, kept fresh with a pump and filter. Teals and mallards brought to her from the man-made lake in town paddle through it, completing their convalescence. Besides improving the quality of life for the waterfowl, the pond adds a sense of serenity appropriate for this wilderness retreat. But Elizabeth, who cared for over 1500 animals and birds last year, takes little time for reflection; she's got lots more plans ready for the next generous benefactor.

Wildlife in the Kitchen

She lavishes tenderness on all the patients that come through her door, but her mission is clear: to rehabilitate them and send them back to their natural environment. She handles all of them with gentle care, clucking and patting, smoothing and stroking, but they are not pets. It's essential for their survival that they remain wary of humans, so she ensures they get no more exposure than necessary and then releases them as quickly as possible.

But no matter how large and efficient her centre becomes, there will always be wildlife in the kitchen. Today, a cage with two baby cottontail rabbits sits beside the home of the opossum babies. "The rabbits are both about the same age," she says, "but they didn't come in together." One hops out toward the grass she puts in. The other stays hidden inside the little cardboard box provided for shelter. Both bunnies are barely bigger than hamsters. "I don't know about this one," she muses, scooping one shy bunny out of the box. "He came in bleeding from his nose and mouth. His eyes were all bloodshot and red and his breathing was so rattly, it sounded like he had a hole in his chest." His face is clear now though. She holds him to her ear and listens. "He sounds better," she reports. She sets him back in the cage and he hops inside the box.

Baby rabbits are notoriously fragile, with delicate skin easily pierced by the teeth or claws of cats. While they may survive a physical attack, they are particularly vulnerable to infection from their wounds. Elizabeth has a phenomenal success rate with these tiny creatures. She fully expects these bunnies to recover and estimates she'll be able to release them into the wild within another couple of weeks.

Inside her little clinic building, a domestic rabbit lies quietly in a crate in the corner, a piece of latex sewn into his skin. "He was skin and bone when he came in," says Elizabeth. "He had such a big mass in his abdomen I thought for sure it would be a tumour." But upon further exploration she found a wound, probably from a cat-bite. The wound had abscessed, creating an enormous swelling. "We drained a third of a litre of pus from that abscess," she says. The latex drain will remain in place until she's sure the infection is gone. If he recovers, Elizabeth will take him to a veterinarian to be neutered and then try to find him a home.

When domestic rabbits grow up and lose their appeal they are sometimes abandoned by careless owners to fare as best they can in the wild. Unfortunately, they don't fare well at all and usually fall prey to dogs, cats, or wild predators. Although dependent on humans for food, they can usually manage to feed themselves in the summer, but food sources become scarce in winter. Elizabeth does what she can. "Our rescued domestic rabbits are spayed and neutered to help control the unwanted rabbit population," she says. "Rabbits make wonderful pets in the right home."

• • •

Wildlife in the Kitchen

As our cities expand ever outward, many species of wildlife are displaced, forced either to relocate or to find ways of living amongst people. The Wildlife Rescue Association in Burnaby, British Columbia, deals with 3000 to 4000 birds and animals each year, many injured as a result of some sort of contact with humans. They see everything from the coyotes that skulk in the city shadows, often being hit by cars, to the tiny hummingbirds that flit boldly among the hanging flower baskets and sometimes smash into windows. "The length of time an animal stays varies a lot," says Jackie Ward, team leader of animal care. "It might be overnight or it could be several months." Because special permission is required to keep wild animals for longer than nine months, most patients are released before then. And the goal is always to get them back into their own homes as quickly as possible. The longer a wild creature is kept in captivity, the less likely its chances of successful re-release into the wild.

When they admitted a badly injured raccoon in August 2001, they weren't even sure it would survive, let alone be fit to live in the wild again. "It was a male, probably a yearling, and he'd been hit by a car," says Jackie. A severe concussion had left him blind and nearly comatose. They suspected he might have been lying injured at the side of the road for up to 12 hours before his rescue. Jackie began an aggressive treatment protocol, hoping against hope that the raccoon would recover. He needed hand-feeding three times daily and his jaw actually had to be manipulated to help him chew. He

Wildlife in the Kitchen

was too badly injured to be aggressive, so there was no risk to the workers of being bitten. Within a few days his appetite returned and he appeared more responsive. But he had a long way to go yet.

The raccoon had sustained a brain injury resulting in neurological damage that left him with rigidly curled, clenched paws. To counteract this muscle spasticity he was prescribed a rigorous program of physical therapy. "We'd stretch the tendons and muscles, putting him through range-of-motion exercises," says Jackie. Hydrotherapy or water exercises had long been used in human medicine; would they be helpful here? Warm water was known to increase blood circulation, and might encourage the raccoon's natural tendency to stretch his arms out and reach for objects in water. They decided to give it a try, putting him in the pool and moving his limbs. Very soon they started to see improvement. His mobility increased, he was more alert, and he responded when people entered the room. This was exactly what they were hoping for — except that it made their job more difficult. Within about a month he was exhibiting hints of the normal fear and aggression expected in a wild raccoon. "Even after he started to become more alert we kept on with the hydrotherapy for another couple of weeks," says Jackie. "Then he became too aggressive and we had to discontinue it."

They put him in a larger pen so he would have more space to move around on his own. They also consulted a herbalist, who designed a nutritional program that not only

Wildlife in the Kitchen

corresponded to a raccoon's diet, but also included a combination of oils and nutrients to assist in the repair of damage sustained from the accident. And a special blend of herbs was given to strengthen his immune system, increase blood flow to the brain, promote muscle fibre relaxation, and generally support the nerve tissue. As time went on, it was apparent that at least some of his vision had returned. He began walking again, slowly, and without full control of his movements at first. But his recovery continued. "After the third month," reports Jackie, "he was climbing again."

Occasionally staff members sedated him so they could give him a proper physical examination. But for the most part, their role was to allow him time to finish healing. "A lot of what we do is providing a safe place to recover, so injured animals aren't picked off by predators," says Jackie. They had specific criteria against which to judge his recovery: he needed to be able to climb, move with speed and agility, be aggressive to humans, and be able to feed himself by catching live prey. Eventually they were confident of everything but the last. He'd been at the shelter for several months, and winter had arrived. To give him the best chance of survival they wouldn't release him until spring, when food sources would be more abundant. But first they needed to be sure he could still recognize a food source when he found one.

So they put goldfish into the pond in his enclosure. With the extent of his injury, they weren't sure what to expect; any number of steps could prove problematic to him. He needed

Wildlife in the Kitchen

to be able to see the fish, recognize them as food, catch them without slipping and falling, and hold onto them to eat them. It was the last hurdle ... but he passed. This raccoon that had come to them near death was ready to be released back into the wild. It had taken them the better part of eight months, but they'd done it. Nearly a year after his injury, the raccoon was taken to Golden Ears Provincial Park and sent off to make his own way in the world. "We were so happy," remembers Jackie, "because a lot of times the brain damage is so bad they never recover."

Jackie loves her job. She started in wildlife rescue over seven years ago as a volunteer. After she received her Bachelor of Science in Biology, she got a full-time position at the Wildlife Rescue Association and has been there ever since. "It's so rewarding to actually be able to take care of the animals that most people never even see," she says. "But it's also the environment I work in. Everyone here is phenomenal!" She's one of three full-time and two part-time paid employees, but the centre would be lost without the 80 to 100 volunteers that help out during the course of each week. "These people are doing it because it's something they're interested in doing," emphasizes Jackie. "A lot of it is grunt work. It's dirty. It's not fun."

Sometimes it's much, much worse than that. In July 2004, North Shore Fire and Rescue called the centre about a skunk that had been found stuck in a dumpster. "It was the third time in about two years that I'd been called out to this

Wildlife in the Kitchen

situation," recalls Jackie. "The skunks put their heads through the drainage holes in the bottoms of the dumpsters and they get stuck. By the time we get there they've been fighting all night to get out." They estimate that if the skunk had been left another hour or two, he'd have died of dehydration. "He was so exhausted he couldn't even spray anymore," Jackie recalls ruefully. "But it still wasn't the most pleasant aroma!" At 10 a.m. it was already unbearably hot, with temperatures close to 30°C. Rotting garbage competed with the pungent odour of the struggling animal. But Jackie just plugged her nose, climbed into the dumpster, and went to work.

The first thing they did was sedate the little skunk so they could assess how badly he was lodged in place. "There was no easy way to get him out," Jackie remembers. "His head and neck were swollen by then." Another goal of sedation was to help him relax and reduce some of his pain so they could help free him. They lubricated the fur and skin around his head and neck. Then, using a piece of gauze, they wrapped his head in a sort of sling, passing it through the opening in the dumpster. "This distributes the pressure a bit more equally," explains Jackie. With gentle traction, pushing from the inside and pulling from the outside, they were finally able to free him and take a good look at his injuries. The poor fellow wasn't a pretty sight. "He was dehydrated. His head was swollen. Both of his corneas and the skin around his neck were badly abraded." They immediately removed him to the centre for first aid: subcutaneous fluids to rehydrate him, antibiotics, steroids to

Wildlife in the Kitchen

counteract the swelling, and ointment for his eyes.

Skunks are common visitors to the centre, especially in the summer, when staff admit one every couple of weeks. It's often the youngsters who get trapped like this. If they survive, they'll likely remember the lesson the rest of their lives. But it's frustrating for Jackie to see this type of incident over and over again. "Dumpster drainage holes are the perfect size for a skunk's head," she says. "If they could put a small bit of mesh over the openings, the problem would be solved."

Wildlife rescue and rehabilitation workers like Elizabeth and Jackie never know if the animal they save today will survive until tomorrow. Much of their work is necessary as a result of human thoughtlessness and irresponsibility. Most facilities struggle constantly to make ends meet, and the majority of their compassionate volunteers are never compensated for their time. But all of them, without fail, say their work is a reward in itself. For these dedicated people, to help one animal live as nature intended, to undo even a bit of the damage wrought by human progress, is reason enough to continue.

Chapter 8
The Last Wild Horses in Canada

The late afternoon sun slants lazily into the baked earth beneath the dry brush. Doreen and Bob Henderson park their camper near a stand of trees and stake their horses loosely nearby to rest and graze. Two massive Akitas, Japanese guard dogs, lie panting in the shade. The dogs are along for more than companionship; they run interference between their owners and wilderness inhabitants. "They've saved our lives on several occasions when we've encountered aggressive bears and moose," says Doreen.

The quarry they seek isn't as aggressive as it is elusive. They're looking for wild horses, animals that are justifiably wary of humans and could be roaming anywhere in an area roughly 325 square kilometres. Bands of these horses may be as small as three or four or as large as 18 or 20, each led by a stallion. It takes great skill to even see them, let alone get close to them, for the stallions are extremely alert. At the slightest alarm they round up their band and take them off into the trees.

In the morning, Doreen and Bob will saddle up and begin their search throughout the lonely hills southwest of Sundre, Alberta. The Hendersons, founders of the Wild Horses of Alberta Society, know that in order to advocate effectively for the protection of these magnificent animals they must know first-hand how they live. And that means trekking into the wilderness several times each year. Sometimes they ride for days without a glimpse. Other times, they get lucky.

On a recent expedition they were setting up camp and preparing to settle in for the night when something caught Doreen's eye. She paused from collecting rocks for their campfire and glanced toward their horses. That's when she saw the wary figure of a wild sorrel stallion, nose to nose with their gelding. "I shrieked," Doreen remembers. "He'd already nosed in to move the mare away." The stallion had slipped up silently, planning to steal the mare for his harem, but he bolted when Doreen yelled. Already, it appeared, this trip was a definite success.

The Hendersons have always been horse lovers, but it wasn't until 1998 that the plight of the wild horse grabbed their attention. "That's when we saw our first wild horses," says Doreen. "We just fell in love with them. They've got tails that

The Last Wild Horses in Canada

flow down to the ground and massive manes. They don't look domestic at all. I guess they appealed to our romantic side."

There's little romance remaining in the lives of these "Spaghetti Western" remnants. Wild horses are found in 10 western states, in remote regions of Canada, and on several barrier islands off the Atlantic Coast. The United States has approximately 40,000 mustangs, officially protected there since 1971, but wild horses in Canada probably number just in the hundreds. Only the wild ponies of Newfoundland and Sable Island have protected status in Canada, and even that might be in question. On Sable Island off the coast of Nova Scotia, 200 to 350 head are protected by both limited access to the island and official regulations. These ponies have great cultural and scientific interest, but the popular notion that they are descended from shipwreck survivors is based more on romance than on reality; present-day horses came from those brought to the island between the late 1700s and the early 1900s. The Sable Island horses are entirely unmanaged and have had legal protection since 1961 under the Sable Island Regulations of the Canada Shipping Act. But this protection depends upon the horses and their habitat being monitored, as they have been since lifesaving stations (originally set up in 1801) guaranteed a continuous government presence on the island. If these government-run stations are withdrawn from Sable Island, its horses will no longer have legal protection. They will join the wild horses of western Canada in fighting for their survival.

Wildlife in the Kitchen

• • •

The threat of animal predation is a natural part of a wild horse's life. But it isn't other wild animals that primarily jeopardize their survival. Their existence is threatened most by humans.

Wild horses are thought by some to be nuisance animals, good for nothing but target practice. Opponents claim they foul local water supplies, displace native species, and compete with domesticated cattle. They're also accused of hastening erosion by overgrazing land, and interfering with reforestation efforts by trampling or eating newly planted tree saplings. The Hendersons say wild horses are innocent of such crimes. "We've never seen evidence of this," says Doreen. "Far more damage is done by all-terrain vehicles." Wild horses can't be held responsible for overgrazing, she adds, because they're constantly on the move. Unlike fenced cattle that will stay in an area and eat until it's scoured clean, wild horses graze lightly and move on. In winter, they even help the deer and elk access food by pawing away snow from the ground. "We believe they've created a nice little ecosystem for themselves," says Doreen. "And they're prey, too. Wolf, cougar, and bear hunt them."

The slaughter of wild horses by humans has been going on unchecked for decades as they've been shot or rounded up for shipment to rendering plants. In fact, until recently there was a bounty on wild horses. But the case that spurred the Hendersons into action was a particularly grisly killing in which a horse was shot, sawed in half, and gutted. The extreme cruelty and senselessness of it lit a fire in them. "No one seemed to be doing anything to protect them," says Doreen. "The SPCA wouldn't get involved, probably because they're not considered domestic animals. Fish and Wildlife officials wouldn't get involved because they said they're not wild animals." So the wild horse fell into a grey area, with the result that they could be hunted and killed at will.

"We decided to do something instead of just complaining," says Doreen. In April 2002 the Hendersons officially established their society, to function mainly as "a lobby group trying to get some changes through the government, specifically legal protection for the horses." Ideally, the Hendersons hope for legislation similar to the Wild Horses and Burro Act in the United States. That 1971 bill states that "... wild free-roaming horses and burros are living symbols of the historic and pioneer spirit of the West; that they contribute to the diversity of life forms within the Nation and enrich the lives of the American people; and that these horses and burros are fast disappearing from the American scene." The act ensures that free-roaming horses and burros are protected from capture, branding, harassment, or death and also says these animals should be considered an integral part of the natural system of public lands.

Wild, free-roaming horses in Canada have no such protection at this time.

Wildlife in the Kitchen

In British Columbia, the Chilcotin Forest District holds the other last major population of wild horses. Recent estimates indicate that there are about 400, including a large group of possibly up to 150 head in the Brittany Triangle. It's a pristine wilderness paradise, filled with lodgepole pines, spruce, aspen, sparkling lakes and streams, and abundant wildlife. The horse population appears stable, thanks in part to mild winters but mostly due to the extreme isolation of the area; it was 1973 before the first logging road reached the valley.

But the majestic trees that provide shelter for the horses also put them at risk as logging companies constantly seek new commercial stands of timber. If this continues unchecked and more forests disappear, the Brittany could be destroyed as wildlife habitat and as a refuge for some of the last wild horses of Canada. Clear-cutting, the logging practice of harvesting vast swaths of timber from a large area, exposes horses to human predation by introducing access roads and traffic, and further disrupts the natural balance by discouraging predators that help keep the horse population in check.

For wild horse advocates, the distinction between true wild horses and feral horses — those that have escaped from farms or ranches — is mainly a political one. While ranchers claim they are feral, descended from escaped settlement horses, champions of the wild horses argue that at least some of them bear genetic proof of descent from Spanish horses brought to North America by Cortez in 1519. It stands

The Last Wild Horses in Canada

to reason that some bands will have formerly domesticated horses among them, but the majority of those observed by the Hendersons appear to have been born wild. Certainly their behaviour is that of wild animals.

Wild horse bands are usually made up of a single stallion and a group of mares and their foals, who live together year-round. Larger bands may have more than one stallion and it's not unusual to find that some stallions and their harems have been together for many years. "Even a few years ago we saw herds with 25-plus horses," says Doreen, "but not now. The numbers are going down."

Wild horses can be fiercely protective of the weak among them. They will surround an injured herd member, and even maintain a slower pace if necessary, to keep him shielded. And they're extremely solicitous of their newborns. The mortality rate for foals is high, and with a gestation period of 11 months it can take years to build up a herd.

Because of this, Doreen and Bob are always excited to see youngsters. In particular, they keep their eyes peeled for one special mare who, without fail, has a new foal every spring. They recognize her because wild horses tend to have unique colour patterns. "She's odd-looking, with a brown head and whitish grey body," observes Doreen. "You wouldn't call her pretty!" But she's healthy and strong and she's a good mother.

When male foals reach sexual maturity they are either driven out by the stallion to join bands of other bachelors, or

Wildlife in the Kitchen

they challenge a reigning stallion for control of a herd. Most of the time, posturing and bluffing decide the winner. But if neither contender concedes defeat, they will fight — to the death if necessary. There's no such thing as dirty fighting; they purposely aim for the vulnerable areas. A broken leg or a severed tendon means game over, and control of the harem is awarded to the winning male.

When the Hendersons saw a limping black stallion, they immediately guessed he was the loser of one such battle. "His front leg had been severely broken. It looked like he had an elbow joint high above his knee," Doreen says. They suspected the injury might have been a couple of years old. But the bone had healed enough that he could run awkwardly and was able to eat, although he was underweight. Since it's unusual for a horse to survive such an injury, they wondered how he'd managed. Then they saw his friend. "A young dun-coloured stallion stayed with him all the time, helping him eat and protecting him."

It's hard for them to see such an injury and not intervene, but they know the horses need to be left alone. They will protect them from human harm, but they also have to protect them from well-intentioned human interference. History has proven that domestication attempts can have devastating results. If the horses are captured for any reason, many will starve themselves, refusing food and water until they simply collapse. For every three captured, Doreen estimates two will die. "They just want to be free," she emphasizes. "They don't

The Last Wild Horses in Canada

want care. They don't need rescuing."

"We go out almost every weekend," says Bob, "riding our horses and visiting and observing the 'wildies' in their natural habitat. After all these years they still get me excited as I watch in awe at their beauty."

•••

No one has ever officially studied the wild horses of western Canada. But decades ago, when Vancouver journalist James Martindale discovered the existence of these horses, he quickly became fascinated and knew he had to learn more.

"Being a history buff, I began to think about the people who lived here on this shining, big-sky land before us. Who were they? Where did they go?" James, who lived in Alberta at the time, spent entire days in the archives of Calgary's Glenbow Museum, pouring over maps, examining old photographs, and learning about the people who first occupied this country.

He found arrowheads in the soil and, in certain spots, centuries-old teepee rings. He discovered that millions of buffalo once roamed the prairies, pursued by aboriginal hunters. "Then it dawned on me," he says. "Once upon a time, the Native peoples depended on dog power to move around the country. Dogs were harnessed to travois, dragging all the peoples' earthly possessions across the countryside. But then along came horses — and everything changed."

Wildlife in the Kitchen

Full-blown horse culture had become dominant by the middle of the 19th century, explains James. Suddenly people were able to travel like the wind, hunt across wider territories, and expand ancient trade routes continent-wide. They became formidable warriors. Inter-tribal horse stealing was the greatest of adventures. Every family kept a herd of ponies, and a man with a few hundred head of horses was a very rich man. "I was hooked. I had hundreds of questions." And, as a journalist, James's motto is, "If you know how to get information, you can find out nearly anything."

He discovered that in the late Pleistocene Era, 1.8 million to 11,000 years ago, a series of devastating events killed off most of the New World's large mammals. Climatic changes and overly enthusiastic human hunters led to the extinction of the mammoth, the saber-toothed tiger, and horses. It wasn't until the 1500s that Spanish explorers reintroduced mustangs to the American continent. These horses were small and squat with long hairy manes, and were extraordinarily tough and hardy.

One of the earliest European reports associating Native peoples with horses comes from the mid-18th century journals of explorer Pierre La Vérendrye. According to La Vérendrye, at that time both dogs and horses were used only as beasts of burden. Although various tribes lay claim to being the first equestrians, the answer is lost in the mists of legend.

James was left with one big question: Where did all the

horses go? "At one time they numbered in the millions on the prairies," he says. "Where are they now? Does anyone know? Are they extinct?"

In his research, James kept coming across newspaper clippings from the 1950s and 60s highlighting the ongoing fight of activist cowboy Slim Davis to protect wild mustangs. Slim testified to the existence of a few remaining herds of purebred Spanish mustang stock still roaming the Alberta foothills, where he owned a ranch. In his lifetime, he pointed out, he'd seen many species of mountain fauna dwindle, citing the nearly lost mountain sheep as an example. He persistently claimed that "his" horses were unique, a heritage animal, and needed protection from the hunters and ranchers who were shooting them down like vermin. Authorities decried Slim as a "crank." This only made him push harder. In 1973 he took a petition to the Alberta Legislature proposing the creation of a wild horse reserve in the foothills country. His petition was barely even given an audience. But with his stubborn cowboy will still intact, Slim continued to court the media at every opportunity, hoping he might eventually grab enough popular support to make a difference.

In 1979 James crossed paths with Slim Davis. "I called him up one sunny day and asked to have a meeting with him," he recalls. "It was an offer he couldn't refuse."

Slim's Hummingbird Ranch home was in a remote area of the foothill country, accessible only by dirt roads. In this wild land without street signs, navigation is strictly by land-

Wildlife in the Kitchen

marks such as large rocks, fences, and trees. Based on Slim's directions, James found his way to Hummingbird Ranch. "His spread looked really lonely and rugged," he comments, as he recalls his meeting with the old cowboy — a natural charmer who loved a good story and even recited poetry when the spirit moved him. After dinner, Slim took James out into the darkness with the promise that they would see something special. "We stepped out into a stunningly fresh, starlit night," remembers James, "and walked about 30 minutes toward a corral hugging a dark forested area." Slim motioned for James to keep quiet and look in the direction he pointed. In the shadows near the far fence James discerned a hesitant, dark presence and heard a low, nickered greeting. Slowly, haltingly, a small wild mare materialized out of the shadows and approached the men. James watched in awe as the mare nuzzled Slim's outstretched hand.

"It was an 'Aha!' moment for me," says James. "Here was a man who shared my own sense of the romance of the old West. We both appreciated wild things from a distant time."

Slim's mustang mare was neither captive nor fully wild, James discovered. She dropped in and out seasonally, finding her way around the fences. Slim fed her well when she needed it, and together they developed an extraordinary, trusting relationship.

James visited Slim Davis once more, in 1980. He was determined to see more of these amazing horses. "He took me out on a ride to look for a herd of mustangs. He said very

The Last Wild Horses in Canada

matter-of-factly that he knew their exact location." Some miles back into the foothills James and Slim located a small group of ponies grazing on bunch grass. "We approached downwind. Slim's dog gave chase, though, blowing our cover. We were within 30 metres of the horses, so I whipped out my camera. But wild mustangs don't immediately run from danger. They stand stock still, frozen. It's a well-recorded behaviour, and one that has helped to endanger them. As if caught in headlights, they're utterly vulnerable at this point. Once assured we were not going to harm them, they returned to their grazing, carefree. Dog or no dog, they had business of their own to do. We only stayed a few minutes."

Slim has since passed away, but James will never forget the sights this remarkable cowboy shared with him.

• • •

The horses of 400 years ago were very different from our modern-day horses. Those free-living mustangs descended from pure Spanish colonial stock that arrived in the 1500s and which, in turn, hailed from ancient Arab Moorish stock. Through contact with escaped domestic horses, herds grew and the mustang gene was diluted. Modern biologists are able to distinguish the mustang from "European" quarter horse stock by means of unique genetic markers.

Many wild horse bands in Alberta and British Columbia display Spanish characteristics. Some people say they show superior conformation, intelligence, and conditioning to ranch and domestic saddle horses.

Only one Canadian horse has had genetic testing done, a little dun mare owned by Steve Howlett of Cooks Creek, Manitoba.

From the moment he first saw her Steve knew she wasn't an ordinary horse, but it wasn't until much, much later — after many months of painstaking effort, phone calls, letters, and conversations — that he was able to patch together her checkered history.

In 1976, during one of the last wild horse round-ups, a dun mare was captured from a herd in the Siffleur Wilderness Area of Alberta's Kootenay Plains. Unbeknownst to her new owners, this mare, purchased for the unlikely purpose of pleasure riding, was carrying a foal of unknown sire when she left the wilderness area. "Little Orphan Annie," born in the spring of 1977, was sold to a man who ran a riding and boarding stable and had a reputation for being abusive. His harsh philosophy backfired with this filly, however, as all she did when saddled or harnessed was rebel, pinning her ears back and trying to bite.

"One day," recounts Steve, "while in harness pulling a sleigh carrying 20 people, she exploded, ripping her harness to the point where you couldn't find two pieces to stitch back together." That got her sold to an unsuspecting family who wanted a riding horse for their son. Although they treated her well, they weren't experienced enough with horses to handle

The Last Wild Horses in Canada

Annie, and she knew it. Since they couldn't ride her, they decided to let her have a foal and bred her to a paint stallion. Annie and her owners then moved to St. Adolphe, Manitoba.

Steve met Annie in the spring of 1984. "She was 10 months in foal and her feet had not been done in over six months," he remembers. But in spite of her untrimmed hooves and somewhat ragged physical condition, he fell in love with her immediately. It was her colour that did it. The mustang colour palette ranges from the usual solid black, brown, chestnut, and sorrel colours, to the elegant chestnut body with black mane and tail of the bay, to the flashy blonde-over-gold of the palomino. They may also have patches, blankets, or spots. Some exhibit more exotic patterns: zebra, red dun, and a pattern called *grulla*. "A *grulla* (or *grullo*, if it's a male) is usually a black horse with a dun gene," explains Steve. "In this dilution, the gene acts on the black body of the horse to make it a mousy grey colour." Each individual hair is greyish coloured, instead of the mixture of dark and white hairs seen in roans.

Steve had always loved the soft grey-brown dun colour Annie inherited from her wild mother, and in late October of that same year he became Annie's new owner. "I felt 'Annie' was not a suitable name for a horse," he says (even though he knew nothing at the time about her wild heritage), "so she was renamed Shandi." Steve's new horse had been described as a renegade, for whom the only safe place would be "in a tin." But he sensed she had been mistreated at some point, and was just misunderstood. "Shandi could be moody and always needed a good reason to do something," he concedes. "It's difficult to describe her personality accurately, as she was quite an individual, not fitting into any category." In any event, her new name, which means "mischievous one" in its original Celtic, seemed appropriate, and it stuck.

Originally from Alberta, Steve was working at the time as a guide on a Manitoba ranch. He'd recently had to relinquish his horse to a newer staff member and had no alternative but to try Shandi out at work. Few mustangs exceed 14.2 hands tall, and most weigh less than 500 kilograms. Although Shandi was big for a "wildie," she was still a fairly small horse. Steve is 6'1" tall and weighs almost 90 kilograms. He knew it would be a challenge for this little mustang to carry him. "I was worried that the long hours and constant riding would break her down," he says. "But although she lost weight no matter how well I fed her, she never missed a day of work. She was always there when I called on her, always willing."

Shandi and Steve worked 5 days a week, up to 10 hours a day, in hot and dusty or humid and bug-infested environments. She developed a reputation for being a tough, smart, fast little horse. Steve was impressed. "There wasn't much this little mare wouldn't do for me, and I really respected her." After working with her day in and day out, logging thousands of miles on her back and finding out just how resilient she was, he became curious about her history and the source of her strength.

The Last Wild Horses in Canada

Shandi

He was astounded when his search for her roots led him to the discovery that Shandi was a bona fide wild horse from his own home province. Eventually he became interested in pursuing the possibility that she might actually have Spanish heritage, and got in contact with the Canadian Wild Horse Society. After seeing pictures of Shandi, society representatives encouraged Steve to have her evaluated as a possible Spanish Mustang/Colonial Spanish Horse. "They sort of follow the theory that if it looks like a duck, walks like a duck, and sounds like a duck, it's probably a duck," quips Steve.

Steve hoped that Shandi could be officially registered with the American Mustang Association. The criteria are simple: confirmed birth in the wild, matching physical and temperamental characteristics, and the ability to breed true. Shandi fit on two of the three. She was the foal of a wild mare captured in an extremely remote area untouched by humans for decades. Her physique was typical of wild Mustangs of Spanish stock: small size, short back, and deep body. She also exhibited the dorsal stripe, Spanish mask face, and shoulder patch, and her spirited temperament was indicative. The only thing she hadn't done was produce a foal sired by a wild stallion, so they couldn't evaluate her ability to breed true, or to pass on these wild characteristics to a new generation.

Steve felt sure Shandi fit enough of the criteria, but would DNA testing confirm what he believed? He contacted the University of Kentucky, where genetic research was being done on wild horses, and requested a blood sampling kit. Steve duly collected the sample, completed the paperwork, and sent off the information. Then he tried to put it out of his mind. It wasn't easy. "It took months of waiting on pins and needles for the results," he says. When the results arrived, they were encouraging but not definitive. "They told me Shandi had significant Spanish Genetic Blood markers,

Andalusian being one of them."

Steve continued his pursuit for information and when he heard about the mitochondrial DNA test, he jumped on it. "All I had to do was send a sample of Shandi's mane hair, including the roots, to Germany." And ... another long wait. But this time the results were clear. Shandi had an unmistakable Iberian mtDNA pattern, the same pattern showing up in the majority of Spanish Mustangs tested in the United States.

Steve and his wife, Lynn, were overjoyed. They had been hoping the Canadian government would recognize the heritage value of Shandi and the other wild horses, so their first reaction was a feeling of vindication. But even with scientific evidence supporting the existence of Mustangs in Canada, the government has yet to take specific protective action.

Shandi (and her home herd of "wildies") are carriers of the genetic heritage of Spanish mustang stock in the Canadian wilderness. Because this has been confirmed, Shandi became the only Canadian horse registered with the American Mustang Association. "She is also the first Canadian horse registered with the Sorraia Mustang Studbook," adds Steve. "Her registry number is 'T94-C Shandi,' the 'C' standing for 'Canada.'"

A proud horse, Shandi carried herself with the dignity of one who knew her lineage. And although she became domesticated, she always retained her natural independence. "She could do it all ... good cow sense ... quiet, yet full of life ... mischievous, yet eager to please," says Steve. "In the forest she was

Wildlife in the Kitchen

level-headed, never shying, and wanting to lead. When you sat in the saddle it was like turning on a switch beneath you."

And just as quickly, on October 2, 2004, that switch turned off. The night before, Shandi pranced happily, awaiting her supper. "When I went to feed her in the morning," says Steve, "I found her down. Silvertip, her friend and companion for the last three years, was standing guard over her. My heart sank and I knew immediately she'd passed away. Shandi, in the last few years, never would lie down. As I entered the shelter, Silvertip nickered softly and moved away as if he knew his vigil was over. He left her in my care, watching from a respectful distance."

Shandi stirred many wild horse advocates to action, allowing people to see at close range the beauty and heritage at risk. But as public as her life had been, for Steve and Lynn Howlett the loss was personal. "Weeks after burying her, I would almost trade that legacy to have her back," Steve says. "We were privileged to have her enter our lives and are utterly heartbroken at losing her. She shall be missed."

Steve, James, Bob, and Doreen have the same questions. What do we owe these horses? Do we help them continue to exist and prosper, or do we let them perish? Are there sufficient numbers left for a healthy gene pool?

Nobody knows for sure exactly how many wild horses are left, but James says his pal Slim felt pessimistic toward the end of his life. "He thought the 1970s estimates of 'a few thousand head' were way too high. He thought a few

The Last Wild Horses in Canada

hundred was more likely," says Jim. "Those numbers don't add up to a sustainable gene pool. I think we are seeing the last wild mustangs now before our very eyes." He adds, "Our children won't see them, ever."

Epilogue

The last rays of sunlight are dim on the horizon. Elizabeth places the carrier near a fat tree trunk and unlatches the wire door. She stands back, waiting. In a moment or two, a whiskered pink nose pokes out. Then another. Then a third. The noses are followed by beady black eyes and delicate, seashell ears. The young opossums move deliberately, sniffing their way out of the crate and into the forest.

It's been a long journey from the roadside death of their mother to the sanctuary of Elizabeth's kitchen. They understand neither the tragedy that brought them together nor the compassion of her care. There are many events Elizabeth hopes animals can't remember either. She will miss these joeys, but it's a fleeting emotion. Many other needy wild creatures, unfortunately, will arrive in the months and years ahead to take their places. But this, right now, is why she does it. All the midnight feedings, the bites and scratches, the cleaning and medicating, everything is done so the creatures she cares for might live as they were meant to live: wild.

The opossums glance in Elizabeth's direction, but only perfunctorily; their journey now is away from her care and toward a second chance at life. As they amble into the wilderness she allows herself a brief smile. And a wistful but contented sigh.

Further Reading

Wildlife Rescue Association of BC
www.wildliferescue.ca

Northern Lights Wildlife Centre
www.northernlightswildlife.com

Bowmanville Zoological Park
www.bowmanvillezoo.com

For the Birds
www.rivernet.ca/~nbiggs/

Wild Horses of Alberta Society
www.northernhorse.com

The Last of the Wild Horses, by James Martindale
http://members.shaw.ca/save-wild-horses/index2.htm

The National Wild Horse and Burro Program
http://www.wildhorseandburro.blm.gov/index.php

Acknowledgments

To the many people who generously shared their experiences with me for this book: Elizabeth Melnick, Jackie Ward, Shelley and Casey Black, Michael Hackenberger, Joan and Neil Biggs, Mike and Doreen Macri, Sam Kayra, Richard Romaniuk, Dave and Valerie Daley, Kim Daley, Bob and Doreen Henderson, James Martindale, and Steve Howlett. My sincere thanks for your enthusiastic participation! I'd also like to thank my family: Ray, Stephanie, Andrea, and Megan for caring enough to check in on me now and then and ask, "How's it going?"

A special thank you to my gifted editor, Deborah Lawson, who smoothed out the rough edges of this manuscript and is always a pleasure to work with!

Photo Credits

Cover: photos.com; Steve Howlett: page 117; photos.com: page 73; Roxanne Willems Snopek: page 90; Stephanie L. Snopek: page 125; Lisa Weir, Elizabeth's Wildlife Centre: page 15.

About the Author

Roxanne Willems Snopek lives and writes in Abbotsford, British Columbia, where she shares her home with her family and many animals, both domestic and wild. Their mountain backyard is populated with deer, squirrels, rabbits, hummingbirds, jays, songbirds of all kinds, and high above them, eagles. She knows how lucky she is.

To read more about her, see her website at www.roxannesnopek.smartwriters.com. She loves to hear from readers!

Amazing Author Question and Answer

What was your inspiration for writing these animal stories?

I'm an animal lover, of course, and I have great admiration for people who work in wildlife rescue and rehabilitation. These animals are not pets; they are not tame and the object is usually to return them to the wild. It's one thing to care for an animal that obviously adores you, like my dog. It's another thing to care for an animal that would rather remove your fingers than accept your help.

Who do you most admire in this Amazing Story?

I think Elizabeth Melnick of Elizabeth's Wildlife Centre in Abbotsford would have to be the person I most admire in this book. Because we both live in the same city, I've known about her for many years, but didn't really get to know her properly until interviewing her for this book. She's such a natural caregiver! And she never complains about the unglamorous parts of her work — she has nothing but compassion for her patients.

What part of the writing process did you enjoy most?

Visiting Elizabeth's shelter, seeing and photographing her patients up close.

Amazing Author Question and Answer

Why did you become a writer? Who inspired you?

I've been an avid reader as long as I can remember but it didn't occur to me that I might be a writer, too, until I was in my twenties. I'd always kept journals, though, and during an episode of young adult career angst I remember telling a friend, "I'm going to write a book one day. I don't know what it will be about, but I know I'm going to write one.".

Who are your Canadian heroes?

Where do I start? Emily Carr, for courageously pursuing her art. Carol Shields, for writing *The Stone Diaries*. David Suzuki, for inspiring and challenging us to care for the environment. Sarah McLachlan, for music that helps me write. Emily Stowe, first Canadian woman doctor. Guy Laliberté, founder and CEO of Cirque du Soleil, the best show ever!

Which other Amazing Stories would you recommend?

I really enjoyed Susan McNicoll's *BC Murders* and *Ontario Murders*. Being a murder mystery buff, I enjoy true crime and Susan's got some great stories.

OTHER AMAZING STORIES

ISBN	Title	ISBN	Title
1-55153-959-4	A War Bride's Story	1-55153-951-9	Ontario Murders
1-55153-794-X	Calgary Flames	1-55153-790-7	Ottawa Senators
1-55153-947-0	Canada's Rumrunners	1-55153-960-8	Ottawa Titans
1-55153-966-7	Canadian Spies	1-55153-945-4	Pierre Elliot Trudeau
1-55153-795-8	D-Day	1-55153-981-0	Rattenbury
1-55153-972-1	David Thompson	1-55153-991-8	Rebel Women
1-55153-982-9	Dinosaur Hunters	1-55153-995-0	Rescue Dogs
1-55153-970-5	Early Voyageurs	1-55153-985-3	Riding on the Wild Side
1-55153-798-2	Edmonton Oilers	1-55153-974-8	Risk Takers and Innovators
1-55153-968-3	Edwin Alonzo Boyd	1-55153-956-X	Robert Service
1-55153-996-9	Emily Carr	1-55153-799-0	Roberta Bondar
1-55153-961-6	Étienne Brûlé	1-55153-997-7	Sam Steele
1-55153-791-5	Extraordinary Accounts of Native Life on the West Coast	1-55153-954-3	Snowmobile Adventures
		1-55153-971-3	Stolen Horses
		1-55153-952-7	Strange Events
1-55153-992-6	Ghost Town Stories II	1-55153-783-4	Strange Events and More
1-55153-984-5	Ghost Town Stories III	1-55153-986-1	Tales from the West Coast
1-55153-993-4	Ghost Town Stories	1-55153-978-0	The Avro Arrow Story
1-55153-973-X	Great Canadian Love Stories	1-55153-943-8	The Black Donnellys
		1-55153-942-X	The Halifax Explosion
1-55153-777-X	Great Cat Stories	1-55153-994-2	The Heart of a Horse
1-55153-946-2	Great Dog Stories	1-55153-944-6	The Life of a Loyalist
1-55153-773-7	Great Military Leaders	1-55153-787-7	The Mad Trapper
1-55153-785-0	Grey Owl	1-55153-789-3	The Mounties
1-55153-958-6	Hudson's Bay Company Adventures	1-55153-948-9	The War of 1812 Against the States
1-55153-969-1	Klondike Joe Boyle	1-55153-788-5	Toronto Maple Leafs
1-55153-980-2	Legendary Show Jumpers	1-55153-976-4	Trailblazing Sports Heroes
1-55153-775-3	Lucy Maud Montgomery		
1-55153-967-5	Marie-Anne Lagimodière	1-55153-977-2	Unsung Heroes of the Royal Canadian Air Force
1-55153-964-0	Marilyn Bell		
1-55153-999-3	Mary Schäffer	1-55153-792-3	Vancouver Canucks
1-55153-953-5	Moe Norman	1-55153-989-6	Vancouver's Old-Time Scoundrels
1-55153-965-9	Native Chiefs and Famous Métis		
		1-55153-990-X	West Coast Adventures
1-55153-962-4	Niagara Daredevils	1-55153-987-X	Wilderness Tales
1-55153-793-1	Norman Bethune	1-55153-873-3	Women Explorers

These titles are available wherever you buy books. If you have trouble finding the book you want, call the Altitude order desk at **1-800-957-6888**, e-mail your request to: **orderdesk@altitudepublishing.com** or visit our Web site **at www.amazingstories.ca**

New AMAZING STORIES titles are published every month.

Comments on other *Amazing Stories* from readers & reviewers

"*Tightly written volumes filled with lots of wit and humour about famous and infamous Canadians.*"
Eric Shackleton, *The Globe and Mail*

"*The heightened sense of drama and intrigue, combined with a good dose of human interest is what sets* Amazing Stories *apart.*"
Pamela Klaffke, *Calgary Herald*

"*This is popular history as it should be... For this price, buy two and give one to a friend.*"
Terry Cook, a reader from Ottawa, on **Rebel Women**

"*Glasner creates the moment of the explosion itself in graphic detail...she builds detail upon gruesome detail to create a convincingly authentic picture.*"
Peggy McKinnon, *The Sunday Herald*, on **The Halifax Explosion**

"*It was wonderful...I found I could not put it down. I was sorry when it was completed.*"
Dorothy F. from Manitoba on **Marie-Anne Lagimodière**

"*Stories are rich in description, and bristle with a clever, stylish realness.*"
Mark Weber, *Central Alberta Advisor*, on **Ghost Town Stories II**

"*A compelling read. Bertin...has selected only the most intriguing tales, which she narrates with a wealth of detail.*"
Joyce Glasner, *New Brunswick Reader*, on **Strange Events**

"*The resulting book is one readers will want to share with all the women in their lives.*"
Lynn Martel, *Rocky Mountain Outlook*, on **Women Explorers**

AMAZING STORIES

GREAT DOG STORIES

AMAZING STORIES

GREAT DOG STORIES
Inspirational Tales About Exceptional Dogs

ANIMAL/HUMAN INTEREST

by Roxanne Willems Snopek

PUBLISHED BY ALTITUDE PUBLISHING CANADA LTD.
1500 Railway Avenue, Canmore, Alberta T1W 1P6
www.altitudepublishing.com
1-800-957-6888

Copyright 2003 © Roxanne Willems Snopek
All rights reserved

Extreme care has been taken to ensure that all information presented in this book is accurate and up to date. Neither the author nor the publisher can be held responsible for any errors.

Publisher	Stephen Hutchings
Associate Publisher	Kara Turner
Project Editor	Jill Foran
Editor	Geoff McKenzie

We acknowledge the financial support of the Government of Canada through the Book Publishing Industry Development Program (BPIDP) for our publishing activities.

Altitude GreenTree Program
Altitude Publishing will plant twice as many trees as were used in the manufacturing of this product.

National Library of Canada Cataloguing in Publication Data

Snopek, Roxanne
 Great dog stories / Roxanne Snopek.

(Amazing stories)
Includes bibliographical references.
ISBN 1-55153-946-2

 1. Great dog stories--Anecdotes. I. Title. II. Series: Amazing stories (Canmore, Alta.)

SF428.2.S56 2003   636.73   C2003-904882-9

An application for the trademark for Amazing Stories™
has been made and the registered trademark is pending.

Printed and bound in Canada by Friesens
6 8 9 7 5

To Molly, our retired racing greyhound who, since the day we got her, hasn't done a single useful thing…except love us.

Max (left) and Dakota (right), heroes of
the story "Terror in Moose Country"

Contents

Prologue 11
Chapter 1 On Centre Stage 13
Chapter 2 On the Force 22
Chapter 3 Faith, Hope, and Healing 36
Chapter 4 In the Classroom 45
Chapter 5 My Eyes Have Four Legs 55
Chapter 6 In the Water 68
Chapter 7 Trigger Happy 77
Chapter 8 Terror in Moose Country 87
Chapter 9 Collies Against the Odds 98
Bibliography 113

Prologue

LeeAnn O'Reilly glanced through the woods into the late autumn sky. Daylight was fading, and a dense chill was setting in the Newfoundland air. It was time to head back.

"Dakota!" she called, "Max!"

She searched the forest for a pair of friendly shadows ambling through the bush, but her Rottweilers were nowhere in sight. LeeAnn took a few tentative steps into the woods, and then she heard it: the telltale jingle — the bells she had fastened to her dogs' collars to warn away wild animals. But the sound grew fainter even as she walked towards it. Again, she called for the dogs, an edge of annoyance in her voice now. This time they burst out of the trees, muscles rippling and tongues lolling as they flung themselves on her. They rubbed their massive heads against her legs and she broke into a laugh.

"Forgiven," she murmured fondly.

Then, as suddenly as they had arrived, the dogs tensed. Pulling away, they stood swiveling their ears, their noses lifted to the wind. A long, low growl rolled from Dakota's throat and her hackles rose. Max froze, his attention trained on a clump of bush ahead, his body poised to leap. LeeAnn could see no sign of danger, but she felt the terror rise deep in her belly.

As the snarls of the dogs began to build, LeeAnn took stock. She had no weapons, no phone, and no radio. She had nowhere to hide. Max gave a single, short bark and it happened: the woods exploded with the fury of a beast enraged.

Only her two Rottweilers stood between LeeAnn and the black bull moose charging straight for her.

Chapter 1
On Centre Stage

From birth, Jammie was destined to be a star. Her bright eyes, elegant bone structure, luscious coat, and regal bearing all pointed to a career in that competitive world of canine beauty contests: the show ring. Indeed, before her first birthday, Jammie (pronounced Jay-me) was a titled conformation champion, beautifully exhibiting the sought-after traits of the ideal silky terrier. She had already lived up to her distinguished registered name, Champion Kedwell's Silk Pajamas.

But success didn't sit well with Jammie. When campaigning for titles, dogs and their owners might spend every weekend on the road, travelling to shows. They meet with hundreds of strangers in new surroundings filled with unfamiliar sights, sounds, and smells. On the judging table, dogs must stand calmly while strangers handle them. If necessary, judges will touch every part of the dog's body.

It got to be too much for Jammie. Her owner, Ros Scott of London, Ontario, watched her dog's happy personality gradually give way to anxiety. Jammie began avoiding strangers. In competition, she would watch the judges over her shoulder, her eyes narrowed in suspicion. Worst of all, she grew suspicious of children. As a result, Ros had to find ways to keep children from touching Jammie unexpectedly. She did what she could, hoping the problem was temporary. But Jammie became more and more anxious and unpredictable around strangers — to the point of growling and snapping if approached by surprise. With great reluctance, Ros admitted that although her dog was a stunning example of the silky terrier physique, Jammie's temperament was less than ideal. Jammie had an aggression problem.

Ros Scott had problems of her own. A decade earlier, she'd had surgery to fuse two vertebrae in her lumbar spine. Now she was beginning to experience pain in her hip. But Ros ignored her increasing discomfort and redoubled her efforts to quell Jammie's anxieties. Ros took the terrier out of the show ring and began agility training — an activity involving a demanding obstacle course run by both dog and handler. It was just what Jammie needed; she was challenged both physically and mentally, but her exposure to strangers was greatly reduced. Within a year, Jammie achieved her Canadian

On Centre Stage

Kennel Club Novice Agility title.

With the title under their belts, Ros sought new challenges. She had always toyed with the idea of trying musical freestyle, a type of obedience-dance competition often compared to pairs figure skating.

Music has long been a part of dog training; in obedience classes, it adds an element of fun to the task of perfecting rhythmic pace. Obedience drill team demonstrations are often performed to music. But musical freestyle obedience as a sport in its own right only began to emerge in the late 1980s. Inspired by the musical routines of equine dressage, demonstrations of this new dog sport began to pop up at various dog shows across the United Kingdom and North America. Since that time, the sport has exploded in popularity. Audiences and competitors alike thrill over the delight the dogs take in performing their routines, and over the vivid evidence of the bonds dogs share with their owners.

Ros thought that musical freestyle obedience, like agility, might be another way to help Jammie overcome her anxiety. Ros hoped she could find something they both enjoyed that she could manage in spite of her diminishing mobility. So, in January 2002, Ros drove with Jammie to a workshop in Michigan. There, they discovered that not only was the event a lot of fun, but that they were considerably better than Ros had expected. In order to compete, however, they had a lot of work to do. The best-case scenario for success in the sport of musical freestyle obedience involves two things: a temperamentally well-adjusted dog who loves to work (preferably a border collie), and an athletic owner (preferably 20 to 30 years old) with a background in dance. Ros and Jammie didn't fit these criteria. But Ros still wanted to give it a try, and she and Jammie started to develop their routine.

Ros quickly learned that this activity was no easier on her back than agility. Her body began to protest in earnest, and after one lengthy road trip to Denver for another workshop, she arrived at the hotel barely able to walk. She began to use a wheelchair whenever possible to save her energy for demonstrations. In spite of anti-inflammatories and painkillers, some days the back pain was barely tolerable.

Still, nothing ever came between her and the terrier. Ros soon realized, in fact, that their bond had become stronger and more intuitive than ever. Jammie seemed to know when her dance partner was in pain. It shouldn't have been a surprise; musical freestyle relies heavily on unspoken signals such as body language and facial expression. Dogs and handlers work in synch, constantly adapting to the slightest change in each other's movements. On the days when Ros wasn't able to move as freely, Jammie moved more, compensating for her partner and drawing the eyes of their audience onto herself.

Ros's health continued to deteriorate rapidly until she was using a wheelchair constantly at home. In addition to the medications, she began getting regular massage therapy, but still the pain increased. In an attempt to help her understand

On Centre Stage

the seriousness of her condition, the therapist explained to Ros what was happening in her body: the muscles in her legs had shortened and rotated, pulling her spine out of alignment. Sitting only made the pain worse. Carefully chosen activity would help, but she had to start gradually. Most likely, the sudden immersion into agility was what had started the domino effect of damage.

So Ros began focusing on the demanding and sometimes excruciating work of rehabilitating and strengthening her muscles — she also continued to practise the musical freestyle routines she loved to do with Jammie. It was a difficult time for Ros. Inadvertent contact with a sensitive spot sometimes brought such intense pain it nearly made Ros pass out. Jammie learned to accommodate her partner even more, picking up on the subtle changes in movement dictated by discomfort and moving carefully to avoid hurting her. As a result, their performance got even better.

Ros and Jammie began to compete. Ros will never forget their performance at the first World Canine Freestyle Organization event in May 2002. The crowd fell silent as the pair entered the ring. They took their spots and stood poised, eyes locked on each other, listening for the music. For a moment, the air hung hushed and expectant, and suddenly, the music began. With a leap, the little dog came to life, rolling, twirling and jumping, stepping backward and forward, executing a series of intricate moves in perfect harmony with her human partner. It all fit into a perfectly choreographed pattern that, by the end of the performance, brought everyone in the audience to their feet. Ros Scott and her silky terrier Champion Kedwell's Silk Pajamas had, once more, made magic. They took their bows and walked to the edge of the ring. Ros immediately reached for her wheelchair and dropped into it, exhausted. Jammie leaped up and settled into her owner's lap, panting happily. When the judges tallied up their marks, success overshadowed pain. Ros and Jammie placed first in the beginners class, receiving high marks for both technical merit and artistic impression.

Later that year, Ros met with a surgeon again to discuss fusing two more vertebrae. It needed to be done, but the surgeon explained that until her muscles had developed greater strength and flexibility, the operation was destined to fail. Ros had a lot of work ahead of her.

The harder Ros worked, the harder Jammie worked. Soon, the awards were piling up. Jammie received her Agility Dog Canada title, points towards her Beginners Musical Freestyle title, and even a trophy for the highest scoring toy dog in musical freestyle. Jammie just wouldn't quit.

In fact, now she leads. "She doesn't always want to follow the practiced routine," says Ros with a laugh. "If she goes from plan A to plan B, you have to go with the flow and keep smiling. No one else knows if she does three spins instead of two."

Ros admits to being apprehensive before each performance, wondering each time what new thing her dog will try,

On Centre Stage

but Jammie clearly knows what she's doing. She's good at it because she loves it and has become a star. If Jammie recognizes a song on the radio, she has been known to jump off the couch and dive into her routine. Ros has even caught Jammie twirling in front of the mirror! Like many dogs, she hates having her feet touched; it's a fight to the finish to get her nails trimmed. But get out the nail polish and the story changes. Jammie loves having sparkly gold nails and she sits calmly for her manicure, like any good diva.

She recognizes "her" music, but Ros knows better than to use a certain song too long. Jammie needs variety and if she becomes bored with a routine, her moves show it. She rolls her eyes and Ros can imagine her thoughts: "Oh for Pete's sake. Not this one again!"

Jammie might be a star but she also seems to understand that stardom demands professional behaviour. When Ros pulls out the frilly collar that indicates it's "show time" Jammie tucks all her anxieties away. The little dog knows that she must tolerate a certain amount of adoration from her fans, and she is especially aware of people with mental disabilities, allowing them to hug and pet her. When once she might have snarled or snapped, now she accepts the attention calmly, if not enthusiastically. To her, it's a small price to pay for success.

Just as Jammie has learned to read Ros, Ros has learned to work around Jammie's sensitivities. Kids still find the little dog irresistible and, tired of body-blocking hoards of affectionate pint-sized fans, Ros came up with a couple of ways around it.

"I tell them she doesn't like to be touched, but she'll do a trick for them," says Ros. Now, when a child approaches, Jammie immediately starts spinning. She's also learned to "say hello" to children: she runs up to them, licks their hands, then returns to Ros for a treat. For most kids — and for Jammie — it's an acceptable compromise.

But Ros knows better than to push it. By a hundred tiny signals, she can tell when Jammie has reached her limit. The tension in her back, the tilt of her head, the set of her ears all give clues to her comfort level. Ros particularly notes how aggressively Jammie takes her treat. "When she snaps it out of my hand," she says, "I know her stress level is getting too high."

Ros and Jammie are so attuned to each other, it sometimes seems like they can read each other's minds. Perhaps this is part of the magic that makes them such a successful team. "When we're dancing," Ros says, "Jammie's eyes lock with mine. She grins at me. I grin at her. It's like we're lovers dancing together." Audiences and judges alike melt in the face of such a relationship. Among Ros's most treasured awards are several trophies for most bonded dog and handler.

By all accounts, the duo shouldn't be successful in dog sports: a 50-year-old woman with mobility problems and a toy dog with aggression problems. But by accepting their limitations and working together, they've both achieved more than most of their competitors. Just recently, the pair received the

On Centre Stage

coveted High in Trial title in an agility competition in Andover, Massachusetts. Ros could choose to compete in handicapped divisions, but she doesn't want to. She doesn't need to. She'll always have to be careful with her back, even though her fitness has improved enough to allow her to exchange the wheelchair for a cane. Surgery will help, but only to a certain extent. Ros knows this. She also knows that unless she challenges herself, she'll never know what she can accomplish.

And she's quick to give the credit to Jammie. "It's all due to a dog who gives her heart and soul."

Chapter 2
On the Force

Everyone knows that no crime can be solved without evidence linking the suspect to the event. Naturally, suspects go to great lengths to dispose of such evidence, but there's one thing they can never remove: their scent.

In Maple Ridge, British Columbia, during the spring of 1995, Corporal Rick Chaulk and his canine partner, Police Service Dog Jake, were called to assist in solving a horrific crime. The body of a man had been discovered, stabbed and beaten to death the previous night. Investigators at the scene quickly identified two suspects.

"They called me to do a search because they hadn't found a murder weapon or any other related evidence," says

On the Force

Chaulk. He knew that the chance of finding clues was best while the trail was fresh. Human beings are constantly shedding scent particles, leaving an invisible cone-shaped olfactory trail marking their movements. The particles hover in the air like dust, before settling on the ground and eventually disappearing. A brisk wind can disturb the trail, as can rain, snow or the overlay of other scents. So Chaulk and Jake wasted no time combing through the residential neighbourhood where the murder had occurred, looking for any evidence that might help them solve the crime. Systematically, inch-by-inch, the pair went over a three-block area near the victim's home.

"The first day turned up nothing related to the crime," says Chaulk. "So we came back the next day and expanded the search area to a one square block radius of the crime scene." They'd worked their way over most of this larger area when suddenly Jake picked up something. He began moving back and forth, narrowing the trail down, looking for the strongest source of the scent. About seven houses away from the victim's home, he began to whine in excitement, sniffing furiously until he reached a hedge. It was clear to Chaulk that Jake had found something with human scent on it. "You learn to read your dog," explains Chaulk. "You look for body language. When Jake indicates, he becomes very animated: his tail starts wagging, he tries to get at the article."

Something lay hidden deep in the hedge and Jake was determined to get at it. Chaulk quickly climbed into the hedge too, trying to see what Jake was so excited about. He also needed to make sure that if they had found something important, Jake wouldn't contaminate it. Chaulk peered through the thicket and then he saw it: a baseball bat.

During training sessions, the dogs are rewarded in a variety of ways. They always receive enthusiastic praise from their human partner. Sometimes they get a brief play session with a favourite toy. Occasionally, they get to play with the search object itself. During a real evidence search, however, the handler tries to keep the dog away from the article for fear he will destroy some vital clue. Jake worked solely for Chaulk's approval and Chaulk piled it on. "Atta-boy, Jake! Good boy!"

But Jake was a new dog, barely out of training. In fact, this was his first official search. How would Jake know the difference between a baseball bat used in a crime two days ago and one lost by schoolboys the previous summer? "Human scent evaporates in time," explains Chaulk. "Jake's indication was so strong I knew the bat had been recently deposited there." And, as a new dog, Jake would be less likely to pick up an old scent. Experienced dogs can learn to distinguish "cold" trails, but Chaulk knew that Jake wasn't likely to do this. Whoever had stuffed this bat into the hedge had done it recently.

They'd made good progress, but more work had to be done and the clock was ticking. Police surveillance noted that the two suspects had been seen walking along the railroad tracks near the Fraser River under the cover of night. They appeared to be carrying something, but it was too dark to see

On the Force

what it was. When the pair left the area a short time later, they were empty-handed, so Chaulk and Jake went in to see what they could find. By this time, the light was quickly fading, but the canine sense of smell is so much more powerful than sight that nightfall makes little difference. Under bushes, behind trees, and up and down the railroad tracks Jake searched off leash while Chaulk stumbled along behind, flashlight in hand, hoping his dog knew what he was doing.

After only a few minutes, Jake began to focus on a gravel area near the tracks. Again, he pawed and dug until his quarry was revealed. When Chaulk caught up, he pulled Jake back to look for himself and saw, glinting through the gravel, the tip of a gun. Jake was on a roll. He'd found a missing pair of rifles.

Instinct is a strange thing, and Corporal Chaulk's instincts told him they weren't finished yet. "A gut feeling told me we should be thorough, and I just figured there was more to it than that," he recalls. Although no official order had sent them out, five days after the murder, he and Jake did a "speculative search." They went back to the river, had a good run, and then made their way back to where they'd found the guns. "Search!" Chaulk commanded. Instantly, Jake went to work, searching back and forth over the rough ground, collecting information, and looking for the particular scents that identified the suspects.

Jake reached a clearing and again, his head went up and his tail started beating the rhythm of success. His find? A stained pair of old blue sweatpants. Chaulk praised Jake, but privately he doubted that the item had any value. Many people used these trails, after all, and they were a favourite place for late-night parties. Who knew by what dubious means those pants had gotten there?

Nevertheless, procedure dictated that the forensic team be called in to retrieve the garment for preservation and analysis. While Chaulk impatiently awaited their arrival, he asked Jake to search one last time, just in case. Within minutes, Jake began to dig beneath a nearby stump. Chaulk ran to check the area himself. "I pushed the dirt with my foot and that's when a knife was exposed," he says.

Chaulk didn't know it at the time, but the last piece of the puzzle had just fallen into place. Jake had uncovered the knife that was used to stab the victim. Forensic tests later revealed that the stains on the sweatpants came from the blood of the murder victim. They had everything they needed to build a strong case against the two suspects. The sweatpants belonged to one of the suspects, and had been worn during the killing. The victim had been killed by a blow to the head, stabbed, and robbed. Without the meticulous work of Corporal Chaulk and his canine partner, Police Service Dog Jake, the offenders might have gone unpunished. Instead, both men were convicted for their parts in the crime and sentenced to time in prison.

Jake's career was launched, inaugurating a brilliant partnership that would continue until his retirement at the age of eight. Chaulk still works as a police dog handler, but no dog will ever fully replace Jake. "I raised Jake from an eight-week-old puppy," he remembers. Chaulk did all the necessary pre-training to prepare Jake for the formal work at the RCMP Police Dog Training Centre in Innisfail, Alberta. For six years, Jake and Chaulk were barely separated, working together and living together. But then came the moment when something changed and Chaulk knew his partner had had enough. "It was a tough call because he was still working fine," says Chaulk, "but you could see it in his eyes. He was tired."

Chaulk knew that retiring Jake meant losing Jake. Although breaking their partnership was devastating, he knew only a complete separation would give Jake the best opportunity to enjoy his old age. Retired police dogs rarely stay with their handlers, unless the handler also retires from the dog unit. "These dogs live to work," Chaulk says. "If I kept him but every morning walked past him with a new dog on our way to work, while he stayed home in the kennel, it would kill him." Instead, Chaulk made the agonizing decision to say goodbye while Jake was still young and healthy enough to enjoy a few years of ordinary life. "It only takes that one call that maybe finishes their career or ruins their health," he adds. He didn't want to take that chance with Jake.

Chaulk handpicked a family that he knew would give his partner the retirement he'd earned, and while he hears about Jake occasionally, he's never visited him. It took Jake a few months to adjust, but he's happy now in his new home, and Chaulk doesn't want to remind him of their old life together. It would be too hard on both of them.

"Jake worked hard," he says. "I told him 'go be a dog, eat table scraps and lie by the fire. You deserve it.' But it's tough."

* * *

The danger of police service dog work takes many different forms. One night in November of 1978, a reckless driving complaint was called in — a deceptively innocuous call. Police officers attempted to apprehend the driver but he fled in a high-speed chase, finally screeching to a stop in front of a house where a large, raucous party was in progress. He leapt out of his car and disappeared into the woods behind the house. RCMP Corporal Terry Barter of Chilliwack, British Columbia, and Police Service Dog Major were called in with the request to "apprehend as many suspects as possible."

Major quickly identified the trail of the driver, found him, and brought him down. But while Corporal Barter was handcuffing the man, several hostile-looking young men suddenly appeared. "When we caught our guy, he started screaming, attracting people from the party," says Barter. Two men jumped Barter from behind, and someone else bootkicked Major viciously in the side, hard enough that a veterinary examination later revealed a ruptured spleen. Not knowing who had kicked him, Major reacted by biting the suspect on the ground. The suspect began screaming again and his companions escalated their attack. Fearing for

On the Force

Major's life, Barter pulled him out of the fray and locked him in the police car.

Other police officers quickly helped subdue the group, but as the officers returned to their vehicles, more young people poured out of the house, shouting taunts and threats. "At one point we had about 50 to 80 people outside chanting 'kill the pigs, kill the pigs,'" says Barter.

The driver and two other men were taken into custody and charged with assaulting a peace officer. One of them, the one who had kicked Major, vented his fury in a particularly ominous way: "I know where you live!" he shouted at Barter. "I'm coming to kill the dog!" Unfortunately, when the young man was released early the next morning, the first item on his agenda was revenge — and he wasted no time. At 6:19 a.m., Barter heard the crunch of tires near his house. Major was resting safely inside instead of in his kennel in the yard, but no one else knew this. While Barter was hurriedly pulling on some clothes, he heard voices outside calling for the dog, and he realized that the young man and his friend were trying to get Major to reveal himself. "I knew why they were there," he says. "I was prepared to defend my residence if they got out of the vehicle armed."

But something spooked them. Just as Barter went outside, the truck roared away. Moments later, five shotgun blasts exploded through the morning air. Barter suspected they'd be back, and he was right. Later that day, neighbours reported the same truck lurking near Barter's home. This time, police nailed the young man before he could get away. Major was safe again. For now. But the unsettling incident reminded Barter that every job he and Major tackled could be the last. And a year earlier, it almost was.

One spring morning in 1977, a prisoner from Agassiz Mountain Prison escaped during a fishing trip on British Columbia's Fraser River. Barter and Major were brought to the location where the prisoner had last been seen, a wooded area near the riverbank. The prisoner had chosen his path deliberately, travelling over rocky ground that was the least likely to carry tracks and the most difficult to follow. He'd taken weather, daylight, and terrain into account, and had probably thought he had a good chance of escaping successfully. Indeed, he might very well have been successful if it hadn't been for Major.

By that time, Barter and Major had been partners on the RCMP dog unit for about six years. They had gone into every kind of situation, from avalanche rescue, missing person searches, and body recovery, to chasing escaped convicts. This was nothing new.

Major immediately picked up the prisoner's scent and started straining at the leash, eager to begin pursuit over the rough mountainous terrain. Police dogs normally work on a long tracking leash, but about two-thirds of the way into the chase, the grade angled up sharply and Barter knew that Major needed his freedom. Barter himself needed both hands to navigate the incline, which by then exceeded

On the Force

50 degrees. Plus, he had another worry: in the back of his mind nagged the thought that they might need to defend themselves against an ambush from above.

Major leapt ahead, scrambling over the rocky terrain, and the officer hoped his dog's strength and agility was equal to the task at hand. Then, through the brush and rocky outcroppings in front of him, Barter heard the unmistakable sound of slipping shale, followed by a heavy thud, a yelp, and then silence. Barter hurried over the jagged ground, frantic to catch up with his dog. When he reached him, he saw that Major had taken a nasty fall. Major looked shaken, but when Barter ran his hands quickly over the dog, he could find no obvious injuries. He hoped that Major's thick coat had protected him from the worst of the biting rocks.

Barter felt sure they were close on the heels of their quarry, but now he worried that his partner had been injured. Major hid any signs of pain, however, and clearly had no intention of quitting, so they continued upward.

About 60 metres below the snow line, Major turned abruptly, crossing a field and doubling back into the woods. He was on to something! Barter rushed to where he found the dog standing, excitedly indicating his find: a carefully hidden cache of three tobacco tins, a book, and a box of biscuits. Barter put the items in a safe place for recovery later on, and they continued the hunt. Once again the track angled sharply upwards, and as Major bounded ahead, Barter lost sight of him.

Suddenly he heard the dog cry out again, but this time something was different. Instinctively, Barter knew that Major had cornered the convict, which meant the dog was in danger. Barter scrambled towards the sound, shouting for Major to return. Finally, as he crested the ridge, he caught a glimpse of the prisoner disappearing into the woods. But where was Major? Barter scanned the area frantically, but when he caught sight of his dog it wasn't relief he felt. Major staggered towards him, trying desperately to obey the recall command, his chest and shoulders covered with blood. Before he made it back to his handler, he stumbled and collapsed. As Barter rushed to his dog's side, Major suddenly heaved himself up again to go after the prisoner. Barter hadn't had a chance to see the wound but he guessed his dog had been stabbed, probably deeply, judging from the blood loss. The officer commanded him to return. Major ignored the command.

All Corporal Barter could do was follow the trail of blood and hope he reached his dog in time. He braced himself for the worst, but when he burst through the trees into a small clearing, nothing could have prepared him for the sight ahead. On the ground lay the prisoner, terrified but unharmed, with a snarling, blood-soaked Major standing guard over him.

The pursuit was over, but now Barter was faced with a desperate escapee armed with an unknown weapon, and a police dog rapidly going into shock from blood loss. Barter needed to get the prisoner disarmed and restrained, but what he wanted to do was attend to his dog. As the corporal reached for his handcuffs, the prisoner lunged into his bag. Instantly, Barter knew what he had to do: he shot the prisoner in the leg.

The next 15 minutes before back-up arrived seemed to stretch on endlessly, the wait punctuated by the moans of the injured prisoner and Major's shallow breathing. Later, Barter would face harsh reprimand for shooting the prisoner in his care, but in those moments, Barter's only concern was for his canine partner. He knew the prisoner was not in danger of dying from his injury, but Major, who was growing weaker by the moment, might very well be. Barter packed the gaping wound in Major's neck as well as he could; all that remained was to wait for the helicopter and pray that his dog would survive. The distant sound of helicopter blades was never more welcome!

But where does a helicopter land on a mountain? "We had to walk more than a kilometre to where the helicopter could hover over a large rock," recalls Barter. Both Major and the prisoner had to be loaded into the aircraft while it hung in mid-air, officers pushing and pulling them into position as best they could. When they finally left the bush and made it back into town, Barter rushed Major to the veterinary hospital, where an examination revealed a nine-centimetre deep stab wound that had severed the dog's jugular vein and a large nerve in his throat. Major had suffered severe blood loss. In a two-hour surgical procedure, the veterinary team did the best they could, but they weren't optimistic. "They told me to take him home to die," recalls Barter. But the corporal crossed his fingers. Only an incredibly strong, determined dog would complete his task in spite of life-threatening injury. Barter clung to the idea that if Major was strong enough to corner the prisoner, he was strong enough to pull through his injury.

And he did. Day by day, Major regained more strength until Barter knew that, incredibly, he was going to recover. "They kept testing him for nerve damage, but they never found any," adds Barter. Exactly two weeks after the event, Major was reinstated to full, active duty. He'd learned something important about knives, though, a lesson he never forgot. "He was always careful about suspects on the ground after that," says Barter. "He was only going to be stabbed once."

Major lived with Barter and his family for his entire adult life. As tough as he was with criminals, Major was overwhelmingly patient and gentle with children. Both of Barter's newborn children were brought home from the hospital in the police cruiser, car seats belted alongside Major. At one point, the family's yard was unfenced except for Major's large dog run, so when Barter's little daughter wanted to play outside, they let her toddle around after Major inside the run. No playground could be more secure and she clearly loved it, perhaps too much. "Our daughter started to bark along with Major," Barter laughs.

On the Force

Major would have retired with Barter, but cancer cut his life short just before his 10th birthday. He worked right up until the morning of his death.

Corporal Barter knows that his job is risky. It's fraught with frustration, and the rewards can be few and far between. But the bond he shares with his canine partners means everything to him. "I joined the RCMP to be a dog handler," he says. "I stayed at this job because it's what I wanted to do."

Chapter 3
Faith, Hope, and Healing

For most of her adult life, Heather MacLeod of Fredericton, New Brunswick, has been heavily involved in dog sports, competing with her German shepherd Bailey in conformation shows, obedience, and tracking. Bailey's successes have made history in the German shepherd world: in 1998, she became the first white German shepherd to earn a Tracking Dog Excellent title in both Canada and the United States. But it was her win in the conformation ring that really threw people for a loop. "White shepherds," Heather explains, "are sort of the 'black sheep' of the German shepherd breed."

When Bailey was about three years old, a good age to have puppies, Heather began making tentative plans to

Faith, Hope, and Healing

breed her. She knew exactly which male she wanted for the father but he lived in Michigan. The logistics of timing and travel were complicated, and the window of opportunity during which a dog can become pregnant is only open a short time — twice each year. Heather didn't want to put Bailey through the stress of being shipped out to where the male lived, so she briefly considered artificial insemination. "Males are hardly ever shipped, but semen can be," she explains. "But that is very costly and the success rate isn't as high as with a natural breeding." She resigned herself to a long puppy-less wait. It wasn't entirely hopeless; the male was being actively campaigned on the show circuit so there was a chance they'd be able to meet. But Heather didn't get her hopes up.

Then, out of the blue, she was contacted with the news: the male she liked was going to be competing in a nearby show right during the time Heather expected Bailey to be in season. Was she still interested in getting them together?

She certainly was, and the romance was duly arranged and consummated. On December 10, 1998, Bailey gave birth to the much-anticipated litter of puppies, including one that Heather would later keep. Heather was ecstatic. The puppies were every bit as beautiful as she'd hoped, and Bailey appeared to be enjoying her pampered status as a new mother.

But the joy was short-lived. On December 11, Heather received a phone call that brought her abruptly down to earth and signalled the beginning of her own private nightmare. It was her doctor, calling with the results of some laboratory tests she'd had recently after complaining of a persistent cough. The chest X-ray indicated that she had a mass in her lung. A naturally healthy, optimistic person, Heather struggled numbly to make sense of the news. The doctors couldn't say what the mass was or what it would mean for her. Until further tests were done, she'd simply have to hope for the best. Heather continued to care for Bailey and the puppies but it was hard to think of the future. She was scheduled for surgery.

The pups were four weeks old in January 1999 when Heather went into surgery to have the mass removed. She had been warned ahead of time that she could lose part or all of her lung in the procedure. When Heather was rolled into the operating theatre that day, she had no idea what kind of news she'd wake up to, but it didn't take long to find out. The mass, along with a lobe of her lung, was removed and sent to the pathology lab for tests. The results were clear: Heather had Hodgkin's lymphoma. Her doctors, however, were cautiously optimistic; as cancers go, this one has a relatively high cure rate.

The tumour itself had been successfully removed, but Heather would need chemotherapy to destroy any cancer cells still circulating in her lymphatic system. Heather assimilated all the information she could find about her condition while trying to keep the fear at bay. As soon as she recovered sufficiently from her surgery, she began the first course of chemotherapy.

Faith, Hope, and Healing

Throughout the ordeal, Bailey's puppies continued to grow fatter and more rambunctious until, in February, they were old enough to go to their new homes. By this time, Heather had decided she would keep one for herself; she named her puppy Faith.

It was a challenging time in her life to have a puppy, and Heather hoped she knew what she was doing. Her experience in dog sports, particularly the tracking she and Bailey loved, was something she thought might help her through this difficult time. But dog sports are physically demanding, and she had a long way to go in her recovery. Six months of chemotherapy had sapped her energy, and only a few months after her last round, she was devastated to learn that it hadn't achieved what they'd hoped for. Her lymphoma was back. Heather faced a difficult decision, but ultimately, there was no choice to be made.

At the end of 1999, when everyone else around her was preparing to celebrate the coming of the new millennium, Heather was in the hospital again, sequestered in the isolation ward. In a world full of champagne-toasting revellers, one woman struggled to keep down popsicles and wondered if she'd still be around to celebrate properly next year. Before the advent of the New Year, Heather would receive another stronger form of high-dose chemotherapy, followed by a bone marrow transplant.

At this high intensity, the chemotherapy destroys all fast-growing cells. It's a kind of last-ditch, scorched-earth strategy. Cancer cells are wiped out, but vital red and white blood cells, platelets, and stem cells are obliterated along with them. "Essentially," explains Heather, "they kill your immune system with the high-dose chemo, as a sort of collateral damage, and then they 'rescue' you with the bone marrow transplant."

Heather remained isolated in the hospital until mid January 2000, while her body fought to rebuild its immune system. This time, the treatment worked, but the roller coaster ride wasn't over yet. Heather had one last trial to overcome. The chronic exhaustion that accompanies bone marrow transplant recovery left her unable to do more than the simplest tasks. Even when she finally came home, although she was anxious to work with Bailey again and start training Faith, she could do very little. Frustrated at times, she struggled to be patient, reminding herself that this was a normal part of the process. "I try very hard not to make people afraid of chemo," she emphasizes. "Chemo saved my life. It was no picnic but I'd do it all over again, no question."

Then spring rolled around, bringing with it a hint of her old energy. "By the end of March, I was growing some hair back and feeling almost human," she recalls. "I'd had my 38th birthday and wished to have a few more!" The future beckoned. It was time to push herself, force her body and mind to recover. She even set herself a goal: that fall, she intended to take the American Tracking Dog test with Faith. She didn't know if the puppy would be ready, but all she could do was try.

Faith, Hope, and Healing

She started by taking Faith out into the field on very short beginner tracking exercises. Gradually, as her condition improved and Faith became more competent, Heather laid longer scent tracks for the pup to follow. In the early days she would sometimes stay out for only a few minutes at a time, but that's all Faith needed. "It fit in so well with my recovery," says Heather. "I told people 'tracking with her is my therapy. It's getting me better!'"

From her past involvement in pet visitation with Bailey, Heather knew about the many positive effects animals have on hospital and nursing home patients. Now she intended to reap the benefits of animal-assisted therapy herself, as much as possible. She continued at home in the field that summer, tracking with Faith. She was determined to meet her goal of taking the test in September. Their performance was beside the point, rather, Heather focused on doing the work and making progress.

That fall, they were as ready as they could be. Heather crossed her fingers and they took the test. Faith passed. "I was thrilled!" she remembers. "I can't even explain the feeling when we passed the test. I thought 'That's it, we're back, baby!'" Their success continued into the following month, when Faith got her Canadian Tracking Dog title.

For Heather, 2000 was "the year back from hell." The physical challenges were tremendous, but the ordeal of riding such emotional highs and lows was at least as difficult. Without the tasks associated with the sport of tracking, and the joy she gets from it, Heather doubts she'd have coped so well. "A major part of my recovery was the work with my dogs. I do so much with them! That's why it was so important when I hit that first title with Faith. I felt like I was back in the world of the living again."

The three-year mark is the point at which a person is considered cured of Hodgkin's lymphoma. "I just had my three-year check up and I'm all clear," Heather reports with quiet joy.

Life was almost back to normal for Heather and her family. She continued working with the dogs and challenging them with new things: obedience, advanced tracking, and agility, which Faith loves. "She's fast but I'm not!" laughs Heather. "The chemo actually damaged what's left of my lungs, so I get out of breath really quickly." In May 2003, Bailey, who was spayed after her second litter, earned both her Flyball Dog and her Flyball Dog Excellent titles. "She would really like to enter squirrel-chasing competitions," says Heather, "but I just can't find any, so she's settling for flyball instead." Flyball is a rapid-fire relay in which dogs run to a ball, trigger its release, catch the ball, and race back with it to the next dog in line. Heather loved it almost as much as Bailey did.

Still, one thing was missing. During Heather's illness, her much-loved old cat, Buckwheat, died. Although she missed his company and wanted a kitten, the doctors advised her to wait for two years after her bone marrow

Faith, Hope, and Healing

Faith, a white German shepherd, and Hope

transplant. Because some cats carry an organism called *toxoplasma* that can be dangerous to immune-compromised people, they wanted to let her fully regain her health before taking any chances.

The month her two-year time limit was up, during the drive home from work, Heather's eye caught a flash of white moving at the side of the road. To her alarm, she saw a kitten stagger out of the brush, directly into the path of her car. She swerved to avoid hitting the animal, then pulled over and got out of her car to search for it. When she found the kitten, she quickly realized that the poor animal was practically frozen, weak and starving, and that it seemed to have given up fighting for life. She gathered the fragile creature into her jacket, hoping it wasn't too late. "I didn't even want to pat her; she was just fur over bones," says Heather.

Heather raced to the local veterinary clinic, where she was told the kitten was severely malnourished, dehydrated, and hypothermic. The young animal would need special care to survive, and without an owner, its chances were slim. Heather decided instantly: the kitten would come home with her. "I knew this kitten was a gift sent especially for me," she says. "Before I had her home, I had already named her: Hope."

Heather wondered how the new kitten would get along with Bailey and Faith, but soon realized her worries were needless. Not long after Hope's arrival, Heather smiled as she watched Faith tenderly nuzzle and lick the tiny animal then stretch out on her side, exposing her flank. Although she's never had puppies, Faith is a natural caregiver. It looked as though the big dog was playing wet-nurse to Hope. Then Heather looked again. Faith *was* nursing Hope! The kitten nosed into the soft fur of Faith's belly, kneading her paws in ecstasy, while the dog lay there as if this were nothing out of the ordinary. Heather leaned down and gently squeezed one of Faith's nipples. Milk. Faith looked up at her as if to say, "What did you expect?"

Faith and her mother Bailey had helped their beloved owner through a difficult health crisis. It was only natural that now Faith would nurture Hope, too.

Chapter 4
In the Classroom

On a bright Sunday morning in Coalhurst, Alberta, teacher Judith Snowdon sat at the sidelines of Perfect Pooches' obedience ring, holding her breath. In a moment, all eyes would be on her German shepherd, Tuxedo Rose. But Snowdon had no worries about that. Already titled in obedience, draft work, scent hurdling, and agility, Rose had earned more degrees than most people ever would. Snowdon had no doubt that Rose would perform well once again. It was Rose's handler, a young student named Kathleen, who Snowdon was concerned about. This obedience match, an afternoon of fun for most participants, was the final culmination of a major school project for Kathleen, who was born with spina bifida.

Great Dog Stories

Judi Snowdon and Rose

In the Classroom

Over the years, Rose had played a number of roles in her job as canine assistant to Snowden, who is a teacher and counsellor at the junior high school in Blairmore, Alberta. The dog patiently modelled for art students, striking various poses while they scrambled to capture her graceful lines on paper. She also frequently accompanied Snowdon to her classes, where as part of the health curriculum, as many as 75 students at a time would practice the proper way to meet a new dog and learn what to do when approached by a stray.

Aside from health education, Snowdon taught Humane Education, a class in which students learned to interact and care for animals with compassion and empathy. Snowdon also instructed the basics of dog training: how to modify an animal's behaviour using the same methods professional trainers use. In Rose, Snowdon had the perfect visual aid to illustrate how and why animals enrich our lives. Students tried their newfound skills out on Rose, and then went home to practise them on their own dogs, choosing specific tasks to teach. Young Kathleen, however, had neither a dog nor a project.

Kathleen's physical challenges meant she needed the aid of arm-brace crutches or her wheelchair to navigate the school's long hallways. Perhaps more difficult than her physical obstacles were the social and academic differences between her and the other students, differences that too often left Kathleen sitting apart from her classmates, on the outside looking in. Snowdon, however, had noticed that in Humane Ed class the social barriers didn't seem as high. She hoped that an interesting and successful project might increase Kathleen's confidence and make it easier for her to connect with the other kids. But what, Snowdon wondered, could they assign that Kathleen could do?

"Can I use Rose for my project?" Kathleen asked Snowdon.

Snowdon hesitated. This was more participation than the dog was used to and she might balk. Besides, what could Kathleen train Rose to do that the dog didn't already know? And how would the girl juggle a leash with her crutches? Then Snowdon had an idea: Rose had never specifically been taught to assist someone in a wheelchair. Perhaps Kathleen could train Rose to assist her with specific tasks — like pushing the handicap button to open doors — and to do it only when Kathleen was in her wheelchair instead of her braces. They formed a plan and got started.

Within a matter of days, Kathleen had taught Rose to retrieve dropped items and to open doors. But as their work progressed, the first snag in the plan became apparent: the two weren't bonded. Rose's attitude quickly deteriorated into, "Why should I do anything for you, kid?" And it was hard to blame her. Dog and wheelchair moved awkwardly side by side; on more than one occasion, Rose's tail got run over. Rose would yelp and run across the hall to Snowdon and they'd have to start all over again.

Of course, as an experienced draft dog, Rose had no problem learning to tow Kathleen in her wheelchair. The

In the Classroom

problem, they quickly discovered, was getting her to stop! On their first attempt, Kathleen and Rose started down the hallway calmly enough, but as Rose saw the familiar door to Snowdon's office, her head pushed forward and her pace quickened. "Rose, slow down," begged Kathleen. But Rose was determined. Kathleen yanked and hauled on the harness, but to no avail. The girl braced herself as the chair crashed against the side of the door and they finally wobbled to a halt. It became a common routine, and students quickly learned to get out of the way when they saw the pair careening towards them.

There was another problem with towing the wheelchair, too. A split second after Rose would finally pull up, the chair would crash into her from behind. Rose would yelp, Kathleen would shriek, and Snowdon would sigh. Snowdon's casual thought of having Rose assist a wheelchair-bound handler was turning out to be more of a hurdle than she expected.

"It took the better part of 12 weeks off and on for part of every day," says Judi. "During their practice sessions, I would see them heading down the hall, Kathleen holding on for dear life, brakes on, yelling 'Rose, easy, *Rose, easy!*' while Rose, her head down, her shoulders set, doggedly made her way to my office." It took time — and a lot of liver treats — but eventually the pair learned to travel together, safely and under control.

And the training had the unexpected benefit of raising Kathleen's profile with the other students. She began to enjoy being noticed by her classmates. They started talking to her, asking how the assignment was progressing, or teasing her good-heartedly about hearing her whiz past on another of her death-defying rides.

The dog and the student had overcome one hurdle, but had Kathleen been challenged enough? The other students in the class reported various problems in teaching their dogs at home. Rose already knew so much; in terms of training, Kathleen's work had been too easy. They needed to take it up a notch, and after a little thought, Judi came up with the perfect plan. A long-time obedience competitor herself, Judi assigned Kathleen the task of training Rose to complete all the necessary requirements for a leg towards an obedience title — with a wheelchair-bound handler. As part of the assignment, she gave Kathleen a copy of the Canadian Kennel Club rulebook for obedience competitions and told her to study it carefully. As Judi pointed out, Rose already knew the rules, but Kathleen had to learn them as well. Kathleen and Judi watched countless videotaped competitions, memorizing various moves and watching for the subtle details that can mean the difference between a passing mark and failure. Training to compete would be Kathleen's final project for Humane Education; as a bonus, studying the written rules would meet some of her English class requirements.

"I didn't cut her any slack," recalls Judi. "I told her, 'You said you were going to do this so you have to make it happen. When — and if — you get good enough I'll tell you and you

In the Classroom

can go in a fun match.'" Then Judi added another incentive: she told Kathleen that if she and Rose entered, Judi herself would enter with another dog and compete against them. Judi knew Kathleen was motivated by the challenge, but worried how she might be affected by failure. After all, Judi was an accomplished trainer and competitor. "How will you feel about losing?" she asked Kathleen. "If I'm good enough to be there," answered Kathleen, "then that's good enough."

Kathleen redoubled her efforts. Because they would be competing against able-bodied handlers and their dogs, Rose and Kathleen needed to learn how to manage tight turns and pace changes from the wheelchair. With the help of a teacher assistant, Kathleen did daily upper body exercises to strengthen her arms enough to handle the workload. They didn't want Rose to be penalized for not being able to change quickly enough from "normal" to "fast" pace. "For Rose," says Judi, "the hardest exercise was the 'figure eight,' and she learned to keep her eyes on that wheelchair, no matter what."

But dogs work best when they love their handler, and Rose belonged heart and soul to Judi. How could Kathleen win her over? Judi knew that Rose's performance depended entirely on Kathleen's ability as a handler, so she pushed Kathleen constantly to improve. Be firm. Be clear. Be consistent. Give the dog lots of praise. Finally, Kathleen got angry. "How come it's always me?" she demanded one day. "You never tell her what she should be doing!"

"Well, Katheen," Judi responded, "Rose can only do what you direct her to do. She needs to have the commands and signals given the same way every time. She needs to have the wheelchair move the same speed and change direction exactly the same each time. She needs for you to be a bit more encouraging and a bit less demanding. When you call Rose, I want to see her run to you like she used to, not walk towards you like it's an effort."

Kathleen looked completely discouraged, but Judi wasn't finished. "You are going to be competing against people like me in that fun match, not against people like you. And that takes more work. You have the best dog, so treat her like she's the best dog and she'll work for you. You're doing okay but you need to do better if you're going to compete. This isn't about marks. This is about life."

Suddenly something changed in Kathleen. When she looked at Rose, she saw another creature who got discouraged sometimes. She realized that Rose needed to be appreciated and praised just as much as she did. "Sorry, Rose," she said. It was the breakthrough Judi had hoped for.

The training progressed to the point where Judi felt Kathleen and Rose were ready to participate in an actual competition, so she entered them in an upcoming event. Still, Judi couldn't help but worry; she knew that a dog's performance during obedience trials is always unpredictable. Kathleen said she would be okay with a low mark, but would she really?

In the Classroom

On the morning of the Perfect Pooches obedience fun match, in spite of their progress, Kathleen was petrified. She sat waiting her turn, trembling and fidgeting, when suddenly the door opened and a man with a television camera came in and made his way towards her. He wanted to interview her for a special news segment. Not only was Kathleen going to compete, but she was also going to be on television! In spite of her nervousness, Kathleen rose to the occasion, answering the reporter's questions with unexpected poise.

But it was Kathleen and Rose's performance itself that truly amazed Judi. "Her 'figure eight' was wonderful," she says. "The 'stand for exam' was perfect, the 'sits' and 'downs' were perfect." The only thing Rose still balked at was the "finish" — returning to the heel position. Kathleen had to be very firm with Rose, insisting that she obey. "I stood there and thought 'please Rose, please let this happen!'" says Judi.

And Rose did. When the judging was complete and the total scores were added up, Kathleen and Rose were awarded a mark of 184 out of a possible 200 for their performance. Not only had they passed, they had passed with flying colours! Judi's own higher-scoring performance with Tuxedo Rose's sister, Smokey Rose, couldn't hold a candle to what Kathleen had just accomplished.

For Rose, that day was just one of a string of shining moments that would end all too soon. After a summer of prize-winning agility and sheep-herding competitions, Judi decided Rose needed a rest. They'd get back into their beloved dog sports next season, after a long quiet winter. But Rose never had another summer. When Snowden noticed Rose seemed to be feeling under the weather, she took her to visit the veterinarian. After much poking and prodding, the veterinarian ordered blood tests and X-rays but Judi wasn't overly concerned. Rose was only seven years old and a strong, stoic dog. It never occurred to Judi that Rose could be sick.

But she was. On March 20, 2002, the first day of spring, Judi Snowdon and the students of Isabelle Sellon School lost their beloved Tuxedo Rose to leukemia. "I received over 200 messages of sympathy from the students, who truly shared my sorrow," recalls Judi. It was a harsh blow for Judi but she's grateful that Rose was able to touch so many lives and so vividly illustrate the value of the human–animal bond.

For Kathleen, life continues to hold many challenges. But no matter what she faces, nothing can take away the gift she received from Rose that day in the ring: the gift of success.

Chapter 5
My Eyes Have Four Legs

The work of a Seeing Eye dog is often misunderstood. Guide dogs, according to celebrated children's author Jean Little, aren't heroes. Instead, they save their people from needing heroes. Legally blind from birth, Jean knows what she's talking about. "A good guide dog keeps you from getting into a dangerous situation," she says. "They don't pull you from beneath the wheels of a bus. They keep you from getting in front of the bus in the first place."

Jean's present guide dog, Pippa, is a quiet Labrador retriever who does her job without fanfare. During one recent visit to a friend's home, Jean noticed that every time she got up to move from one room to another, Pippa would get up, amble to a certain spot, then stand there and wait for Jean to come back. Jean didn't think anything of it until she realized that there was an open staircase at that spot. Pippa was just making sure that Jean didn't tumble down a flight of stairs on her way to the bathroom.

Sighted people sometimes underestimate the importance of the concentration required for guide dogs to do their work. Jean's dogs wear the harness of working guide dogs, which identifies them, but she wishes people would explain more clearly to children what that means. "People say, 'don't pet him, he's a working dog.' It doesn't make sense." Better, she argues, to say "Don't *distract* him, he needs to concentrate."

Actually, both the dog and the handler need to concentrate. It takes careful observation of a dog's behaviour to catch all the cues, and Jean has had her share of mishaps. Rarely, though, have the dogs been to blame. Most of the time, Jean takes full responsibility herself. Several times when she's walked into something or fallen, she's been ready to snap out a reprimand, only to discover that the dog had already stopped. Had she been paying attention, she would have known she was supposed to stop also. On one occasion however, Jean was almost involved in a deadly traffic accident and it wasn't due to an error on the part of either herself or her dog. Instead, it was because a sighted woman she knew had seen the pair and called to them. The dog looked up, and missed the curb. As a result, Jean missed the curb as well, and stumbled forward into the path of oncoming cars.

My Eyes Have Four Legs

Jean recalls how angry she was at her close call. "I can just see the headlines: Woman Led to Death by Guide Dog," she says. "Not what it should have been: Blind Person Dies Because Stupid Sighted Woman Distracted Guide Dog."

Although she was born with a visual disability, Jean didn't use a guide dog until relatively late in life. But then, she had always been extremely independent. Born in Taiwan in 1932 to missionary-doctor parents, Jean moved to Canada at the age of seven. Despite her disability, she attended regular classes in elementary and secondary school and went on to receive her BA in English Language and Literature from the University of Toronto. Books and stories had always been important in her life, and it was only natural for her to seek to share this love with young people. When she finished her studies, she took a teaching position at the Guelph Crippled Children's Centre in Guelph, Ontario.

Because she understood what it meant to be a handicapped child, Jean quickly developed a rapport with her students. She knew what it was like to be left out or overlooked, to feel different, angry and embarrassed. She remembered how it had helped her as a child to know the clinical terms for her condition, so she taught her students to face insensitive questions with straight answers. Soon the children in her classroom could reel off complicated medical terms such as "muscular dystrophy," "cerebral palsy," and "spastic quadriplegia." If you live with it, her motto seemed to be, you should also be able to name it.

Jean encouraged the children to read widely, often bringing in her own childhood favourites to read aloud. Characters with handicaps were of great interest, of course, but after teaching for several years, she realized that all the children's books dealing with disability focused on the characters overcoming their condition somehow. Usually, they were either cured or they died. "It's as if book publishers didn't think that a book could have a happy ending if the person was still in a wheelchair at the end," she says wryly.

So, Jean set out to change that. Her first novel, *Mine for Keeps*, is about the adventures of a child with cerebral palsy — who still has cerebral palsy at the end of the book. It was published in 1962, and won the Little, Brown Canadian Children's Book Award. "People think handicapped people are always sad," Jean says, "but I'm happier than most people I know who aren't handicapped."

Both teaching and writing are demanding occupations, and Jean soon admitted she couldn't do both. Writing won out and, reluctantly, she left the classroom. She never, however, left children. Since *Mine for Keeps*, she has published 36 books for young readers. Her books have been translated into 10 different languages and she has won eight literary awards. She's taught children's literature at the University of Guelph and is adjunct professor in the department of English. She's been the featured speaker at countless conferences, and she travels widely, talking about her dearest love: stories. Children line up for hours to get autographed copies of her books and ask questions. One she hears frequently is why someone who clearly enjoys the company of children never married and had some of her own. To the delight of parents and teachers in the audience, she answers, straight-faced, "Some mistakes, I've never made."

But while she never had children, Jean usually had a variety of animals in her life. Still, she couldn't have predicted how much her four-footed companions would one day mean to her.

By 1963, the birth defect that had scarred both her eyes had progressed to glaucoma. The pressure and swelling led to acutely painful corneal blisters, and as more time passed it became apparent that her left eye had to be removed. She wasn't left totally blind; the vision in her right eye came and went, sometimes allowing her to distinguish shapes and patches of light and dark. However, every eye pain or migraine headache reminded her of the very real possibility of losing her right eye to glaucoma as well.

An unexpectedly severe depression hit. Jean had always been able to cope with the limited vision she had; the possibility of going totally blind terrified her. The only thing that might possibly be good about blindness, she admitted grudgingly, would be getting a guide dog. Friends and family suggested that she might be eligible for a Seeing Eye dog. Why didn't she apply and find out? Finally, in 1982, she filled out an application form. In April of that year, she received word that she'd been accepted to receive a dog and needed to be in

Morristown, New Jersey, on August 15 for training. Her adventure with her first guide dog — Zephyr — was about to begin.

And what an adventure it was! Jean had never imagined that having a guide dog would make her life anything but easier. Why should she expect any problems? After all, she'd had dogs most of her life, and she'd been legally blind most of her life. She was good with dogs, and she was accustomed to her disability. But when Zephyr entered her life, he brought more than guidance. He brought challenge, fear, and despair. He also brought inspiration: Jean's book *Stars Come Out Within* tells, among other things, the story of how she and Zephyr finally overcame their problems and learned to work together.

By the time he first met Jean, Zephyr, a naturally big-hearted dog, had already formed — and lost — two strong attachments in his young life. He'd been lovingly cared for by both the family who had raised him for the first year and the trainer who had prepared him for his new job. He was friendly with Jean, but reserved. She sensed it would take some time for him to risk further heartbreak.

Jean, however, had no such reservations. Awestruck by the intelligence this big dog exhibited, she had a hard time reprimanding him for anything. He already knew so much and obeyed so readily that nothing prepared her for the problems they'd face once they left the training centre.

Like all dogs, guide dogs for the blind need time and training to become accustomed to their new life. But because guide dogs have already had so much specialized training,

My Eyes Have Four Legs

people often expect too much of them. Zephyr, a powerful yellow Labrador retriever, had the problem-solving abilities needed to be an exceptional guide dog. Unfortunately, he was also an "alpha" dog, waiting for the opportunity to assert himself and wrest control from his handler.

His opportunity came shortly after he and Jean left the training facility. Jean, thrilled with her new canine companion, couldn't wait to show off the independence he provided. When Zephyr first began to test her authority, she was so afraid of having to admit failure, so terrified that all her hopes of independence would be dashed, that she ignored the warning signs. These signs started slowly: an unhurried response here, an ignored command there. But soon, Zephyr had the bit between his teeth. Although he'd been raised and trained in the company of other dogs, now he found, in the more tolerant atmosphere of Jean's home, the opportunity to show off his superior power to every dog he met. His dominant personality rose to the surface, making him unwilling or unable to resist letting other dogs know who was boss.

At first, strange dogs merely distracted him. But as more time passed, he began to bark and growl at them. Eventually, he became obsessed with even a glimpse of other dogs, straining at the harness, leaping up and doing everything in his power to get at them. Jean began to dread going for walks. She avoided streets where she knew dogs lived. She tried everything she could think of to correct his behaviour but nothing had any effect. In every other way, however, he was a perfect guide dog. "I almost gave up on Zephyr," recalls Jean, who at 50 was older than most first-time guide dog recipients. "When you get a dog and have problems it's a great shock." However, Jean had grown to love Zephyr and couldn't bear the thought of losing him. She knew they couldn't go on as they were, but she couldn't give up on him either.

Then came the winter day when Zephyr saw a poodle inside a passing car. He went berserk, dragging Jean into five lanes of traffic, barely missing cars, deaf to screeching tires, blaring horns, and the screams of his owner.

When she finally made it home that day, shaken and fighting back tears, she went straight to the phone and called the centre where she and Zephyr had trained. Seeing Eye, Inc., in Morristown, New Jersey, is the oldest guide dog school in North America. The behaviour problems Jean described to them sounded so severe that they immediately offered her a new dog. Jean begged for another option. Couldn't someone come down and help them? In a last-ditch effort, trainer Dan Boeke stepped in to work with the pair. Jean told him about Zephyr's tendencies, and then the three of them went for a walk. Zephyr wasted no time disgracing himself, and Boeke was appalled. Grimly, he warned Jean not to get her hopes up, then he took hold of the harness himself. He knew that their only chance lay in drastic measures — and he was merciless. Zephyr had met his match.

Within a day, everything changed. "Zephyr just needed somebody strong who knew what to do," Jean says. The strategy was simple: Zephyr had to be shown, in no uncertain terms, that he was not the boss. Jean was horrified to see her big dog jerked off his feet, slammed to the ground, yanked into position and hollered at like a cadet at boot camp. The slightest growl earned him a terrific punishment, both verbal and physical, and the more he resisted, the more Boeke piled it on. Finally, Zephyr admitted defeat. Jean began to believe there might be hope after all.

But only, Boeke emphasised, if she used the same techniques herself. Jean steeled herself to dominate Zephyr and ignore his beseeching appeals for leniency. It had to be done and it was hard, but it worked. Zephyr reluctantly deferred to Jean's authority. The next step was rewarding him for good behaviour. For Zephyr this meant one thing: food. They practised incessantly, walking up and down every dog-filled street Jean could find. Whenever she heard another dog bark, she knew Zephyr was working hard to control himself. Praising him extravagantly, she'd give him a treat. Zephyr had been reminded of his job and was willing, once again, to do it whole-heartedly. "It got to where he was making faces at the other dogs, trying to get them to bark so I'd give him a treat," she laughs.

It was the turning point in their relationship. Jean, already well published by then, did what she always did with the significant events in her life. She wrote about them, with typical honesty. "No one was talking about the problems," she says. "I decided it was time someone wrote about the first year with a dog, from the perspective of the blind person." *Stars Come Out Within* continues the autobiographical tale begun in *Little by Little*, which tells the story of her adolescent years as a blind child.

After Jean and Zephyr's rough start, an amazing tale of teamwork began. Jean had learned to be firm with Zephyr, and soon she would learn to trust him.

One afternoon, during a sweltering Ontario summer, Jean made the mistake of going shopping downtown with Zephyr. "We were outside, just walking along, and the heat was burning my feet," she recalls. "I figured it must be torture for Zephyr's feet." She decided to turn around and head for home. But Zephyr had a better idea. Although he was familiar with the route they'd taken, he suddenly took a different turn. "He had no reason to turn," says Jean. "I should have corrected him but I was curious."

She let him walk, wondering what he had in mind. He kept on going, purposefully walking across the sidewalk and up a set of steps until Jean realized they were inside a city bus. He flopped down and turned towards her, waiting patiently for her to catch on. "He looked at me as if to say, 'Lady if you want to walk, walk. I'm taking the bus.'" But you can't just get on any bus — it has to be the right one. Jean imagined herself and the dog lost, travelling back and forth across the city for the rest of the day. She approached the driver apologetically, asking which bus she was on and where it was headed. "Turns out it went right past my corner! So, we just sat down and took the bus home." From then on, Jean enjoyed telling everyone that because her dog had chosen the right bus out of a line-up, he must be able to read. But, she adds, when she got home and tried to get him to read something else to her, he wasn't interested. "He told me it wasn't in his job description," she jokes.

The job of learning to trust Zephyr was more difficult than Jean expected, and sometimes it was hard to know whether or not he really knew what he was doing. One time when the pair was walking to the library, Zephyr refused to take Jean across the street at the usual corner. At that particular corner, five streets came together, making a wheel-like intersection. "I said to Zephyr, forward!" says Jean. "He stood there and looked to where I was pointing. Then he turned and went the other way — four crossings over — until he got to the same spot." Jean bit back her annoyance. The trainers, after all, had reminded them constantly to put their faith in the dogs so she repeated to herself what they told her: "Your dog can see. You cannot." When they finally got across the street a woman stopped her to comment on how smart Zephyr was. "Smart dog? Smart?" Jean responded indignantly. "He should have crossed way back there!" Then the woman explained what Zephyr already knew: a road construction crew was working on the sewer right where they usually crossed, making the path too narrow for both to cross safely. "He'd have fit through but I'd have been hit," Jean says. "He wouldn't go because of me."

Zephyr lived with Jean for 10 years, at which time guide dogs are usually retired. By then, the duo had naturally become extremely close, but Jean needed a dog young and strong enough to do the job. Many retired guide dogs live out their senior years with their owners, but Jean lived alone at that time and felt she couldn't handle two dogs by herself. She found him a home with a family who wanted a big dog for their children and who would still let her visit him. She feared he'd pine for her and was rather taken aback to discover that, while he was always thrilled to see her, the sociable dog enjoyed life with his new family.

Since Zephyr, Jean rarely travels without a dog at her side. After him came Ritz, and then Pippa, and each guide dog has found a special spot in Jean's heart. But the challenges she faced with Zephyr created something unique. "He was my first so there was a deeper bond," she says. "You spend more time with a guide dog than you do with any human being."

Jean, who has been the recipient of numerous prestigious awards, including the Order of Canada, doesn't take herself too seriously. Perhaps attending awards ceremonies with her dogs helps keep her grounded. "You should see these guide dogs walking in honorary procession," she laughs. "They certainly behave themselves. But then they'll start chewing their foot in the middle of it, or licking themselves."

Perhaps more than anything else, Jean values the way her dogs have helped her make connections with those around her. Many people, she's found, are afraid to initiate a conversation with a blind person. In her pre-dog days when she'd attend one of her frequent conferences or speaking engagements, she often felt lonely. "I didn't know where anyone was or if anyone was looking at me," she remembers. But now that a guide dog always accompanies her, people readily approach her to comment on how beautiful her dog is.

A dog, she says, acts as a wonderful bridge between her and the sighted world. "Now, if no one's talking to me, I talk to my dog. It makes me look engaged, rather than pitiable." If anything, she adds, she feels enviable. "A lot of people would love to have one of these dogs."

Chapter 6
In the Water

If you don't want to be dragged back to shore, say Newfoundland dog enthusiasts, don't go swimming with a Newf. As far as these big dogs are concerned, people belong on dry land. If they think someone is in danger of drowning, they'll do everything in their power to come to the rescue.

When a warm body hits cold water, the muscles contract with shock, making it impossible to draw breath. Even strong swimmers can be virtually paralysed within moments, certain to drown without aid. And, unless dressed in protective gear, would-be rescuers are at risk of suffering the same fate. But for the huge, sea-loving Newfoundlands, with their naturally water-repellent fur and tremendous lung capacity,

In the Water

making a rescue in frigid water is a piece of cake.

Denise Castonguay of CastaNewf Kennels in Maple Ridge, British Columbia, saw vivid proof of this skill several years ago during a lakeside training session with Mister, a young Newfoundland male bred at her kennel and sold to close family friends. Castonguay works on her dogs' water rescue skills each year at beautiful Buntzen Lake, between Coquitlam and Port Moody. A popular tourist destination, the lake is clear, clean, and stocked with fish. It's also one of the few lakes that allows dogs and has a boat launch, two essentials for water work training.

Although all the dogs are worked in each session, Castonguay focuses on achieving a title with one specific dog every summer. This is no small task. Newfoundlands who have reached Junior Water Dog status title have already learned to perform a number of small tasks on command: retrieving a life jacket from the water; taking a rope to a stranger who is pretending to drown; and towing to shore a stranded boat, four to five meters long, made of heavy aluminium. Senior Water Dog titleholders have learned to do the more difficult tasks of distinguishing between several items to be retrieved, or people needing to be rescued. They also must take a rope out to a stranded boat and tow it ashore, and they must find and retrieve an item dropped to the lake floor. These underwater retrieves are tricky because some dogs resist getting their heads wet.

But the most difficult task to teach is what's called a

"swim with handler." In this task, dog and trainer swim side by side within an arm's length of each other. After swimming about six metres, the handler goes into a limp free-float. The handler then grabs on to the dog, who must tow his "victim" back to shore. Usually, the dogs happily perform the return trip but really resist the swim out. "It's one of the hardest things to train, because a really instinctual dog will do anything he can to keep you out of the water," says Castonguay. "Including body blocking you or herding you back to shore."

Castonguay will never forget one particular day at Buntzen Lake. It was a hot, cloudless morning, and she knew the sun-worshippers would be out in force. Castonguay and her group of dogs and trainers arrived early in an attempt to avoid the crowds, but by the time they'd finished their work the park was already filled to capacity.

They had just finished loading their boat back onto the trailer when a group of teenagers arrived on the dock. The dogs watched them, whining and pulling at their leads. Because they would never come out of the water voluntarily, the dogs were all tied to trees until their handlers were free to put them into the vehicles. As the dogs waited, each teenaged whoop and holler, and every splash off the dock, wound them up a little more until they were all pining to get back into the lake. "The dogs were very focused on this group who were jumping and diving off the end of the dock," says Castonguay. "They were a rowdy bunch, racing each other back and forth from the dock area to a rocky outpoint a few

In the Water

hundred yards away." Castonguay and the other handlers tried to ignore the barking and whining. The dogs were only following their instinctive drive; they had no way of knowing the commotion was nothing more than kids having fun. Still, it was quite a racket and Castonguay and her friends hurried to pack up and get away before the dogs became more upset.

Mister, in particular, could barely contain himself. Although he's now the most successful of her dogs, currently holding 17 titles for his various skills, at that time he was just getting started. The temptation was more than his youthful enthusiasm and energy could withstand. Finally, in a frenzy, he broke free and flew straight for the end of the dock, full speed, all 100-plus pounds of him. By that time, the rest of the dogs had caught his excitement and as he plunged into the water, they increased their chorus of frantic barking.

Castonguay tried everything she could think of to get Mister back to shore but he ignored her. "He was not coming," she says. "He was circling at the end of the dock, whining. We couldn't entice him with anything, not toys, not cookies, nothing."

The teenagers had formed a circle at the end of the dock, yelling and screaming, and Castonguay knew she needed to get Mister out of there as soon as possible. The only thing left to do was head back into the water and drag him out. "We had to unload the boat from the trailer, row out, and physically grab him by the collar," she says.

There were by then so many people at the dock that

Castonguay suspected something else must have happened. Even after being unceremoniously hauled out of the water, Mister remained intent on the crowd near the dock, so as soon as they reached the shore, Castonguay locked him securely inside her vehicle. "By the time we got the boat secured again," recalls Castonguay, "an ambulance had arrived." It was much later in the day that they learned the full story of what had happened, the incident Mister and the other dogs had sensed. One of the teenage boys had dived off the end of the dock and hadn't come up. "They had to call in divers to retrieve his body," she says.

Castonguay was astonished to learn that Mister had been circling the water over exactly the same place where the body was later recovered. "Mister knew where to go but not what to do once he got there," she says. "An older, more experienced dog might have attempted to dive."

Castonguay, who currently has 14 Newfoundlands of varying ages, has almost 20 years of experience in breeding and training, and in achieving championships in the conformation ring. In addition to water work, she also trains her dogs in obedience and draft work, striving to preserve the purpose for which her dogs were originally bred. "We strive to do it all with our Newfs," she says. But still, Mister's exhibit of natural talent left her awestruck. "I've seen them do some pretty basic things that other people think are amazing, but this to me was a real indication of their real life-saving ability," she says. "Pure instinct told him to disregard his restraint

In the Water

and ignore our commands."

For well over 200 years, the Newfoundland breed's instinct has been invaluable to fishermen and sailors who work in and around the frigid waters of the northeastern Canadian coast. Various theories exist to explain the appearance of these big, black dogs on their native island of Newfoundland. Dog experts speculate that their ancestry includes everything from early European explorers' dogs, to mastiffs and sheepdogs, to wolves. Lewis and Clark, in their famous expedition to the Pacific Northwest of the United States, had a dog with them named Scannon who is thought to have been a Newfoundland. By the 18th century, the breed had gained some uniformity in appearance and had begun to increase in both numbers and popularity, but it was during the 19th century that breeders developed the characteristics we recognise in today's Newfoundland dog.

No matter what the origins of the breed, their early purpose was clear: to assist fishermen in their work in and around the water. The dogs were used for a variety of tasks. They helped to haul in heavy wet nets loaded with fish, and spent a fair amount of time retrieving items such as ropes from the water. But often, they did much more. One famous Newf named Tang received the Lloyd's Medal for Meritorious Service in 1919 after performing a dramatic rescue off the coast of Nova Scotia. When the ship Tang was on was being dashed against the rocky shoreline by a vicious December storm, the last hope of survival for the 92 people on board

An Italian dry-point by Amos Nattini illustrating the
Newfoundland as "ship dog."

was for someone to carry a line to shore. One sailor attempted it but was quickly lost in the gale. Tang saw this and stepped up to grab the line. When his captain gave the command, Tang leapt into the ocean and managed to bring the

In the Water

line to a group of people on shore, who were then able to complete the rescue. Everyone on board was saved.

On the open ocean, making rope connection to land can mean the difference between life and death. But sometimes it's simply a matter of convenience. At Buntzen Lake, Castonguay has often seen vacationers in their rental canoes, paddling in circles and sitting on their lifejackets, with no idea what they're doing. Usually they make it back to the dock awkwardly but in one piece. But one time, she saw two young girls stranded motionless in their canoe, about 45 metres from shore. They'd lost their paddles and, to make things worse, they spoke almost no English. Castonguay was preparing a dog named Sunny for her Senior Water Dog certification that year and thought it was a perfect opportunity for the dog to get some real-life practice. "We were yelling at them, trying to explain that we'd send a dog out with a line to tow them in," laughs Castonguay. But the girls didn't understand and were terrified of the dog. A hiker happened by just then who was able to translate, and he also tried to explain. "He shouted at them and they nodded, so we sent the dog out."

Sunny took the line and began swimming towards the boat. But when she got within range, the girls refused to take the line. They couldn't bring themselves to get close enough to the big dog. Sunny turned around to start towing them back, but stopped when she didn't feel the weight of the boat. She then swam back to the canoe to offer the rope again. Puzzled but determined, Sunny circled the boat several times until finally, when her back was turned, the girls gathered their courage and snatched the end of the rope. "The boat was a little different and the people were a little different," says Castonguay, "but other than that, it was exactly like what we do in our training exercises." Even with uncooperative "victims," Sunny knew what to do and she did it. Who knows, she may have given them a story they'll tell for the rest of their lives.

Chapter 7
Trigger Happy

Marsha Armstrong had heard of seeing-eye dogs, but she never supposed dogs could help people with other disabilities. Indeed, she had no reason to even consider the notion — she had been healthy all her life.

But in 1993, Marsha sat in her doctor's office in Burlington, Ontario, struggling to make sense of the words she was hearing. She'd just been diagnosed with an acoustic neuroma, an egg-yolk-sized brain tumour that occurs in about one out of 500,000 people. The growth sat nestled on the eighth cranial nerve leading from the brain to the inner ear, an area affecting the muscles of the face as well as those that control balance. A tumour in this delicate area can have devastating results.

Several years earlier, Marsha, who works in the construction industry, noticed that she was losing some of her hearing ability in one ear. She wasn't surprised; it's a common occupational hazard. What she didn't realize was that single-sided hearing loss, accompanied by ringing or buzzing — called tinnitus — is also the first symptom of this rare brain tumour. And the symptoms don't stop there.

Intermittent episodes of facial nerve paralysis, also called Bell's palsy, made Marsha suspect something more serious. "They figure I had the tumour for 10 years," Marsha says. It was a good news, bad news situation; acoustic neuromas are usually benign, but slowly and surely, they grow deeper into the brain stem, which is "command central" for the entire body. Marsha's surgeon told her that without surgery, she'd be dead within the year. However, he also warned her that surgery in this part of the brain was risky, and there was no guarantee that, even in the best-case scenario, her symptoms would disappear. When Marsha signed the consent form the day of the surgery, she knew it was a delicate procedure with potential for problems. She had no idea what sort of world she'd wake up to.

The procedure seemed to go well, and her tumour was successfully removed. She would live. But the surgeon's warnings proved prophetic. Marsha was left completely deaf in her left ear, and partially blind in her left eye. As another after-effect of the surgery, she also developed a condition

Trigger Happy

called Meniere's syndrome. Its most frightening symptom is severe vertigo, a balance disorder common in people with acoustic neuromas.

Balance problems, partial deafness, and partial blindness may not seem debilitating; many people suffer worse disabilities, after all. But these conditions had profound effects on Marsha, partly, she thinks, because her handicaps aren't obvious. "I look perfectly fine," she says. "But I'll be walking down the hallway and suddenly drop to the floor." The simplest things suddenly became difficult. "The elevator, for instance," she says. "I have to think the whole way up and when I'm getting off." No longer could she drive her car or go dancing on Friday nights. Even a quiet walk outside was fraught with difficulty. On a couple of occasions, she misjudged the direction of sound and inadvertently moved right into the path of joggers approaching from behind — both times she was flattened as a result. Crawling into bed exhausted, she often found she couldn't relax enough to sleep. "It's scary to lie down at night and not be able to hear anything," she admits.

Under stress, her symptoms worsened, affecting her speech and causing one eyelid to droop. That's when people would notice something was wrong, but they still wouldn't necessarily suspect a disability. Instead, they'd treat her as if she was drunk, absent-minded, or just plain thoughtless. "When people approach me from my left side or behind me I don't hear or see them," she says. "People would speak to me in grocery stores, for example, perhaps wanting to get past me, and when I didn't respond I'd be bumped with carts or called rude names."

For several years, Marsha tried to adjust to her new life, but her once outgoing, extroverted personality began to fade under the weight of misunderstanding and prejudice. Even casual conversations were so difficult they seemed hardly worth the effort. "I lost my confidence and stopped going out in public," she remembers.

Then, one weekend in 1997, she had an experience that changed the rest of her life. She saw a group of people and dogs doing a demonstration for National Service Dogs (NSD). Marsha was surprised to learn that NSD trained hearing ear dogs. Eagerly, she grabbed all the brochures and information pamphlets she could find and immediately contacted the organization to request a spot on its waiting list.

A long and anxious waiting period began. It takes a full year of training — at a cost of about $8000 to $10,000 — to teach an assistance dog all the specific tasks he'll be required to perform. NSD tries to find the best dog to fit each owner, and sometimes it takes additional time to make an appropriate match. Larger dogs such as Labrador retrievers, Golden retrievers, and German shepherds are well known for their abilities as assistance dogs. But Marsha worried about having such a large dog. "You're only too happy to get a dog at all," she says, "but I hoped it would work with my small home and my two cats."

Trigger Happy

Then the people at NSD introduced her to Trigger, a handsome Jack Russell terrier. Although he was large for his breed, he was much smaller than the Labrador retriever Marsha had been expecting. She was overjoyed! They were only allowed a brief period of time to get acquainted before Trigger was taken back to be trained in the specific tasks Marsha needed help with.

Marsha would soon discover there was a lot of dog packed into the compact breed NSD had chosen for her. The word *terrier* has its roots in the Latin *terre*, which means "earth." Like most terriers, Jack Russells were originally bred to "go to ground," hunting small rodents such as rats and mice. But these alert, feisty dogs have many other capabilities. They excel in sports such as flyball and agility and are popular companions for children. One Jack Russell terrier named Rats even attained international celebrity in the 1970s after "joining" a Northern Ireland army unit and surviving numerous bombings and sniper attacks. Today these terriers are becoming more common as assistance and alert dogs, especially when a smaller dog is needed.

After three long months, Marsha and Trigger met again, this time to begin their training together. Professional trainers lay the foundation of general knowledge for each dog, but once a match is made the dog has to learn the specific tasks required by his new owner. For an intensive six weeks, five days each week, Marsha and Trigger took instruction from trainers on how to work together as a team. Trigger had to learn that

Great Dog Stories

Marsha Armstrong and Trigger

Trigger Happy

Marsha, and only Marsha, was boss. Wherever Marsha went — even if it was to the bathroom — Trigger went too. "Trigger was attached to me all the time, even sleeping, by a long lead around my waist," she says. "He came to work with me for two weeks as well." It was hard, time-consuming work, but ultimately, it cemented the bond necessary to form a successful working relationship. Marsha, however, is quick to credit her and Trigger's success to NSD trainers Heather Fowler and Danielle Forbes, whose patience and dedication have enriched the lives of so many people affected by disability.

What are Trigger's daily tasks? He is trained to alert Marsha to any important sounds that she might not hear herself. He informs her when the telephone, doorbell, alarm clock, or stove timer rings. He's also trained to indicate the sound of the smoke detector, and he even taught himself to let her know when the buzzer on the clothes dryer goes off. Sometimes he'll even let Marsha know when trucks are beeping to back up. His method is simple, with a few variations. When the phone rings, Trigger runs to Marsha and jumps against her to let her know something's happening. Then he runs back, jumps onto the chair beside the phone and puts both paws on it. To alert her to the smoke detector, he jumps up against her to get her attention then spins in circles. When the doorbell rings, he comes to her, then goes to the door and jumps up against it. And when the alarm clock rings in the morning, he jumps onto the bed and starts tugging at the blankets.

He's also trained to recognize her name. When Trigger is out with Marsha's grandson Taylor, for instance, the boy can say "Marsha, Marsha! Get Marsha!" and Trigger will take him to wherever Marsha is. He's also learned Taylor's name, so Marsha can always find her grandson.

Although Trigger is not specifically trained to assist Marsha with her balance problems, he's taught himself to do what she needs. "He stays on my weaker side, as a buffer to keep me from bumping into people," she says. When fatigue causes her pace or step to change, Trigger adjusts his positioning. He makes sure he's slightly in front of her so she won't trip over him.

He's smart and strong, but he's still terrier to the core, which means he's also very stubborn. When guests are in the house, Trigger likes to lie down on the job, secure in the knowledge that others are there to help Marsha and alert her to various sounds. Even though she could let him off the hook, Marsha knows she has to be firm with him, and he grudgingly complies.

But one day in the grocery store, Marsha couldn't reprimand him. She had left Trigger in the truck, with the sliding window cracked for ventilation. He waited until she was out of sight, then nosed the window open, jumped out, and found his way to the dairy section at the back of the store. Marsha reached for a jug of milk, looked down, and there he was, casually trotting along behind her. She had thought she could do this one little job on her own, but the assistance dog who

Trigger Happy

had changed her life thought different. He had no intention of being left alone in the truck while she went shopping, not if he could avoid it. Helping her was his job and nothing would stand in his way. "He just took his place without any fanfare," she says. "I didn't leave him very often and he was familiar with the store. He thought he should be there with me."

Marsha has come a long way from those dark days after surgery. Between medication, therapy, and Trigger's help, her physical abilities have improved dramatically and she is once again able to tackle life with confidence. "He has a marvellous personality and he entertains me daily," she laughs. She's even able to drive during the day now. Trigger rides shotgun, ready and waiting for his next task. If she leaves him in the car, he waits for her to return, eyes straight ahead, even ignoring people who try to talk to him. "Then when I come back he turns around and barks at them like mad!" she laughs.

Marsha's emotional healing has been just as significant as her physical healing. Where once her life seemed to be an uphill battle full of bad days that kept getting worse, Trigger has brought a sense of competence, good-fortune, and even joy. "I'm not afraid to go out at night anymore," she says. "I am happy and healthy and outgoing again."

Marsha hit the jackpot with her little dog and she knows it. Each day she is more grateful for Trigger's enthusiastic help and companionship. She's also become something of a crusader, educating people on the symptoms of acoustic neuroma and Meniere's syndrome. She hopes no one else will have to go through the lonely years of confusion and despair that she did. She also encourages people with less common disabilities to consider the benefits that an assistance dog could bring to their lives.

"It's hard to reflect on the sadness I felt at that time," she says. "I think I have done much better than a lot of people without dogs. I can't imagine not having a service dog."

Chapter 8
Terror in Moose Country

LeAnn O'Reilly walked through the quiet forest, keeping step to the rhythmic clang of the cowbell attached to her backpack. Her dogs, Rottweilers named Dakota and Max, ranged slightly ahead of her, circling back periodically. It was a chilly, late October afternoon in 1999, and they were just about ready to head back home when LeeAnn heard a crashing noise on the trail above her. She figured a falling tree branch had caused the noise, but then she saw that her dogs had stiffened. Watching them growl, their hackles raised, LeeAnn realized the noise must have been something else — something dangerous. A moment later, the blood froze in her veins as she came face to face with one of the most frightening eventualities of wilderness hiking: an angry timber moose charging straight towards her.

LeeAnn knows all about wilderness hazards. Moose, bear, caribou, bottomless bogs, disorienting forest, and unpredictable weather — they're all considered by this long-time resident of Corner Brook, Newfoundland, as part of the beauty of life on the "Rock". As an experienced outdoor adventurer and dog sport enthusiast, LeeAnn loves having access to new areas to take her dogs hiking and tracking. Although she was born in Ontario, she can't imagine living anywhere else. "I stay here because of the environment," she says. "It's ideal for dogs."

And dogs are her life. LeeAnn works nights as a psychiatric nurse so that she's home during the day to run her private dog charity, By the Bay Rescue. In the past six years, she estimates that she and her volunteers have rescued over 500 homeless, unwanted, or abused dogs. She tries not to think of the money it costs her to do this work; because By the Bay Rescue is not a registered charity, expenses are paid for out of pocket — usually *her* pocket. So why is she so dedicated? She's an ardent advocate for large breed dogs and seeks to educate potential owners of their needs so that they don't end up with more than they bargained for. "Larger breeds require so much more caution and care than most people know about," LeeAnn says.

But beneath her formal answer is a more personal reason. "I do it for the love of Max and Dakota."

Terror in Moose Country

LeeAnn never expected to become a fan of Rottweilers. The breed, developed in Rottweil, Germany, in the 1800s, was intended to be powerful and muscular, with a strong protective instinct. Their original purpose was to drive herds of cattle between farms and butcher, guarding the cattle from thieves along the way. Although the breed almost died out at one point, the Rottweiler is one of the most popular breeds today. Unfortunately, their trendy status, and the irresponsible breeding and training that accompany it, has damaged the breed, earning the dogs a reputation for viciousness that doesn't apply to most carefully bred Rottweilers. LeeAnn knows that owning a large, powerful dog is not a responsibility to take lightly. She also knows that in Max and Dakota, she got far more back than she ever gave.

Dakota, a well-bred, strapping female puppy, arrived from a reputable breeder in southern Ontario on schedule, just as promised. She grew into a calm, intelligent dog who did everything "by the book." She listened carefully and obeyed commands promptly, displaying caution and reliability.

Max, on the other hand, couldn't have been more different. He was shipped from a breeder in Cleveland, Ohio, and right from the start, he kept LeeAnn on her toes. "Remember the ice storm in Quebec?" LeeAnn asks. "That's when he arrived." With several unexpected flight changes in his itinerary, he never once landed as scheduled. Due to the extreme weather problems, his flight was delayed first in Ottawa, then again in Halifax. In the end, LeeAnn had to hire a custom's officer to go pick up the puppy from the airport and drive him home. She heard later that flight attendants were frantically trying to stuff him into his crate on the tarmac because they hadn't had the heart to keep the little guy crated during the flight. He'd flown the entire way snuggling with one attendant or another. By the time they finally reached their destination, he had no intention of going from a warm soft jacket to a cold plastic crate!

Max grew into a 140 pound tank of a dog with an agenda all of his own, and the day that LeeAnn encountered the moose, her dogs' unique combination of attributes — Dakota's intelligence and Max's stubbornness — probably saved her life.

LeeAnn always took precautions when hiking and tracking with the dogs. Moose cows are extremely protective of their young — ready and willing to take on a full-grown black bear if necessary. But when they do not feel threatened, they usually keep to themselves, preferring to melt into the background rather than meet up with humans. In her several years of hiking, LeeAnn had never encountered moose.

Still, she knew from experience that moose could be unpredictable. Once, as she was driving home from work at about 4:00 a.m., a yearling calf appeared in front of her vehicle. Usually yearlings aren't so much dangerous as they are disoriented and frightened. Each season when the cows give birth, the previous year's calves are sent out into the world, whether they like it or not. "They're all legs," LeeAnn laughs.

Terror in Moose Country

"They don't know what to do with themselves." But by their first winter, calves can easily weigh over 200 pounds and are capable of inflicting serious damage to anything perceived as a predator. When LeeAnn saw this particular youngster, she slammed on the brakes, turned off her headlights, and hoped he'd make his way out of town. Instead, he fled blindly towards a couple of late-night bar patrons who were staggering down a nearby street. LeeAnn honked her horn to warn them, but they didn't notice and the calf ran right into them. A moment later, she saw the inebriated twosome sit up and look around as if wondering what had hit them.

Meeting a scared juvenile is one thing. A high-speed collision with a 900-pound adult is another, and wandering moose are a well-known Newfoundland road hazard. But the most dangerous time of year by far is the autumn breeding season or "rut." During this season, bull moose can become very aggressive in their search for cows, attacking other bulls and even humans who have the misfortune to cross their paths.

The day that LeeAnn met her moose, she purposely went out in the afternoon, when moose are least active. As her hike wound to an end, the wind picked up and it started to hail. It was definitely time to head for home. The cracking sounds she heard in the bush came from the area where park officials were clearing a new trail, but LeeAnn knew the workers were gone for the day. Suddenly Dakota, who was dancing around anxiously, ran to Max, body-slammed him in the shoulder, and took off into the bush. "Dakota flew off in the direction of the sound," recalls LeeAnn, "and my Max, God love him, for the first time ever sat and stayed in one place." That one place happened to be right on LeeAnn's feet.

LeeAnn was frantic to call Dakota back from wherever she'd gone, but Max wasn't about to let her go. "It's the first time she didn't recall to me," she says. "She wasn't listening; I rang the bell and still she wouldn't return." She screamed for Dakota to come back, trying to push Max out of the way so she could run after her other dog, when suddenly she looked up and discovered what the dogs already knew: a moose was charging down the hill directly towards her. And it wasn't just any moose. It was a huge black timber moose, in full rut and furious.

"This animal was so big, small spruce were falling down around his antlers," says LeeAnn. Behind the moose raced Dakota, nipping at its heels like a herding dog, directing the charge as her German ancestors once did. Dakota seemed to know exactly what she was doing, but LeeAnn was terrified that the moose would turn and aim its deadly hooves or antlers at the dog. She wanted to get Dakota away from the moose, but she couldn't move with the weight of Max against her. Each time she moved, he moved in front of her, blocking her way.

LeeAnn watched the drama unfolding in front of her as if it were happening in slow motion. There was nowhere else for this moose to go but past her. The trail ran alongside the

Terror in Moose Country

river, and suddenly she realized that Dakota was deliberately herding the moose away from her, towards the water's edge. Persistently, Dakota nipped and barked at the animal's heels, always keeping herself between the moose and her owner.

Finally, Dakota drove the moose down through the rough bush of the embankment, pushing it over the rocky ground. The whole time, LeeAnn was screaming at Max, who steadfastly ignored her. Dakota got the moose down into the water and stayed on the beach until the animal was halfway across the river. Then, to LeeAnn's horror, she saw the moose turn around for another pass. "It didn't want to go across the river, for some reason," she says. This time, Dakota went into the river and swam out until she was within three metres of the moose, barking and making a big racket in the water. Max, knowing LeeAnn was out of danger, went down over the embankment to help Dakota. Upon seeing both of the dogs, the moose decided it wasn't worth the fight and turned towards the other side of the river.

Late that night, LeeAnn heard on the radio that in another part of the province, a man had been gored by a timber moose in rut, barely escaping with his life. That's when it hit her. "It takes the wind right out of you," she recalls. "If I'd been hiking by myself I'd have been hurt, without a doubt. If the dogs hadn't done what they did, I'd have been face to face with that moose." The two dogs had worked as a team, independent of LeeAnn. Although she'd trained them, they'd known that they had to disregard her commands in order to protect her.

The next summer, LeeAnn and the dogs encountered another hazard of moose country: bogs. It was a hot July day and they'd gone down an unfamiliar road, hoping to find some shade.

Thinking she could see a little pond ahead that might provide relief from the heat, LeeAnn let the dogs off their leads. Max immediately headed through a patch of scrubby brush in the direction of the water. When LeeAnn called Max to return and he didn't respond, she became worried and sent Dakota to find him.

"She returned in just minutes, grabbed the leash from my hand and took off barking wildly," says LeeAnn. Dakota pulled and whined anxiously until they pushed through the brush and found Max up to his neck in the quagmire and sinking fast. "I knew there were bogs and that some of them are bottomless," LeeAnn says. "But I thought we were on firm footing."

The famous backwoods bogs can be deadly; some are shallow, while others are so deep that trucks can disappear in a matter of minutes. LeeAnn didn't recognize the danger immediately, but Dakota did. The dog ran between her owner and Max, blocking LeeAnn with her body. She dropped the leash at LeeAnn's feet and then did something the woman had never seen her do: she got down onto her belly and crawled towards Max. LeeAnn followed suit, creeping on her belly until she could reach Max. She attached his lead and then grabbed Dakota by the collar. Together, LeeAnn and Dakota began to pull.

Terror in Moose Country

"Within seconds," she says, "I'm up to my armpits in this boggy stuff. Max is still lying there on his side, stuck. Now I'm the one sinking." Dakota lay flat on the ground, distributing her body weight so she wouldn't sink, and dug in her claws. LeeAnn gripped Max's collar in one hand and Dakota's collar in the other and they half crawled, half swam their way to solid ground. "If it wasn't for her thinking," remembers LeeAnn, "I would have gone in, too."

LeeAnn was badly shaken by the incident. Because she hadn't planned to hike the new trail, no one even knew where she'd gone. She and her dogs could have disappeared without a trace. "It changed the way I hiked," she says.

Now, she scouts out her hiking areas and keeps the dogs on leads until she knows it's safe to roam freely. And she always files a "hike plan" with her husband, who was understandably alarmed at her experience. "He told me, 'For God's sake, LeeAnn, tell me where you're going! At least roughly!'"

Wiser for the experiences, LeeAnn continued hiking with Max and Dakota. "What," she often wondered, "would I ever do without them?"

But one night when LeeAnn let the dogs outside, Dakota came back into the house looking distinctly unwell: her body stiff, her head hanging. Panicking, LeeAnn phoned her veterinarian, who guessed that Dakota was reacting to something she'd eaten and would probably be fine by the next day. But the next morning, before LeeAnn could get her to the veterinarian, Dakota took a turn for the worse. LeeAnn was outside the house when she heard her husband screaming at her to hurry in. She dashed back just in time to see Dakota draw her last breath. She gathered the big dog into her arms in disbelief. How could she live without Dakota?

LeeAnn was devastated. How did a perfectly healthy dog become deathly ill seemingly overnight? A veterinary examination on the body gave her the answer: Dakota had a hemangiosarcoma, a large tumour on her spleen. She'd most likely had it for some time without symptoms, until the night it ruptured and she became ill. It was amazing that she lived through the night.

As heartbroken as LeeAnn was, it was even more difficult to watch Max grieve for his friend. Before LeeAnn took Dakota's body away for cremation, she brought Max to the van to let him say goodbye. After LeeAnn returned without her, Max repeatedly sat down next to the van and howled. He searched the house restlessly, looking to LeeAnn as if to say, "where is she?" He couldn't relax. He lost interest in eating.

Five days after Dakota died, LeeAnn looked at Max and her heart filled with foreboding. She saw something in his eye that terrified her. Something, she knew not what, was terribly wrong with him. She rushed him to her veterinary clinic in a panic and told them, "He's dying!" They checked him over thoroughly, taking blood samples and X-rays, but everything turned up normal. "They told me he was fine, not to worry," says LeeAnn. "But I knew he was dying. I didn't leave him for a minute."

Terror in Moose Country

When Max's appetite continued to flag, LeeAnn had him retested. This time there were some minor changes in his blood results and the veterinarian diagnosed hemolytic anemia. Although this is a serious illness, it can usually be successfully managed medically. "We thought we had it nailed," remembers LeeAnn. "We could treat him with prednisone and he'd be fine." But secretly she still feared he wasn't going to make it.

LeeAnn is forever grateful for the patience, dedication and expertise of her veterinarians. They understood her grief for Dakota and knew how it drove her fears for Max. They tried to reassure her but they didn't discount her insistence that something more was wrong. Once again, her instincts were tragically accurate. Max had developed a malignant mast cell tumour, a cancer as deadly as it is difficult to diagnose.

Two weeks to the day after the death of Dakota, Max passed away.

In some ways, it was fitting that he died so soon after her. "He never got over her being gone," says LeeAnn. But the loss of both dogs in such a short time hit hard. LeeAnn continues doing her rescue work, more dedicated than ever to the plight of needy dogs. In her car hangs a silver locket containing ashes from both Max and Dakota, a daily reminder to her of the love the dogs gave her. They threw all their vast abilities into doing whatever needed doing; now their memory inspires her to keep doing what needs to be done.

Chapter 9
Collies Against the Odds

It's training day on the southern Alberta sheep ranch. The gate swings open and as one, the sheep scramble to the far side of the dust-choked corral. They shift nervously from side to side, trying to keep their distance from the mesmerizing eyes of the dogs slinking around them. These dogs, young border collies, don't need training so much as the opportunity to discover and hone the skills lying just beneath the surface. The moment they focus their sharp eyes on the sheep, centuries of breeding click into gear. Marrow-deep instinct stiffens muscles, narrows their gaze, and shifts limbs into the predatory crouch that will bend the churning herd to the dogs' will.

All of the border collies in training are doing what

Collies Against the Odds

comes naturally. All, that is, except for one; a small black and white puppy cowers outside the gate. More frightened than even the sheep, she refuses to join the other dogs.

If ever a breed of dog was meant to work, it's the border collie. They rank at the top of every canine intelligence test; they excel in obedience matches, agility, flyball, and — of course — sheep-herding competitions. But even some border collies have phobias. Some might be scared of lightening or thunder. Others may feel threatened by a broom or a vacuum cleaner.

While a number of phobias are easily explained, others make no human sense whatsoever. Unfortunately, a dog's phobias can cause serious problems for those who live with the animal. Sometimes anti-anxiety drugs help. Desensitization through behaviour-modification techniques can also be effective for many dogs. Some owners simply learn to work around the trigger. But on this busy, sprawling ranch where everyone — human and animal alike — had a job, there was no time to deal with the cowering puppy. For this one little dog named Eve, all the dormant talents in the world didn't compensate for her one vital deficiency: she was a sheepherder who wouldn't herd sheep.

On most ranches, such a situation might be handled with expedient, if reluctant, practicality. But Eve escaped such an end. Unwilling to "dispose" of her, the rancher called the Border Collie Club of Canada and they, in turn, contacted Brenda Kovac and her fiancé Brent Fukuda of Calgary,

Alberta. At that time, the two were actively involved in border collie rescue, often providing foster care for dogs awaiting new homes. Brenda, who had rescued her first border collie from the pound 25 years earlier, had known back then that it would only be a matter of time before she got involved in breed rescue officially. "I've always loved dogs," says Brenda, "so it really didn't have to be a border. But I've always been drawn to any collie-type dog."

Even with all the combined rescue experience that Brenda and Brent shared, the timid little Eve presented something of a challenge. At just past one year of age, Eve hadn't had any training or socialization and was terrified of her new world. "I didn't even get a chance to touch her until she'd been with us for a week," Kovac remembers. "She was terrified of everything in the house, right down to the linoleum." Then one day, Brent showed Eve a ball. Like everything else, this was new to her, but to their relief, it didn't appear to terrify her. Instead, Eve looked interested. "Brent got on all fours, down at her level," says Brenda, "and she woke up and paid attention." The ball was the connection they'd been looking for.

Brenda and Brent began to work with Eve, helping her to get accustomed to life in a home. "We had to train her to do everything," says Brenda. "She wasn't housebroken and she had no manners." It was a huge change for Eve to go from a big, open farm where she spent most of her life surrounded by other dogs, to living in a house in close contact

Collies Against the Odds

with people. She even balked at leaving the yard, trembling at the sight of the leash. Brenda suspects that Eve's early experiences on the ranch were more traumatic for the sensitive dog's temperament than anyone could have expected. "They had to put her on the leash to drag her into the corral," she says, "and to this day she's scared of sheep."

Knowing Eve as she does now, it makes complete sense to Brenda. Sheep are nervous, simple-minded creatures and the sounds they make, especially the lambs, are similar to human cries. "Eve picks up on everything," Brenda emphasizes. "The main thing in her life is she doesn't want to upset anyone." For her, the cacophony of frightened animals, and knowing she was the cause, must have been overwhelming. But Brenda's aim wasn't to help Eve overcome her fear of sheep; it was to prepare her for life as a pet in a permanent home. After three months of foster care and constant, gentle training, Eve was ready. Brenda and Brent said goodbye and hoped for the best, but they knew they'd miss the timid collie. They'd grown attached to her gentle presence. "When the dogs find a home you're happy," Brenda says, "but you're sad, too."

Less than a year later, their paths crossed again, under tragic circumstances. The new owner Eve had quickly grown to love had died suddenly, leaving the dog bereft and homeless yet again. This time when Brenda and Brent saw her, they knew Eve had been through enough. All the progress she'd made was gone. She cowered and shook, afraid of everything, suspecting the worst of the world. They knew Eve needed security so they decided to make her a permanent member of their family. "Brent had really missed her," says Brenda. "She's had such a hard and difficult life, he just said 'no more.'"

They started over with Eve, slowly regaining her trust. "It took some time for her to come to us again," recalls Brenda. "Eve was looking for her owner, grieving for her." But gradually, she settled in and became part of the household, along with Brenda and Brent's two other dogs. Eve even chose her own special place in the living room on the loveseat, next to the window so she could watch passers-by.

Brenda spent the next year helping Eve become more comfortable with strangers and new situations. But Brenda suspected that the shy dog needed even more stimulation. She knew from experience that all border collies need to feel useful, so one weekend the following spring, she took Eve to an introductory tracking seminar run by Marcy Wright, a handler certified with the RCMP Civilian Search Dog Association (CSDA). Although tracking work had always intrigued Brenda, she'd never pursued it. "I never thought I could do it," she says. "Or that I had a good enough dog." She was just there to expose Eve to something new and let her watch the other dogs. But immediately, a change came over Eve. Her eyes lit up; she became alert and focused.

Noting Eve's reaction, Wright and Brenda decided to let her give tracking a try, and Brenda set a scent track. "Our tracking area was a bare field," she explains. "No humans had been in it." Brenda picked out a line about 90 metres long, walked the length of it, set a favourite toy of Eve's down at the end of it, and then left the area without disturbing the line. Next, she took Eve to the beginning of the line, pointed to it, and told Eve to "track it." Eve followed the line perfectly! Wright was impressed but figured it was probably a fluke. "So we set another track, a harder one this time," continues Brenda. "It went around a tree, over here, over there." This time, Wright ran alongside, keeping a close eye on Eve as she worked. By the end, Wright knew Eve had something special. "Marcy said it's quite rare for a dog to perform so well, almost by the book," says Brenda. After the seminar, Wright invited Brenda and Eve to train with the CSDA team in Calgary.

But they were coming into the group at a tremendous disadvantage; everyone else was six months ahead of them in their training. And Eve was still Eve. Her fearful nature didn't inspire confidence. "Everyone said 'I don't know about Eve'," recalls Brenda. "They couldn't even pet her."

Being part of the CSDA isn't a casual commitment; it requires countless volunteer hours of practice. Handlers must undergo rigorous training, learning such skills as first aid, search and rescue fundamentals, global positioning system operations, evidence handling, and courtroom demeanour. In tracking abilities, civilian dogs are trained to the same standards as the RCMP dogs, with a few exceptions: they are *not* trained to search for drugs or explosives, nor are they trained to be aggressive. In the first year, certification tests require dogs to perform exercises in agility, obedience, finding an article, finding a person, and searching a ditch. Dogs are trained to alert their handlers to the presence of human scent in a variety of locations, from wilderness, to alleys and ditches, to water. Experienced dogs may be trained in the more advanced task of locating human remains.

Brenda and Eve had a lot of work ahead of them. Eve had to learn to make subtle distinctions between commands. "Track it" means to follow a scent trail from start to finish. "Small search" means to look for evidence, while "search" is a general command referring to all other types of searching. It takes an average of a year and a half, but sometimes two or three years, to train a dog to pass the certification tests.

Brenda and Eve worked hard and quickly caught up to the rest of their group, several of who were preparing to take the certification tests that spring. "We were told, 'You're probably not ready, but give it a try and see what happens'," says Brenda. So, in April 2002, the pair travelled to Red Deer, Alberta, to see what they could do. The test was a demanding, all-day event. Timid Eve would be required to perform surrounded by strange people in an unknown environment. How would she respond?

Eve gave a stellar performance that day. When she was told to "search," all of her fears and insecurities evaporated. "It was like you'd turned on a light switch," says Brenda. "No matter how shy she was, she was very confident and eager to do this job." In one test activity, two objects are hidden in a field and the dogs must find them both within 30 minutes.

Collies Against the Odds

Eve found the first one in eight seconds, and five minutes later she had uncovered the second one. It was a pivotal moment in her career as a civilian search dog. "Ten of us did the testing," says Brenda proudly, "and Eve and I were the only ones that passed!" Eve became the first civilian-owned dog in Calgary to be certified as an RCMP Civilian Search and Rescue Dog. She'd found her niche.

But talent and knowledge are nothing if they aren't used. Shortly after she received her certification, Eve got her first opportunity to try out her skills in an actual search. Residents of an upscale neighbourhood just outside of Edmonton had reported hearing gunshots in the middle of the night. The local police brought in a search dog to look for bullet casings but they didn't find any, nor did they find anything else that indicated the need for further investigation. The police were satisfied, but the homeowners weren't. They'd heard gunshots and wouldn't rest until they'd received an explanation. At that point, the CSDA was contacted and Brenda and Eve, as well as others in the group, came to do a search of the area. Fifteen minutes into the search, Eve found something that no one had thought to look for: a spent firecracker. "It was the first indication that it wasn't guns but rather firecrackers that had made the noise," says Brenda. The people in the neighbourhood were satisfied, and the case was closed.

Eve continues to make progress, though her basic personality remains the same: shy and submissive. Still, she's come a long way — from the sheep dog who was afraid of sheep to a highly valued member of the Civilian Search Dog Association.

Eve's a lucky dog, but Brenda and Brent feel the good fortune is theirs. They love having her in their lives. Recently, Brenda was invited to do a demonstration with Eve at the world-famous Calgary Stampede. Once more, Eve will be surrounded by the sights and sounds of farm animals, even sheep. She probably won't like it, but she's got more important things to think about these days. "We're all pretty excited," says Brenda proudly. "This little girl is taking us on all sorts of adventures."

* * *

In Baltimore, Maryland, a newborn collie caused her breeder to look on with dismay as the pup nuzzled her mother sleepily. The puppy's two brothers appeared to be developing normally, but something was wrong with this little female. Smaller than usual, she had a slight head tilt, and something looked different about her face. At three weeks of age, when the puppy's eyes still hadn't opened, the breeder took her to the veterinarian. The news wasn't good: the puppy had a condition described as "bilateral agenesis of eyes." Through a fluke of nature, this little female had been born without eyes.

Naturally, the breeder was distressed. Nothing like this had ever cropped up in her bloodline before. Her dogs were healthy show champions; she'd even bred one two-time

Collies Against the Odds

winner of the National Specialty. Distraught, she turned to her computer and posted a message on an Internet newsgroup for collie owners. What should she do?

When Jana Lashmit, also of Baltimore, logged on to the collie owner forum, it was more out of habit than interest. The recent death of her own collie left her grieving and unable to participate with her usual enthusiasm. "I read it every day but after Parker passed away, I was ready to quit the collie list," she says, "except my 'unsubscribe message' had an error so I was still getting mail." The message about the puppy without eyes caught her attention. When other forum members suggested euthanasia, Jana decided to post her own message. She wanted to meet the puppy herself.

"I didn't want another collie," she insists, "but Bonnie was something special. She was as spunky and playful as any eight-week-old."

Jana took Bonnie home with her. Then began the long task of teaching a blind dog to live in a sighted world. "Training her wasn't easy at first," she admits. The open spaces beyond the comfortable walls of the house overwhelmed Bonnie. When carried outdoors, she flopped to the ground and refused to move. Nothing could entice her to do so much as lift her head.

Jana began to wonder if she would ever be able to go for real walks with Bonnie. "Finally," she says, "on a nice warm day in April when Bonnie was three and a half months old, I just out-waited her." She spread a blanket out in the sun and sat down beside Bonnie, patiently waiting for the puppy to gain enough courage to sit up. When Bonnie finally did, Jana praised her lavishly, then rewarded her by taking her back inside her beloved home. The ice was broken. Gently, Jana continued to push Bonnie to explore further. Every tentative venture was followed by a reassuring trip home.

Jana decided that Bonnie needed to be treated like any other puppy. Housetraining followed, as well as learning to accept a leash. Puppy classes and regular obedience training came soon after. Bonnie was quickly turning into a normal dog — almost. "She even chased ducks," remembers Jana. "When she heard them quack, she'd weave her head back and forth like a satellite dish, and when she realized where they were, she'd run toward them at top speed, head still tipped at an angle."

For her blind collie who tended to be shy, Jana knew that socialization would be particularly important, so she made sure Bonnie was exposed to plenty of new situations. Jana's two jobs — one at a veterinary hospital and one at a pet store — allowed her to bring Bonnie to work with her every day. That way, Bonnie could grow accustomed to meeting strangers. The little dog's personality blossomed. Before long, Bonnie had passed her Canine Good Citizen test, a practical, non-competitive evaluation meant to improve manners. As well, she became a certified "therapy dog," able to do hospital and nursing home visitations. Both tests are a wonderful way for ordinary dogs to become better members of society.

"Mixed breeds are also allowed to earn them," explains Jana, "but they aren't recorded on a dog's pedigree like obedience or agility would be."

Still, Jana worried that this would be the extent of Bonnie's achievements. She knew that Bonnie's family tree contained many talented canines, athletes titled in sports that were simply beyond the reach of a blind dog. Bonnie clearly had the necessary intelligence, as well as the desire to work, but the typical collie sports — obedience, agility, and herding — weren't options. "It didn't seem fair," says Jana, "that she should always be an outsider."

So Jana looked into other activities. "Again, the Internet came to the rescue!" she says. In the spring of 2001, she discovered draft work, a sport dominated by large dogs specifically bred for the task of hauling carts. Jana didn't care whether or not Bonnie would win any competitions; she only wanted Bonnie to have something she could enjoy participating in. "I ordered a harness right away and an adapter kit that transforms a child's wagon into a dog-powered vehicle," Jana says. To her surprise, Bonnie took to draft work immediately. Before the first day ended, the dog was happily pulling the wagon behind her, doing wide circles around the yard.

After less than a week, Bonnie was doing so well that Jana decided to enter her in a draft dog competition put on by the American Rottweiler Club. The pair intensified their training. The day of the event, as Jana looked at the more than 20 dogs entered, she silently berated herself. Everywhere she turned, there were big, powerful cart-pullers: Rottweilers, as well as a Bernese mountain dog, a Swiss mountain dog, and a Leonberger. What had she been thinking? Bonnie was the only "non-traditional" draft dog there; the only dog who weighed less than her cart — not to mention the only dog without eyes!

Even the sopping grass surface was different from the dry earth or pavement they'd practised on at home. Nevertheless, the duo had entered the competition, and they would participate. After all, *Bonnie* didn't feel nervous or discouraged. As soon as their turn came, Jana's fears evaporated. "She threw herself into the harness and pulled as well as always," says Jana, "slow and steady." That day, Bonnie did herself proud: of all the dogs entered, she came in second place with a score of 98 out of a possible 100 points.

Jana could see that Bonnie enjoyed the challenge. Next, they set out to train for the Draft Dog test put on by the Saint Bernard Club of America. This time it wasn't quite as easy; during the first test, the cart caught on a turn. However, on the second try, Bonnie passed — the only dog out of seven to succeed. Jana now knew that Bonnie could hold her own — but was she good enough to earn an official title from the American Kennel Club? They'd have to find out.

That's when Jana discovered that official regulations do not permit blind dogs to compete in AKC-sanctioned events. "I was a little disappointed, but not really surprised," says Jana. She and Bonnie would have to be content with participating in the local clubs that accepted Bonnie's disability.

Collies Against the Odds

Jana Lashmit and Bonnie, getting ready to take the Draft Dog test.

Or would they? On a whim, she telephoned the central office of the Canadian Kennel Club to see if, by any chance, they might allow blind dogs to compete. "The nice young man I asked just paused a moment then said, 'Well, I don't see why not!'" Jana remembers. "Then he checked the rules just to be sure." Bonnie, he told her, was welcome to compete for titles in CKC-sanctioned events, just like any other dog.

Jana was thrilled. "I love the idea of Bonnie competing

on equal footing with 'normal' dogs," she says. That autumn, she and Bonnie packed for the trip up north, crossing the border into Ontario, where Bonnie's blindness wasn't a barrier. "It's about a 12-hour drive every time I go up to Canada to compete," says Jana, "but it's a pretty drive, straight up through rural Pennsylvania and New York, and past Niagara Falls." In October 2002, after much work, Bonnie the blind collie received her official Draft Dog title, as bestowed by the Canadian Kennel Club.

Jana and Bonnie are currently planning to take the CKC Draft Dog Excellent test, but meanwhile, Jana keeps Bonnie busy with her other jobs. With a group called Fidos for Freedom, they continue their regular pet visitation therapy to the sick and elderly. Bonnie also works as a "reading dog" with Dogs Educating and Assisting Readers (DEAR). "We go to libraries with 6 to 10 other dog/handler teams and have third-graders come and read to the dogs," she says. "Bonnie has a little green cape and her own ID tag to wear on her visits." These dogs, who listen without judging or correcting, make great reading partners for the children, and Bonnie is as non-threatening as they come.

Bonnie has come a long way from the frightened puppy who once wouldn't even lift her head off the ground. She's handicapped but she doesn't know it. All she knows is that when Jana asks her to do a task, it must be important, so she does it. It's her job.

Bibliography

Alderton, David. *Eyewitness Handbooks: Dogs*. Ontario: Stoddart Publishing Co. Ltd., 1993.

Budiansky, Stephen. *The Truth About Dogs*. New York: Penguin Putnam Inc., 2000.

Owens, Carrie. *Working Dogs*. Rocklin: Prima Publishing, 1999.

Sheldrake, Rupert. *Dogs That Know When Their Owners Are Coming Home*. New York: Three Rivers Press, 1999.

Slowik, Teresa. *The Ultimate Dog Quiz Book*. New York: Howell Book House, 1996.

Acknowledgments

The author extends her sincere thanks to all the dog enthusiasts who generously shared their stories for this book: Cpl. Terry Barter and Cpl. Rick Chaulk of the RCMP Police Dog Service, Marsha Armstrong, Judi Snowdon, Ros Scott, Heather MacLeod, Brenda Kovac, Jana Lashmit, Denise Castonguay, LeeAnn O'Reilly, and Jean Little, who all love their dogs dearly. Your patience and helpful comments were much appreciated!

Also, I'd like to thank my biggest fans: Stephanie, Andrea, and Megan, for reading my stories and making their own lunches, and Ray, for cheerfully taking the smaller office.

About the Author

Roxanne Willems Snopek lives and writes in Abbotsford, British Columbia, surrounded by her family and a variety of dogs, cats, birds, and fish. The human–animal bond is a recurring topic in her writing, which includes fiction and non-fiction. She is currently working on her second novel.

Photo Credits

Cover: www.comstock.com; **Amos Nattini:** page 74; **Andre Cyr:** page 82; **Dorothy Hansen:** page 111; **Heather MacLeod:** page 43; **O'Reilly O'Rotties:** page 8; **Susie Pitman:** page 46.

Every reasonable effort has been made to trace ownership and to obtain permission to reprint copyrighted material. The publishers would be pleased to have any errors or omissions brought to their attention so that they may be corrected in subsequent printings.

AMAZING STORIES
NOW AVAILABLE!

AMAZING STORIES™

GREAT CAT STORIES
Inspirational Tales About Exceptional Cats

ANIMAL/HUMAN INTEREST
by Roxanne Willems Snopek

Great Cat Stories
ISBN 1-55153-777-X

AMAZING STORIES
NOW AVAILABLE!

AMAZING STORIES™

STOLEN HORSES

Intriguing Tales of Rustling and Rescues

ANIMAL/CRIME

by Dorothy Pedersen

Stolen Horses
ISBN 1-55153-971-3

AMAZING STORIES
NOW AVAILABLE!

AMAZING STORIES

RESCUE DOGS

Crime and Rescue Canines in the Canadian Rockies

ANIMAL/ADVENTURE
by Dale Portman

Rescue Dogs
ISBN 1-55153-995-0

AMAZING STORIES
NOW AVAILABLE!

AMAZING STORIES™

THE HEART OF A HORSE

Poignant Tales and Humourous Escapades

ANIMAL/HUMAN INTEREST
by Gayle Bunney

The Heart of a Horse
ISBN 1-55153-994-2

OTHER AMAZING STORIES

ISBN	Title	ISBN	Title
1-55153-959-4	A War Bride's Story	1-55153-951-9	Ontario Murders
1-55153-794-X	Calgary Flames	1-55153-790-7	Ottawa Senators
1-55153-947-0	Canada's Rumrunners	1-55153-960-8	Ottawa Titans
1-55153-966-7	Canadian Spies	1-55153-945-4	Pierre Elliot Trudeau
1-55153-795-8	D-Day	1-55153-981-0	Rattenbury
1-55153-972-1	David Thompson	1-55153-991-8	Rebel Women
1-55153-982-9	Dinosaur Hunters	1-55153-995-0	Rescue Dogs
1-55153-970-5	Early Voyageurs	1-55153-985-3	Riding on the Wild Side
1-55153-798-2	Edmonton Oilers	1-55153-974-8	Risk Takers and Innovators
1-55153-968-3	Edwin Alonzo Boyd	1-55153-956-X	Robert Service
1-55153-996-9	Emily Carr	1-55153-799-0	Roberta Bondar
1-55153-961-6	Étienne Brûlé	1-55153-997-7	Sam Steele
1-55153-791-5	Extraordinary Accounts of Native Life on the West Coast	1-55153-954-3	Snowmobile Adventures
		1-55153-971-3	Stolen Horses
		1-55153-952-7	Strange Events
1-55153-992-6	Ghost Town Stories II	1-55153-783-4	Strange Events and More
1-55153-984-5	Ghost Town Stories III	1-55153-986-1	Tales from the West Coast
1-55153-993-4	Ghost Town Stories	1-55153-978-0	The Avro Arrow Story
1-55153-973-X	Great Canadian Love Stories	1-55153-943-8	The Black Donnellys
		1-55153-942-X	The Halifax Explosion
1-55153-777-X	Great Cat Stories	1-55153-994-2	The Heart of a Horse
1-55153-946-2	Great Dog Stories	1-55153-944-6	The Life of a Loyalist
1-55153-773-7	Great Military Leaders	1-55153-787-7	The Mad Trapper
1-55153-785-0	Grey Owl	1-55153-789-3	The Mounties
1-55153-958-6	Hudson's Bay Company Adventures	1-55153-948-9	The War of 1812 Against the States
1-55153-969-1	Klondike Joe Boyle	1-55153-788-5	Toronto Maple Leafs
1-55153-980-2	Legendary Show Jumpers	1-55153-976-4	Trailblazing Sports Heroes
1-55153-775-3	Lucy Maud Montgomery		
1-55153-967-5	Marie Anne Lagimodière	1-55153-977-2	Unsung Heroes of the Royal Canadian Air Force
1-55153-964-0	Marilyn Bell		
1-55153-999-3	Mary Schäffer	1-55153-792-3	Vancouver Canucks
1-55153-953-5	Moe Norman	1-55153-989-6	Vancouver's Old-Time Scoundrels
1-55153-965-9	Native Chiefs and Famous Métis		
		1-55153-990-X	West Coast Adventures
1-55153-962-4	Niagara Daredevils	1-55153-987-X	Wilderness Tales
1-55153-793-1	Norman Bethune	1-55153-873-3	Women Explorers

These titles are available wherever you buy books. If you have trouble finding the book you want, call the Altitude order desk at **1-800-957-6888**, e-mail your request to: orderdesk@altitudepublishing.com or visit our Web site at www.amazingstories.ca

New AMAZING STORIES titles are published every month.